TH...

"THE PEOPLE"

THE SPECTER OF "THE PEOPLE"

URBAN POVERTY IN NORTHEAST CHINA

MUN YOUNG CHO

CORNELL UNIVERSITY PRESS
Ithaca and London

Cornell University Press gratefully acknowledges receipt
of a Subsidy for Publication Grant from the Chiang
Ching-Kuo Foundation for International Scholarly
Exchange (USA), which generously assisted the publication
of this book.

First published 2013 by Cornell University Press
First printing, Cornell Paperbacks, 2013

Printed in the United States of America

Library of Congress Cataloging-in-Publication Data

Cho, Mun Young, 1975–
    The specter of "the people" : urban poverty in northeast
China / Mun Young Cho.
        p. cm.
    Includes bibliographical references and index.
    ISBN 978-0-8014-5165-2 (cloth : alk. paper)
    ISBN 978-0-8014-7864-2 (pbk. : alk. paper)
    1. Poverty—China—Harbin.   2. Harbin (China)—
Economic conditions—21st century.   3. Socialism and
culture—China—Harbin.   4. Ethnology—China—
Harbin.   I. Title.
    HC428.H34C46   2013
    339.4'6095184—dc23   2012039749

Cloth printing   10 9 8 7 6 5 4 3 2 1
Paperback printing   10 9 8 7 6 5 4 3 2 1

For my parents

Contents

Preface   ix

Acknowledgments   xix

Introduction   1

1. In Search of "the People"   21

2. Gambling on a New Home   46

3. On the Border between "the People"
   and "the Population"   68

4. The Will to Survive   93

5. Inclusive Exclusion   120

6. Dividing the Poor   144

Conclusion   167

Notes   173

References   187

Index   203

PREFACE

        As an anthropologist born in South Korea, I have become both fascinated with and uneasy about the concept of "the people." *Minjung,* a South Korean expression meaning "the people," was a term of exclusion as well as liberation. In the 1970 and 1980s, many intellectuals and activists used *minjung* to refer to factory workers, peasants, street vendors, slum dwellers, and so forth to build solidarity against the political, economic, and social violence under military rule. Whether wittingly or unwittingly, however, the coiners of the term participated in determining who deserved to be designated as *minjung* and who did not. The honorific category, for instance, did not fully embrace angry rioters who reacted to state violence with violence of their own, or female workers who were resisting a gendered hierarchy as well as labor exploitation.

Regardless of such ambiguities, the concept of "the people" was fading away during my high school days in South Korea in the early 1990s. It was a period when the state regime publicly announced the arrival of "democratization" after the implementation of its first direct presidential election. The official announcement was ironically followed by the downfall of the very social activism that had led to the movement itself. Social and political activism was crippled not simply by the "Thermidorian reaction" of the regime but also, more important, by the activists themselves, who became directionless with the fall of the Berlin Wall in 1989, the demise of the Soviet Union in 1991, and the social atmosphere celebrating the end of ideological struggles and the victory of liberal democracy—a historical context detailed in Francis Fukuyama's well-known book *The End of History and the Last Man* (1992). Nevertheless, the early 1990s was also a time when increasing social inequality and political violence clouded the official claim of democratization, thereby challenging many students to grapple painfully with new possibilities for resistance.

Chinese socialism remained one of the ideals we students held on to—and, more precisely, wanted to hold on to—in our quest for viable political and social options. Despite the implementation of its Open Door Policy in the late 1970s, we recognized China as a country that had not abandoned the term "socialism." Above all, in our desperate search for new political possibilities, our eyes were directed less toward the perplexing present embodied by the Tiananmen massacre of 1989 than toward the epic past of the Chinese Revolution and the Long March. We read and widely disseminated the biography of Lei Feng, a model worker in Mao's era; his devotion to the Chinese people reminded us of Chun Tae-il, whose suicide protest in 1970 awoke South Korean workers to a political awareness of their miserable condition. We were not fully aware that Lei Feng, unlike Chun Tae-il, was publicly celebrated not for his defiance of but for his loyalty to sovereign rule. Despite the different names for "the people" in China and in South Korea, Lei Feng's moral purity and his rallying cry "Serve the People" inspired us to revive the rusty slogan "Power to the People" and long for the time when authenticity and idealism had been respected in our society.

Nevertheless, I felt, "the people" (*renmin*) invoked by the Chinese socialist model worker was becoming an outdated and even anachronistic term. In 1997, while living in Beijing for language training, I went to a theater to see *The Days without Lei Feng* (*Likai leifeng de rizi*). Audiences for the movie consisted of only a few foreigners—not "the people" to whom Lei Feng allegedly had devoted himself. "Nobody would go to see the movie except in a group viewing with free tickets," a friend of mine remarked cynically. Colleges at the time were plastered with posters celebrating Hong Kong's return to China. In the memoirs of intellectuals as well as in contemporary official accounts, the period of the Cultural Revolution was portrayed as ten "lost" years of suffering. "The Internationale," the famous anthem of international socialism once sung by protesters in South Korea, was solemnly played at the funeral of Deng Xiaoping, a leading helmsman who helped steer the People's Republic toward a market economy. Hearing the stirring anthem in that new context in Beijing, I decided to temper my emotional attraction to China's socialism and to study carefully what had actually been happening in that nearly unknown land for almost half a century.

Interestingly, two summers of preliminary research in 2004 and 2005 enabled me to witness a deluge of the very same socialist nostalgia that I had chosen to curb personally. I went in search of "the people" haunting the old industrial cities of northeast China. Impoverished workers conjured up the Maoist past as they experienced massive layoffs amidst the restructuring of state sectors. Anger, despair, and sadness loomed large in the streets, factories, and residential compounds when workers witnessed the sudden rise to wealth of those they called "snakes with glasses" (*yanjing she*). These "snakes" were the same intellectuals whose membership in "the people" had always been questioned in Mao's era. Now the "snakes" were profiting while workers despaired of the party-state that had once given them a voice but was now implementing the layoffs. Furthermore, those workers were saddened to find their suffering described as "inevitable" in public accounts and to hear themselves called "useless" by those in power. Accordingly, they ceaselessly brought up the history of "we the people." One laid-off worker told me with a sigh: "These days, the *haves* celebrate Deng Xiaoping while the *have-nots* miss Chairman Mao. In the days of Chairman Mao, we workers were the masters of the country. We had respect in society. Today's society, however, wants us to disappear as soon as possible."

The two summers I spent in China observing widespread layoffs and worker despair may not have revived my withering attachment to the country's socialism, but it did ignite my desire to explore further how "the people" haunted public discourse. Through subsequent fieldwork (2006–2008) in Harbin, a city in northeast China, I witnessed how impoverished workers' invocation of "the people" complicated governmental interventions that attempted to make these workers legible as "the poor." Like *minjung* in South Korea, *renmin* had no fixed referent but was laden with multilayered tensions and temporal shifts of meaning. Unlike *minjung,* however, *renmin* gave both voice and leverage to many impoverished workers as they continued to negotiate with the Chinese state. Originally coined and invoked by the party-state, *renmin* raised legitimate claims that could not be overlooked by the officially socialist state.

In this book I explore China's experience and management of poverty as the fast-growing market economy brought about ever-deeper immiseration among erstwhile socialist workers. My account draws on ethnographic materials collected during twenty-six months of fieldwork in Hadong, a decaying residential area of a former work unit in the city of Harbin. Impoverished workers whom I met in Hadong have not merely been reduced to "the poor." Once celebrated as the ideological representatives of "the people," they are now mocked as ignorant dropouts from the market economy. Once honored as a hub of socialist industrialism, their region—northeast China—now epitomizes the remnants of the planned economy. Such a historical shift matters because, despite several decades of market-oriented reforms, China persists in proclaiming "socialism" to be the nation's official ideological doctrine. Impoverished workers grapple with old socialist signifiers, laying claim to the rubric of "the people," the very name by which the party-state once identified and venerated them.

By making not the standardized category of "the poor" but the histori-cally informed category of "the people" an object of inquiry, I situate the study of poverty in a wider discussion of class, political subjectivity, and state governance. The management of poverty thus becomes not merely a techni-cal project for alleviating individual impoverishment but a contested arena in which the relationship between the nation-state and its subjects is being reconfigured.

By shedding light on the multilayered tensions embedded in the claim of belonging to "the people," my approach also unveils the complex and often contradictory ways in which impoverished workers not only experi-ence and respond to their changing positions but also involve themselves in state projects for governing poverty. Although these workers assert that they exemplify "the people," their claim often contradicts governmental direc-tives regarding how "the people" should be reborn as self-managing sub-jects. When these workers invoke their memories of "equal poverty" in the socialist past, such recollections unexpectedly resonate with and even nour-ish the neoliberal quest for wealth in their economically thriving socialist country. Furthermore, against the backdrop of the nation's enduring urban-rural divide, state governance differentiates between urban workers and rural migrants, as those who once stood separate from each other as claimants to the title of "the people" now stand together under the common condition of the urban poor. Urban workers make "the people" an exclusionary claim, often expressing antagonism toward rural migrants.

In all, "the people" (*renmin*) still haunts the experience of urban poverty and its management in northeast China, whereas "the people" (*minjung*) in South Korea has faded away in the consciousness of both its creators and those who were designated as such. Whom *minjung* should fight against has become unclear owing to "the dual effects of political democratization and economic liberalization" (Shin 2011: 12), particularly after the Asian finan-cial crisis in the late 1990s (Cho 2005; Song 2009). Not only in South Korea but also in many capitalist societies around the globe, the "regime of disap-pearance that seeks to erase poverty from popular and political conscious-ness" has become a neoliberal feature of dealing with poverty (Goode and Maskovsky 2001:15). In the old industrial bases in northeast China, however, impoverished workers are far from invisible despite their marginalization. In the *People's* Republic of China, they are continuously narrating the old his-tory of "we the people" and invoking the old maxim of "Serve the People." In this book, however, I show in detail how laying claim to "the people" ends up being precarious as new possibilities for resistance are sought. It is precarious not just because the concept of "the people" is "unitary" (Hardt and Negri 2004: xiv) but because it is exclusionary and subject to volatile uses by state forces as well as by the poor themselves.

Fieldwork on Poverty in China

While conducting preliminary fieldwork in urban centers of northeast China in 2004 and 2005, I found that research on poverty was mainly conducted in the form of survey sampling (*chouyang diaocha*). Poverty was considered one of the "social problems" (*shehui wenti*) that social scientists—mostly economists or sociologists—were expected to diagnose and solve in partnership with policymakers. The common practice was for researchers to send questionnaires to local governments, or for graduate students to go directly to rural villages or urban shantytowns with survey questions. In most cases they were temporary visitors rather than long-term sojourners.

"Wenying [the Chinese equivalent of my Korean name], you don't have to go find the poor for yourself. Once you make up the questionnaires, I will have students go to several shantytowns to distribute them. No worries!" When the professor in Shenyang, a city in northeast China, simplified my rambling request for access to a fieldwork site in this way, his answer contained two significant implications. First, he assumed that research on poverty does not call for lengthy fieldwork. Particularly in northeast China, where the discipline of anthropology is very rarely taught at the university level, local scholars may be forgiven for assuming that "anthropologists" dig for fossils or conduct surveys on ethnic minorities. Second, and more important, the professor implied that urban poverty is a sensitive topic, and foreigners' straightforward, inquiring presence is not welcome. In the PRC, the party-state remains the primary domain for managing urban poverty. While "antipoverty programs" in the countryside have embraced intervention from international agencies and foreign NGOs, most poverty-related programs in the cities have been run directly through bureaucratic channels of the party-state. Furthermore, taking action on behalf of the poor has been considered one and the same thing as acting in "the nation's general interests," as part of the state's preoccupation with "social stability." No government officials would appreciate a scenario in which a foreign student circulated through shantytowns where laid-off workers might give vent to angry outbursts at any moment.

Given the circumstances, I had to spend two summers searching for a research site. I had decided on northeast China, but where? A good friend of mine in Beijing led me to his hometown—Fushun in Liaoning province—assuring me: "All my family members are laid-off workers. They will help you." Once famous as a pilgrimage site for admirers of Lei Feng, the industrial city was notorious for massive layoffs and sit-down strikes on railways when I visited in 2004. A family of laid-off workers with whom I stayed for two weeks allowed me to glimpse their predicament. Local scholars as well as government officials kindly hosted a feast for a foreign student from the United States. Yet realizing that my interest lay not in investment but in research on poverty, both scholars and officials kept me waiting for permission until I finally gave up after a year. Another attempt in Shenyang, the capital of Liaoning province, also ended in failure. Researchers in the Liaoning Academy of Social Sciences kindly agreed to sponsor a visa for me, but for my "safety," they wanted to impose limitations on where I could visit and with whom I would travel. In fact, the long quest to find (or to be presented with) a research site illuminated some of the ways in which the issue of poverty was problematized among various interlocutors.

My journey finally ended in August 2005, when I visited Harbin, the capital city of Heilongjiang province. Like many in northeast China, Harbin is a city where the collapse of the manufacturing sector inherited from socialist planning has led to high unemployment (Yan 2001; Yin and Guan 2004; Li 2005; Yin 2006; Hsu 2007; Hanser 2008).[1] I was also intrigued by the historical reversal of the city, in which its history as a socialist industrial base became "invisible" while the general public as well as government officials and scholars attempted to restore the city's reputation as the "cosmopolitan" hub it had been prior to 1949 (Wolff 1999; Lahusen 2001; Carter 2002). How can we understand the impoverishment of the representatives of socialism amidst the silencing of their recent past and the celebration of old colonial histories?

Fortune, as usual, arrived by accident. Through a short-term language program in which I participated in Harbin, I was introduced to a sociology professor at the Harbin Institute of Technology who was preparing her own dissertation on social networks among poor residents in Harbin. She often spoke with me about issues of poverty in China and brought me along with her to Harbin's shantytowns, where she had done her research. Intimacy formed by chance eventually superseded the official channels I had followed for two years. The professor invited me to join her department as a research fellow and, furthermore, helped me find a research site by mobilizing her network (*guanxi*). I tried to return the favor by helping graduate students prepare their masters' theses or by introducing them to anthropological theories and methods.

The primary site that this book addresses is Hadong, a decayed residential area (*jiashuqu*) of a former work unit in east Harbin.[2] Like many other residential compounds operating under the aegis of a bankrupt work unit in China, Hadong is a place experiencing spatial upheavals as it declines from honored workers' village to shantytown (*pinminku*). The Fenghuang work unit in Hadong was once a large-scale state-owned enterprise that in its heyday had more than fifteen thousand workers.[3] It announced its official bankruptcy in December 2005, however, after a decade-long downward slide. Most retirees, laid-off workers, and their families were barely managing to survive through the support of meager pensions, temporary work, or other governmental assistance. Furthermore, like many other peripheral urban locales in China, Hadong is a place where impoverished urban workers and rural migrants—who never thought of themselves as sharing a common situation—have had no choice but to live together, given the breakdown of both the household registration system and the urban work unit system. Out of a total population of about 55,000, the number of migrants (*wailai renkou*) was almost equal to that of the urban population (*changzhu renkou*), although the number of migrants was still less than 10 percent of the entire population, according to official data from the local government.

In Hadong I spent most of my time in street-level government offices—one "street office" (*jiedao banshichu*) and eleven "Community committees" (*shequ jumin weiyuanhui*)—as well as residential areas. These venues allowed me to observe the interaction between Community cadres and poor residents, among different levels of government officials, and between poor urbanites and rural migrants, as well as to conduct in-depth interviews with all these informants.[4] Except for participating in a weekly meeting in the street office, where local government officials in Hadong all convened, I conducted my research in highly unpredictable and irregular circumstances—from filing documents about local residents in a Community office all day to tracking unexpected disputes such as "the *shoufei* incident" discussed in chapter 6. Flexibility is the destiny of—and a blessing for—an ethnographer who seeks "the actual performances of social life" rather than "underlying 'real' identities and orientations" (Ferguson 1999: 97–98). To observe the interactions between my informants, I accompanied street-level officials on their field trips, helped them with computer work in local offices, tutored the children of local residents in the neighborhood, and joined other temporary events such as job training, elections, and audits. I also obtained meaningful data while lingering in individual houses, on streets, in retail markets, and in government offices.

This account of my journey begins with Hadong but does not end with it. Increasing doubt about the value of a "fixed" field (Marcus 1995; Gupta and Ferguson 1997) has led many anthropologists to avoid staying within the boundaries of a village rather than commuting among variously inter-connected venues. Nevertheless, the critical emphasis on mobile fields need not cause us to abandon entirely the ritual of thick participant observation, which the "village studies" of classical anthropology achieved in the past. In this book I focus, in a sense, on both a "train station"[5]—Hadong—and "trains" that stop at Hadong, have already left Hadong, or pass by Hadong. Passengers in these trains, to name a few, include urban laid-off workers and retirees who inevitably remain in their dilapidated housing, former residents who left Hadong much earlier than others and grabbed golden opportuni-ties for entrepreneurship, or rural migrants who chose to leave their land and temporarily stay in Hadong. To understand both the changing conditions in Hadong and various trajectories of its people, I often left Hadong for other destinations, among them higher-level government offices, rural vil-lages distant from Harbin, and even luxurious gated communities in down-town Harbin.

Reflecting these concerns, this book consists of an introduction, six num-bered chapters, and a conclusion. The introduction presents my primary arguments as well as theoretical and regional commitments. It situates the specter of "the people" within wider discussions of poverty, class (subjectiv-ity), and state governance in and beyond China.

In chapters 1 and 2 I examine the experiential contradictions of impover-ishment that urban workers and their families are facing in Hadong. In chap-ter 1 I explore impoverished workers' collective nostalgia for the Fenghuang work unit and their invocation of "the people" as these workers try to seize their place in history by highlighting their contributions to and sacrifices for their former work unit. This claim, however, is not sufficient to unite them under the title of "the people." I detail the tensions embedded in invoking "the people" by historicizing work experiences and family lives in Fenghuang as well as the complex relationship between Fenghuang workers and peri-urban farmers in Hadong. This chapter also makes geocultural statements about the book's main stage, northeast China (*dongbei*), as a mirror of the socialist working class. In chapter 2 I illustrate the complexity of "the poor" as a category by examining the crazed pursuit of new housing in Hadong. Impoverished workers often gamble their savings to satisfy their aspirations for new commercial housing despite their de facto inability to afford it. Their pursuit brings to light dynamic and ambivalent processes of impoverishment in the unexpected encounter between the historically unique condition of China's working classes and the recent neoliberal quest for wealth.

In chapters 3 and 4 I look at the complex workings of government pro-grams relating to urban poverty by documenting the mundane interactions between street-level officials and poor residents as well as among different levels of state officials. Chapter 3 builds on my discussion of the minimum livelihood guarantee, the party-state's primary policy for dealing with urban poverty since the late 1990s. This chapter details the resistance of urban laid-off workers in Hadong against attempts by the government to reduce poverty to a technical problem and explores how their resistance has had the unintended outcome of excluding many of them from the scheme. Chapter 4 focuses on the state's campaign of "community self-governance" amidst the collapse of the work unit system. I explore how the remapping of state practices through "community" is made possible not through "the will to empower" of voluntary citizens (Cruikshank 1999) but through "the will to survive" of Community cadres. Mostly female laid-off workers, these cadres attach themselves to the old Maoist doctrine of self-reliance to cope with their liminal, vulnerable position. In both chapters I show how paradoxical outcomes arise when impoverished workers claim that they are exemplary of "the people," contradicting government initiatives that entail new rationales about what and who "the people" should be.

Chapters 5 and 6 move on to the tension between impoverished urban workers and the other poor, that is, rural migrants. Chapter 5, an ethnography of one migrant woman ragpicker in Hadong, examines why and how rural migrants, in contrast to poor urbanites who still give weight to their attachment to the state, have come to identify themselves as social outcasts outside the purview of the state's care. I demonstrate that these rural migrants experience exclusion at the very site where they are formally included. Chapter 6 examines the processes of differential impoverishments, meaning why and in what way poor urban residents and rural migrants have reinforced mutual distinctions instead of recognizing that they share a common situation. This chapter traces the historically accumulated tensions deriving from the lack of communication between the two impoverished groups, and then explores state practices of dividing them, as well as these groups' contrasting responses to state appropriation. The collection of community fees (*shoufei*) by street-level officials in Hadong serves as an ethnographic example. I demonstrate how these officials, who are urban residents as well as state agents, circulate and intensify the fear of, anxiety about, and even antagonism toward rural migrants in their day-to-day lives. Urban laid-off workers and rural migrants now live cheek by jowl in China's cities under severe economic duress but rarely unite as "people" owed common state protection. As this chapter shows, the uncontrollability of rural migrants, which is the very outcome of state governance, opens up a space for resistance that is not entirely controlled by the state.

ACKNOWLEDGMENTS

This book would have been impossible without the enormous patience and unfailing hospitality shown me by numerous people I met in China. People in Hadong and elsewhere, who must remain anonymous, filled my fieldwork with their passion. Yin Haijie, a professor at the Harbin Institute of Technology, deserves special thanks. From finding a research site to solving unexpected difficulties, she literally made my fieldwork possible by her courageous support. Other scholars and friends also helped me immensely, making northeast China my second home. Many thanks to Wang Yalin, Liu Er, Wang Shusheng, Li Songhua, Li Bin, Zhou Lin, Huang Zhe, Mei Mei, Xia Quanwei, Huang Wenyan, Chen Junwei, Chen Zhipu, and Li Yan and her parents. *Xiexie nimen dui wode guanhuai!*

I am truly indebted to James Ferguson. I knocked on his office door and asked him to direct my project because I was so excited by the first class he offered at Stanford, the Anthropology of Neoliberalism. Since then he has been a dedicated adviser to me, and my excitement over his brilliant scholarship has never abated. Matthew Kohrman deserves my bottomless gratitude for challenging me to clarify and sharpen my analysis. Not only his incisive comments but also his genuine support throughout my study kept me from doubting my ability to complete the project. My great thanks also go to Li Zhang. Her dissertation, which I read a long time ago, steered my interest toward the problem of inequality in China. Perhaps the only way to repay her invaluable guidance would be to channel and extend this inspiration toward others.

The Stanford Department of Anthropology provided immense support. I am grateful to Sylvia Yanagisako, Liisa Malkki, Paulla Ebron, Miyako Inoue, Ellen Christensen, and Shelly Coughlan for taking care of me both academically and personally. Many thanks to my cohort and other conversation partners: Tania Ahmad, Kevin O'Neill, Zhanara Nauruzbayeva, Oded Korczyn, Stacey Camp, Rachel Derkits, Serena Love, Ramah McKay, Erica Williams, Thet Win, Yoon-Jung Lee, Tomas Matza, Rania al Sweis, Neta Bar, Jocelyn Chua, Nikhil Anand, Hannah Appel, Elif Babul, Robert Samet, Dolly Kikon, Curtis Murungi, Kutraluk Bolton, Bruce O'Neill, Rachael

Miyung Joo, Hantian Zhang, Chengdiao Fan, Joe Segar, and Yeon Jung Yu. They have taught me what it means to study *together* and how academia can be a friendly and communal place.

The Center for Chinese Studies at UC Berkeley, where I stayed as a post-doctoral fellow, provided a pleasant environment for starting my book project. I miss the thought-provoking conversations and companionship with Aihwa Ong, Andrew Jones, Hong Yung Lee, Kevin O'Brien, Lan-chih Po, Wen-hsin Yeh, Xin Liu, You-Tien Hsing, and Elinor Levine. Special thanks to Aihwa for guiding this book with critical intervention. I am also grateful to Zhanara Nauruzbayeva, Daniel Gallegos, Steven Lee, and Matthew Gil-liland for making Oakland a spiritual shelter and realizing the "community" that we need to achieve.

Yonsei University in Seoul, South Korea, has been an ideal place for completing this book and deepening my thinking process. I thank my new colleagues Cho (Han) Hae-Joang and Kim Hyun-Mee in the Department of Cultural Anthropology for their friendship and support from the bottom of my heart. Their intellectual vigor and unceasing efforts to create "the common" in our society keep me from drowning in self-sufficient elitism. I have benefited greatly from insightful discussions and conversations with other colleagues in the College of Social Science, the Graduate Program in Culture and Gender Studies, and the Institute of Korean Studies at Yonsei University, as well as in warm intellectual communities in Shinchon.

Members of my community in South Korea have remained strong pillars of support throughout my work. I am grateful to my advisers Kim Kwang-Ok, Lee Mun-Woong, and Oh Myung-Suk and to other teachers in the Department of Anthropology at Seoul National University for welcoming me to the forest of anthropology and encouraging me to make my own path through it. This book is, I hope, my small gift for the retirement of Professor Kim Kwang-Ok, who earnestly taught me how to love China as an anthro-pological location. This gratitude also extends to other China specialists in South Korea, to just name a few: Baek Seung-Wook, Baik Young-Seo, Chang Ho-jun, Chang Jung-a, Cho Young Nam, Chung Jae Ho, Jang Soo Hyun, Jang Yoon-mi, Jang Young Seog, Jeong Jong-ho, Lee Hui-ok, Lee Hyeon Jung, Lee Eung-chel, Park Choong Hwan, Seo Jung Min, Won Jae-Yeon, Yang Han-Sun, and Yang Young-Kyun. Special thanks to Jang Soo Hyun, Pak Sunyoung, Juhyung, Sun-ah, Seung Taik, Kyung Mook, Simpei, Heyon Jung, Jeehwan, Hyun Sook, Dongju, Yung-Jin, Kangwon, Gowoon, Geun Young, and Kiho for recharging my energies with cordial advice, challenging critiques, and drinks. I also thank Wang Li, Yu Shujing, and O Seung Min for their sincere assistance in preparing the draft of this book.

I have also benefited from a cluster of colleagues who offered helpful questions and comments at numerous conferences, seminars, and workshops. My thanks to Alan Smart, Andrew Kipnis, Andrew Walder, Dorothy Solinger, Elizabeth Perry, Jean Oi, Jesook Song, Jie Yang, Lisa Hoffman, Lisa Rofel, Philippe Bourgois, Seung-Wook Baek, Liping Sun, and Jun Tang. Roger Haydon, my editor in Cornell University Press, deserves a great deal of credit for his insightful, patient guidance, and enthusiasm for this project. I am deeply fortunate to have had such an attentive and supportive editor in this long journey. I am thankful to Dorothy Solinger and the anonymous reviewer. It was an absolute pleasure to receive extremely detailed comments and suggestions from such capable and thoughtful readers. Thanks also to Susan Specter and Amanda Heller for their brilliant editorial help.

I acknowledge the following financial sources that made my research possible over the years: the National Science Foundation, the Wenner-Gren Foundation, the Stanford University Department of Anthropology, the Stanford University Center for East Asian Studies, the Stanford University School of Humanities and Sciences, the Stanford University Freeman Spogli Institute for International Studies, the UC Berkeley Center for Chinese Studies, and Yonsei University.

Portions of the following were previously published: chapter 3, in "On the Edge between 'the People' and 'the Population': Ethnographic Research on the Minimum Livelihood Guarantee," *China Quarterly* 201 (2010), 20–37; chapter 5, in "Forced Flexibility: A Migrant Woman's Struggle for Settlement," *China Journal* 61 (2009), 51–76; and chapter 6, in "Dividing the Poor: State Governance of Differential Impoverishment in Northeast China," *American Ethnologist* 39, no. 1 (2012), 187–200. I thank the publishers of these journals for permission to include these works in this book.

Finally, I thank my family, with a broad definition of kinship. My aunt's family in Sacramento has made my life in the United States less lonely and more delightful. I owe innumerable debts to Juhyung and his family in Gwangju. I may never be able to repay their enormous support and generous love. My sister Hyun Ju and her family also deserve my thanks. Their life is not easy, but it is full of hope and passion. Thank you for teaching me how to dream in a dreamless world. My gratitude also goes to my longtime friends Hwa-Jung, Yoon-Jung, Jong-Eun, Tania, Zhanara, Daniel, Sun-ah, Seung-ha, Yu-ra, Hoon, Seung-jun, Joo-han, Jun-yong, and Jun-bum. Thank you for filling my life with love, humor, and sincerity. This book is dedicated to my mom and dad. Thanks for allowing me to fly instead of keeping me in a cage. Thanks for making me who I am.

THE SPECTER OF
"THE PEOPLE"

Introduction

It was July 2008. The Beijing Olympics were just ahead. In Harbin, a city in northeast China more than 750 miles from Beijing, no Olympic events were taking place. Nevertheless, the Olympic Games were at the core of everyday conversation in Hadong, one of the city's peripheral shantytowns. People were thrilled, agitated, irritated, and worried about the largest and most extravagant event in the modern history of the country.

As the Olympics drew near, the tone in which street office director Li Yuming spoke to local cadres grew more somber. In a weekly street office assembly (*jiedao banshichu*) he announced: "The antigovernment forces opposed to the Olympics are lying low everywhere. Supporters of Tibetan independence as well as Falun Gong are hiding among vulnerable groups [*ruoshi qunti*]. You should find them. Also, don't forget to visit the families of the poor and disabled once a week. Don't forget to patrol the streets every day. No disreputable incidents should happen around the time of the Olympic Games!"

The anxiety of government officials was not entirely groundless. Among residents, conversations about the Beijing Olympics often extended to critiques against the state. One day in July I was on my way to a street market with Zhou Lin, a laid-off worker in her early fifties. On the streets of Hadong we witnessed a group of older retirees discussing the country's misfortunes. They were talking about a series of upheavals and disasters that had occurred earlier in the year, such as the crippling snowstorms in the southern regions, political unrest in Tibet, a train crash in Shandong, and the monumental earthquake in the province of Sichuan. We overheard one of the retirees attributing these misfortunes to the "wrath of Chairman Mao," saying: "Chairman Mao is as good as a god. Did you hear the rumor that his corpse in the mausoleum in Beijing was put away early this year? That's why all the misfortunes have happened. Look at the fate of our factory. The statue of Chairman Mao on the main building was removed twenty years ago. After that, our factory started to decline. Some factories where his statue stands have survived. How is it possible that Chairman Mao is not angry when we retirees are dying in poverty after three decades of work?"

"That's nothing but superstition," said Zhou Lin, who simply brushed off the remarks of the retiree. Finding a sharp rise in prices at the street market, however, she angrily returned to the topic of the Olympics to criticize the government: "The government has already spent 140 billon yuan on the Olympics. But it's said that we need at least 50 billion yuan to restore Sichuan following the earthquake. We could rebuild Sichuan more than twice over with the money that will be spent on the Olympics. How ridiculous! Yesterday I read in a newspaper that during the Olympics, the horseback riding competition is to be held in Hong Kong. Horses are supposed to be transported from the mainland to Hong Kong. I was shocked at the photo of a container for transporting each horse. The container was much bigger than my house. It even had an air conditioner. Now, our workers' lives are far inferior to the horses'. Look at this neighborhood. Who would believe it used to be an honorable workers' village?"

The anger felt by Zhou Lin and other workers died down on the evening of August 8. At that time everyone in Hadong watched the Olympic opening ceremony with breathless attention. With her eyes fixed on the TV, Zhou Lin said: "Who would've imagined China hosting such a big event? This proves that our country is no longer poor!" The next morning we overheard the same retirees who had brought up the "wrath of Chairman Mao" excitedly praising the ceremony. "It's true that our government spent a great deal of money on it. But we have the capacity to do so," said one. Another predicted: "Our Chinese players should sweep all the medals. Americans won't laugh at us anymore!" One told me: "Wenying, you should find a job in this country. China will defeat America, and soon become the wealthiest country in the world!" This time none of the residents brought up their experience of poverty. Rather, their key theme was that the Olympics would be a great opportunity to proclaim the end of the nation's long humiliation and validate its status as the world's economic superpower.

I went to China to investigate the experience of urban laid-off workers and retirees, who have been left out of the nation's burgeoning prosperity in a state of increasing immiseration. The nation's fast-growing economy has brought deep impoverishment to many urban workers, particularly in the Northeast, where old manufacturing cities, once a socialist industrial base, have become a moribund rustbelt. In the former cradle of socialist industrialism, urban laid-off workers and retirees are experiencing downward mobility at the moment when their country is being heralded as the world's emerging superpower.

How do urban workers experience and respond to their impoverishment? How is their suffering being managed in state projects for governing poverty? China continues to define itself as "socialist," despite having undergone several decades of market-oriented reforms. While statues of Lenin have been demolished in Russia and other eastern European countries, Mao's giant portrait still hangs in Tiananmen Square. Reproductions of his handwritten motto "Serve the People" are still displayed in China's government offices. Against this backdrop, the former socialist representative of "the people"—the urban worker—has been plunged into dispossession. Pointing to the "Serve the People" sign in a government office in Harbin, one laid-off worker remarked to me: "Do you know whose handwriting it is? Our Chairman Mao! The government should not abandon us if it wants to display Mao's handwriting and if China is still to be called a socialist country!"

The management of poverty becomes a challenging task when impoverished workers make legitimate claims that cannot be overlooked by the officially socialist state. In many capitalist countries where sudden prosperity has occurred simultaneously with a deep impoverishment of the masses, the pauperization of some has been held to be an unavoidable and necessary condition for the accumulation of wealth (Marx 1976; Geremek 1994). Seeing poverty as a necessary evil, however, cannot be easily normalized in a socialist country where the ruling party in this case the Chinese Communist Party— persists in promulgating Marxism-Leninism and Mao Zedong Thought as part of its guiding ideology despite increasing marketization. How can the state rationalize incorporating "the people" into "the urban poor" while regulating their poverty?

Yet, as in the instance of enormous popular anger having abated at the time of the Olympic Games, the former representatives of "the people" are not necessarily inclined to rebel against the officially socialist state. Contrary to exaggerated predictions in the global mass media regarding the outcome of Chinese protests, betrayed workers have not threatened the nation's development by causing social unrest. During my two years of fieldwork in this dilapidated shantytown in Harbin, I found that workers' ambivalent feelings about the reemergence of China complicate their perceptions and experiences of living in poverty. Facing appalling stories of corruption as well as the growing gap between rich and poor, my informants often simply sighed, saying, "This is what China is" (*zhongguo jiushi zheyang*). Anger and despair went hand in hand with delight and hope as they recounted the nation's growing GDP, China's important presence in world politics, the number of gold medals won by Chinese athletes, and so on.

These complexities shape the way in which the Chinese state is managing poverty. I argue that the management of urban poverty is not merely a technical project of alleviating individual need but a contested arena for the nation-state and its subjects. I explore this contestation particularly through the changing notion of "the people," a historically informed category that has profoundly shaped subjectivity in the intentionally named People's Republic of China. Since 1949 the PRC has proclaimed that "the people" (*renmin*) are the masters of the country and that the Party represents the interests of "the people." In his essay "On the People's Democratic Dictatorship" (1967: 411–24), Mao Zedong asserts that a People's Republic led by the working class, not a republic of the bourgeoisie, is the only path to save China from imperialist oppression. The People's Republic must be achieved, he writes, through "a people's democratic dictatorship under the leadership of the working class and based on the alliance of workers and peasants." The claim of being "the people" stems from the deeply Maoist ideological doctrine of "Serve the People," which emphasizes the intimate (and often paternalistic) relationship between the party-state and its subjects. Contemporary impoverished workers in northeast China grapple with their claim to be "the people" amidst their deepening impoverishment under market-driven reforms. They engage terms such as "the people" (*renmin*) and "Serve the People" (*wei renmin fuwu*) or otherwise conjure up the aura attached to those terms as they narrate their histories of impoverishment. By invoking "the people," the name by which the party-state once acknowledged them, these workers seek protection and recognition (C. K. Lee 2000, 2007; Baek 2007; Cho 2010).

The central argument of this book is that the invocation by impoverished workers of the category of "the people" has animated historically embedded tensions, creating unavoidable contradictions in China's management of urban poverty. Although many impoverished workers claim that they exemplify "the people," their assertions often contradict governmental initiatives that redefine who "the people" should be in contemporary China. Furthermore, this claim of being "the people" is exclusionary in that it fails to embrace rural migrants, the "peasants" who once constituted a primary component of "the people" along with the urban workers themselves. In short, any claim of belonging to "the people" is contingent, despite the category's semantic centrality in the PRC. "The people" is not fixed in specific referents. It haunts the government's management of urban poverty.

With an eye to the changing face of "the people," this book bridges poverty studies and class studies while challenging some discussions of both. First, my argument centers on the historically layered category of "the people" rather than the conventional category of "the working class." It reinterprets the oft-mentioned uniqueness of China's working classes not simply to point to the limits of collective mobilization but to unfold various ways in which impoverished workers grapple with the ambiguity of their historical position. Second, I incorporate an analysis of class interests into that of the "dispositions, desires, and subjectivity" entailed by the formation of class (Yanagisako 2002: 8, 178). By discussing workers' subjectivity beyond the dichotomy of resistance and submission, I produce a more versatile picture of the downward mobility these workers experience while living in a thriving socialist country. Third, this book, unlike most other empirical studies of poverty, neither reduces individuals living in poverty to the poor "population" for purposes of policy implementation, nor, unlike the conventional Western-based citizenship discourse, does it posit individuals in Chinese society as "citizens." Instead it reclaims the historicity of poverty while problematizing the very process whereby the onetime representatives of "the people" are converted into numbers without history or the autonomy that one is encouraged to cultivate in the name of "the citizen." Finally, this book does not merely address the heterogeneity of poverty. It questions *which* poverty matters in a specific society at a specific moment by paying attention to differential governance of as well as class conflicts between urban laid-off workers and rural migrants in northeast China.

"The People" as a Class versus "the People" as a Nation

By exploring China's impoverished workers not in terms of the classical category of the working class but in terms of the historically informed category of "the people," I situate these workers within the oscillating tension between "the people" as a class and "the people" as a nation. By investigating how government officials as well as impoverished workers are being caught between and negotiating the two, I hope to reveal not only the different styles in which resistant voices speak but also the precariousness of such styles.

Many scholars have addressed the historically unique condition of China's working classes, that is, the fact that the condition of the working class is *not* defined by its relation to production (Kraus 1977; Walder 1984, 1986; Li 1996; Li 1999; Rocca 2002b; Hsu 2007; Lee 2007; Hurst 2009). Richard Kraus, for example, analyzes the shift from class to status society in the Maoist era by giving attention to "the persistence of a class vocabulary designed for application to a pre-socialist society" and its role of concealing new occupational inequalities (Kraus 1977: 55).[1] Jean-Louis Rocca summarizes the singularity of urban labor during the Mao period in two respects. First, Chinese workers were not proletarians in a Marxist sense since they were not seen as people without means of production. As "both workers *and* owners of means of production,"[2] these working classes had no "enemies of class" (Rocca 2002b: 7).[3] And second, across all aspects of social life, workers were entirely dependent on their work unit (*danwei*), in which the life-tenure job was the rule. These workers "constitute a privileged social category and the *danwei* interests seem to override the class interests" (Rocca 2002b: 9). To these observations I would add the ambiguous nature of the "master" (*zhuren*), a title that China's socialist regime once granted workers. Despite their de facto subjection to the work unit system, workers were encouraged to speak as the "masters" of their work unit during frequent political campaigns. Yet these workers were masters without servants—or slaves—who would recognize them as such.[4] The self-certainty of these masters was problematic because it was obtained through the recognition not of servants but of the party-state, which workers often viewed as the "real" master.

Underlining the historical uniqueness of China's working classes, however, does not need to be reduced to demonstrating the limitations of their capacity for resistance.[5] Social scientists engaged in labor studies tend to bring up this uniqueness in order to address the *unmaking* of the working class, that is, the fragmentation or cellularization of workers' resistance. They focus on how Chinese workers, lacking "class enemies," seek different interests in terms of different benefits from different work units, rather than mobilizing cross-unit lateral movements (for example, Walder 1984: 40–41; Zhang and Yin 2000: 34; Rocca 2002b: 7–10; C. K. Lee 2007: 70–73, 111–13). If we no longer limit the idea of workers' resistance to class struggle based on the relation of production, however, what we witness in China is not the absence or incompleteness of resistance but a different style of resistance (cf. Won 2005).

On the urban periphery in northeast China, the impoverished workers whom I met did not just remind me how they used to be celebrated as the masters of the country but also emphasized their sacrifice for and contribution to the nation's development (see chapter 1). Arif Dirlik (1989) asserts that both socialism as an ideology of revolution and socialism as an ideology of national modernization have deep roots in the history of Chinese socialism. Since the reform, however, the regime has promoted only the latter instead of reconciling the two. Most of my informants were keenly aware that "national development" continues to be a powerful signifier amidst the ideological re-articulation of Chinese socialism.

It is in this context that I examine the condition of impoverished workers in terms of the changing face of "the people," thus engaging with "the people" as a nation as well as a class. These workers may be considered "abnormal" if we limit our analytic lens only to the Marxist understanding of the working class. Giorgio Agamben argues that what is called "the people" in Western politics was not a unitary subject but a "dialectical oscillation between two opposite poles," that is, "on the one hand, the set of the People as a whole political body, and on the other, the subset of the people as a fragmentary multiplicity of needy and excluded bodies" (1998: 177). In modern China, the discussion of such duality emerged as part of the project of nation-state building when China's intellectuals newly discovered "the people" as a project of salvation in the late nineteenth and early twentieth centuries (Duara 1995). Sympathy for the anonymous and often excluded *min* (people) was prevalent among early Marxists as well as the New Youth intellectuals.[6] Yet at the same time these intellectuals identified "the people" as the political subject who would salvage the nation from the invasion of imperial powers. When the Chinese Revolution of 1911 led not to a unified form of sovereignty but to the chaotic vicissitudes of local politics, intellectual debates centered on how China might emerge from its humiliating position and rebuild itself as a powerful, modern nation-state.

The figure of "the people" was at the core of these debates. Significantly, it was doubted as well as celebrated. Many intellectuals, including early Marxists, questioned whether "ignorant and backward" people would be qualified to rescue their nation (Anagnost 1997; Judge 1997; Chen 2003). For example, Li Dazhao, one of the founders of the Chinese Communist Party, did not conceal his distrust and anxiety about the people's capacity to build a new society: "We Chinese are beggars rather than robbers. Without working, we only care about how to steal or beg others' meals. Imagine that one large factory is built in the world. Imagine the coming of a day when people all around the world come to work and eat together. Where in the world is the place we Chinese can stand?" (Li 1984: 593–96)

The oscillating tension between "the people" as a class and "the people" as a nation seemed to abate with the founding of the PRC in 1949, when Maoist socialism gave excluded bodies a legitimate voice as "the masters of the country." In official accounts of the PRC, the intellectuals' profound distrust of "the people" was replaced by the Maoists' open celebration. Mao Zedong himself praised the alleged backwardness of "the people" in his famous "poor and blank" thesis: "Apart from their other characteristics, the outstanding thing about China's 600 million people is that they are 'poor and blank.' This may seem a bad thing, but in reality it is a good thing. Poverty gives rise to the desire for change, the desire for action and the desire for revolution. On a blank sheet of paper free from any mark, the freshest and most beautiful characters can be painted" (1990: 36). As historians have fully addressed, China's Maoist socialism invoked and built upon the people's capacity and willingness as well as their openness to engage in the nation's development and in revolutionary struggles. In contrast to orthodox Marxism, it looked for the decisive factor in history not in the objective forces of historical development but in the consciousness of the popular masses (Meisner 1999; Dirlik 1989; Hsu 2007; Anderson 2010).[7]

In post-Mao China, however, the rhetoric surrounding "the people" no longer celebrates the alleged "backwardness" of peasants and workers. The tension between "the people" as a class and "the people" as a nation has intensified as the post-Mao Chinese state has claimed the nation's economic wealth and discarded egalitarianism (Dirlik 1989). The old debates over the so-called character of the Chinese people, a question that many intellectuals raised with suspicion and anxiety a century ago, are being revived in the current discussions over improving the "quality" (*suzhi*) of the Chinese people. Impoverished workers and peasants, who once constituted the primary classes of "the people," are considered the most problematic populations in these debates (Yan 2003b; Anagnost 2004; Greenhalgh and Winckler 2005; Kipnis 2006).

For impoverished workers whose lack of education raises doubts, therefore, invoking "the people" as subjects who are willing to sacrifice themselves for the nation-state is a double-edged sword. Their narratives of sacrifice and contribution seem to harmonize with the regime's current tendency to reduce socialism to "an instrument in the cause of national development" (Dirlik 1989: 38). Sadly, however, these narratives hinge on the Maoist past, not the present. Furthermore, in modern-day post-Mao China, "the people" as a class is overshadowed by "the people" as a nation. The rhetoric of the former celebrates urban workers as the masters of the country. Yet the rhetoric of the latter considers them to be shadowy subjects of a "reemerging"

China (see chapter 4). Workers are affected by this rhetoric because they are intensely attached to both the socialism of the past and the present market economy. How do impoverished workers grapple with the very ambiguity of their historical position while living in a "reemerging" China? To address this question, I now expand the discussion of class, engaging the formation of "class subjectivity" to capture various lived experiences that are not reducible to resistance.

Class Subjectivity and Downward Mobility

What does it mean for the former representatives of "the people" to experience impoverishment while living in a thriving socialist country? When China overtook Japan as the world's second-largest economy in 2010, journalists were busy weighing China's "continued growth" against its "impending collapse." Those who advocated the theory of collapse highlighted the growing gap between rich and poor. Noting how the country still lagged far behind its rivals in per capita GDP,[8] they warned that China's new poor, especially betrayed urban workers, would threaten the nation's development by causing social unrest.

Although their analysis is more nuanced, many social scientists engaged in labor studies also tend to assume that impoverished workers are either potential social threats or revolutionary forces. This is so because they explore the relationship between the poor and the party-state solely in terms of "resistance," for example, by asking: What curbs collective mobilization? Why are some forms of resistance widespread while others are not? (e.g., Chen 2000; Blecher 2002; Cai 2006; Perry and Selden 2003; Rocca 2002b). Paraphrasing Jacques Rancière's words, however, I oppose the assumption that the proletarian has only one thing to do: to create the revolution. Resistance is surely one significant theme for helping us understand the ordinary lives, rituals, and struggles of impoverished workers. Nevertheless, much as I noted in the previous section, the various historical dynamics that complicate the relationship between workers and the state do not have to be reduced to legitimating the limits of collective mobilization. I hope to present a more flexible and complicated picture of impoverished workers and how they encounter "the state" in their daily lives.

Therefore, the question I ask is how these workers construct a particular form of class subjectivity rather than why these workers fail to develop an antagonistic working-class consciousness. Today most scholars would agree that class is as much cultural as economic and that it is not simply a set of self-regulatory structural givens but is "in the making" (see Zhang 2010: 14).

I am reminded of E. P. Thompson's famous words: "The [working] class did not rise like the sun at an appointed time. It was present at its own making" (Thompson 1964: 8). In this vein, Sylvia Yanagisako views the formation of class subjectivity as a series of processes in which "people come to see themselves as having particular goals and interests and particular identities" (2002: 100). Although treating all "interests" as cultural representations risks missing "the distinctiveness of the concept of class through which we make sense of the structure of inequality" (Park 2011: 6), I draw on Yanagisako's insight about the *temporal* dimension of class, that is, "how people's ideas about their identities and their interests are formed in relation to both their past social trajectories and their present location" (2002: 100). Such a temporal dimension of class subjectivity is important because it enables us to explore how workers perceive and experience their downward mobility in their complex relationship with past socialism as well as with the present market economy. To advance this inquiry, let me first provide some comparative contexts for China's shifting political economy.

In many postsocialist countries of the former Soviet Union, industrial workers are considered to have been the hardest-hit victims of economic liberalization during the 1990s. Amidst the wholesale privatization of previously publicly owned assets, workers have seen their longtime worksites sold to private investors, and especially to foreign companies, for their scrap value. Facing situations ranging from job insecurity to overdue wages to massive layoffs, these workers have fallen to near the bottom of the social hierarchy (Wedel 1998; Müller 1999; Desai and Idson 2000; Kideckel 2002).

In China, pro-market restructuring under economic reform was much more gradual than in the former Soviet Union and was, in addition, controlled by the central government. The collapse of the urban work unit system was not simultaneous with the reform that started in the late 1970s.[9] Although some institutional and legal reforms for restructuring state-owned enterprises were designed in the early 1980s, they were not fully implemented right away in consideration of social stability. The dismantling of the "iron rice bowl" in state-owned enterprises did not become conspicuous until the mid-1990s, when the party-state finally began to take strong measures to privatize most enterprises while retaining the state ownership of key defense-related and high-technology industries (Naughton 1997; Rocca 2000; Cai 2006; C. K. Lee 2007). During the period of economic restructuring from 1995 to 2001, the number of workers in the state sector fell from 113 million to 67 million (Giles, Park, and Cai 2006: 61). The number of workers who were owed unpaid wages increased from 2.6 million in 1993 to 14 million in 2000 (C. K. Lee 2007: 5).

Accordingly, despite differential institutional paths taken by each country, one frequently hears of instances of appalling consequences that former socialist workers have faced under a new market economy. It is hardly surprising that ethnographic studies of impoverished workers in postsocialist contexts have described their circumstances in the language of denigration, for instance, "the subalternization of labor" in Romania (Kideckel 2002), "the declining power of worker solidarities" in Poland (Kalb 2009), or "protests of desperation" in northeast China (C. K. Lee 2007).

Yet the processes through which the subjectivity of impoverished workers is being reshaped in post-Mao China are more contradictory and ambiguous than these scholars suggest. In the past, China was one of the socialist countries where the revolutionary consciousness of "the people" was greatly appreciated. China has since become *the* most thriving socialist country that has successfully survived under market-oriented transformations, serving as an engine of the world economy. The reformulation of subjectivity is thus temporarily informed by both the past and the present, or, more specifically, by the interrelation between the two. The reformulation of subjectivity among impoverished workers in northeast China is contradictory, however, because these workers are intensely *and* ambivalently attached to both past socialism and the present market economy.

To begin with, workers' ambivalent attachment to China's socialist past is seen in their claim to be of "the people." From the mid-1960s to the mid-1980s, the Soviet Union was mired in the long "period of stagnation," when the popular vision of socialism completely withered away under the inertia of bureaucracy and the reduction of economic growth (Anderson 2010: 70). During this period, in contrast, China's masses were caught up in the vortex of "revolutionary excess" (Dutton 2005: 4; Feuchtwang 2002: 196). Despite enormous contradictions and grim consequences, the Cultural Revolution provided workers with memorable opportunities to tear down the established social order, including the Party, in the name of "the people." As I show in detail in this book, however, the privileged status of "the people" was always incomplete and problematic. It was often belied by persistent hierarchies dividing urban workers from peasants and male workers from female workers. Insurgent labor politics were frequently overwhelmed by traumatic violence, and welfare secured under the urban work unit system was overshadowed by everyday suffering under a shortage economy.

The nation's revitalization and the growing gap between rich and poor deepen workers' ambivalent attachment to the present market triumphalism. Ethnographies of postsocialist societies including Russia, Central Asia, and eastern Europe often begin with descriptions of collapse, violence, or other sociopolitical crises (Burawoy and Verdery 1999; Nazpary 2001; Volkov 2002; Oushakine 2009; Shevchenko 2009). Such descriptions document the harsh actualities of economic liberalization, under which not just workers but the entire population have suffered from a massive social and economic crisis in their everyday lives. The position of China's impoverished workers in relation to a wider society differs from that of workers in many other postsocialist countries in that Chinese workers are witnessing their status wane while their country is emerging as an economic superpower. They are becoming the new urban poor while their former comrades are enjoying sudden wealth by seizing new opportunities offered by economic reforms. Such arresting contrasts attach impoverished workers to the new market economy in highly ambivalent ways. Hopes and frustrations are inextricably intertwined in their everyday lives: hope that they can catch up with others' success in the nation's swiftly growing economy and frustration that they remain poverty-stricken despite the nation's emerging prosperity; hope that they may enjoy the unprecedented availability of commodities and frustration that they remain mere spectators of the nation's "consumer revolution" (Davis 2000).

These ambivalent attachments lead me to frame the cultural meaning of downward mobility in terms of its relationship to larger social transformations. In her seminal work *Falling from Grace,* Katherine S. Newman provides a cultural analysis of downward mobility by focusing on the lived experience of the American middle class. She articulates the experience of downward mobility as a "fall from grace," which means "to lose your place in the social landscape, to feel that you have no coherent identity, and finally to feel, if not helpless, then at least stymied about how to rectify the situation" (1988: 11). Newman suggests that the analysis of downward mobility should embrace not only economic hardship but also the cultural, social, and psychological consequences of losing one's "proper place" in the world (8). The metaphor "losing one's proper place" aptly describes the sense of loss and frustration that many laid-off workers and retirees whom I met in northeast China come to feel when they are no longer celebrated as honored workers but rather mocked as ignorant dropouts from the market economy. Such a metaphor, however, cannot explain the sense of hope and aspiration that these impoverished workers maintain at the same time in the nation's rapidly growing economy. My analysis complicates the experience of the downwardly mobile by probing how they associate their individual lives with those of other social groups (especially rural migrants) as well as with larger social transformations.

Many impoverished workers I met in Hadong are indeed living in ambiguity. They neither simply resist nor submit.[10] Instead they alternate between frustration, depression, and hope while struggling to survive in the most thriving socialist country in the world. Lived socialism—and its complex encounter with pro-market restructuring—thus raises the problem of governance: How can poverty be managed when impoverished workers make legitimate claims that cannot be overlooked by the socialist regime? Furthermore, are these workers the only poor living in the cities?

When Does Poverty Matter? Whose Poverty Matters?

Why and in what way have "the urban poor" become a target population for policy implementation and scholarly projects in recent years in China? This question may seem odd, as well as less significant, for poverty researchers who measure the poor population empirically and determine its demographic variables. What they are concerned with is how to define "the poor" and depict their complex composition according to a series of variables including income, expenditures, housing, work, location, and so forth. Such an ahistorical approach, however, does not fully answer a number of questions. For example, why do many Chinese, including scholars and government officials, often argue that urban poverty is a "new" phenomenon that has emerged for the first time in the People's Republic? What does it mean that the term "urban poverty" did not appear in official documents until very recently (Wu et al. 2010: 5)?[11] Some studies answer these questions in part by paying particular attention to urban workers—laid-off or unemployed workers, low-income workers, and retirees—as China's "new" urban poor (Kernen and Rocca 2000; Wu et al. 2010; Wu and Webster 2010). With an emphasis on "new," they articulate the institutional and structural forces behind China's urban poverty, linking it to "broader processes of urbanization, economic restructuring and the reorganization of social welfare and provision" (Wu and Webster 2010: 11; cf. Khan and Riskin 2001; Y. Wang 2004; Solinger 2006).

Like those studies, this book focuses on "workers" among the larger category of the poor and situates their predicament within China's shifting political economy. Unlike those studies, however, it centers on the impoverishment of urban workers not because they account for the highest percentage in the composition of the urban poor, but because the particular ways in which these workers are governed enables us to examine the changing relationship between the nation-state and its subjects in this officially socialist country. In other words, my analysis does not simply supplement previous studies on China's urban poverty with ethnographic data; rather than position urban workers among diverse poor groups, I focus on them as the former representatives of "the people," thus problematizing the ways in which scholars and government officials have conceptualized them as "the urban poor" and produced a particular kind of poverty knowledge.

For this purpose I engage meaningful insights that Foucauldian studies have offered in relation to "governing." By loosening governance from its moorings in the nation-state, Foucault's notion of "governmentality" (1991) has allowed scholars to identify various ways in which government programs are articulated through social institutions and even individuals. Beyond the historical account that sees governmentality as a new form of exercising power in European societies, what I find more exciting in this concept is that it seeks to "interrogate the problematizations through which 'being' has been shaped in a thinkable and manageable form" (Rose 1999: 22). This problematization enables me to claim that poverty as a condition of economic impoverishment does not necessarily correspond to poverty as a social problem for government. Likewise, there is "no universal object, the governed," in relation to which policymakers may proceed to act (Rose 1999: 40). I would suggest that only a specific form of poverty and a specific group of the poor matter in a specific society at a specific moment. Scholars have succinctly argued that the birth of "the poor" as a separate class that requires governing is a historical invention (Procacci 1991; Dean 1992; Escobar 1995; Chatterjee 2004). Yet this argument can be applied not only to the birth of "the poor" as a class but also to the way government officials or other agents who manage poverty select a particular form of "the poor" for governing.

This argument is significant for understanding the contested ways in which urban poverty has been formulated and managed in the PRC in recent times. Although the main players in my ethnography are urban workers, they are not the only poor in Chinese cities. In fact, mainstream academic histories tell us that Chinese cities have always contained large numbers of disadvantaged groups throughout the socialist regime. In the Maoist period, many seasonal, temporary, and contract workers had only very limited access to labor insurance benefits that were fully enjoyed by permanent workers in state-owned enterprises (Whyte and Parish 1984; Walder 1986; Lü and Perry 1997). Many of these workers held a rural household permit (*hukou*), which made their presence in the city contingent and precarious (Meisner 1999). In addition, there have always been people without any sources of support, that is, orphans, the elderly, widows, or the disabled. These people formed the majority of the "three no's," those who traditionally received meager, if any, relief from the government (Wong 1998: 113). More important, since the early 1980s, about 150 million rural migrants, those other key players in my ethnography, have flooded China's cities in search of work.[12]

Excluded from the government's urban antipoverty schemes, many of these migrants live in conditions far worse than those endured by the "new" urban poor and former outsiders (Solinger 1999, 2003; Khan and Riskin 2001; Lu 2004; Ngai 2005; Yan 2008).

Despite such multiple forms of the poor, it is important to note that nationwide governmental interventions for dealing with urban poverty in the post-Mao era started not in the early 1980s, when numerous rural migrants began to flood into the cities, but in the mid-1990s, when urban workers began to experience massive layoffs amidst the country's widespread restructuring of state-owned enterprises. Such governmental interventions initially centered not on all the poor but on urban workers. Many policies such as the reemployment project, the urban minimum livelihood guarantee (*dibao*), unemployment allowances, and housing subsidies reached their full-fledged form in the late 1990s, when massive layoffs of urban workers led to widespread social unrest (Cho 2010: 24–27).

Significantly, it was these laid-off workers, not other categories of the poor, who had been both the ideological representatives and the main beneficiaries of the socialist regime. Although both urban workers and peasants were celebrated as "the people" in the Mao period, however, socioeconomic benefits fell only to the urban workers, in keeping with the state's concentration on heavy industry at the expense of agriculture (Oi 1989; Meisner 1999; Yang and Fang 2003; Naughton 2007). Many urban laid-off workers have protested against local governments and their work units by invoking the very language with which the party-state once acknowledged them. Most prominently in northeast China, an old industrial base of the planned economy, these workers have mobilized historical discourses and performances that have evolved around the socialist concept of "the people" (C. K. Lee 2000, 2007; Weston 2004; Hurst 2004, 2009; Baek 2007; Cho 2010). It is in this context that the Chinese state has given more attention to urban laid-off workers than to other categories of the poor, thus buttressing both the claims to morality and the stability of the socialist regime.

In comparison, rural migrants were not a crucial target for state welfare policies until the mid-2000s, when China's new leaders realized their significance in upholding the nation's economic position as the world's factory. Not since China's economic reforms began in the late 1970s had there been such an outpouring of heartfelt concern and attention given to rural migrants, who used to be widely stigmatized as "dirty, silly, poor, aimless, uncivil, congregating, and money-driven" (Zhang 2001: 32). Aiding and protecting migrant workers in the city was the linchpin of the leaders' overall push to pursue growth based on a low-wage strategy.

This book shows how, against the backdrop of the nation's enduring urban-rural divide, impoverished urban workers and rural migrants are not viewed together as the urban poor but instead are often governed differentially (see chapter 6). The governing of poverty perpetuates their differences not merely by excluding these poor people from the wider society but by dividing them against each other. Such division is made possible not by a singular, intentional project of specific bureaucrats but through the "porous array of intersections" (Rosaldo 1993) of various governmental interventions. Expanding an anthropological "field" both temporally and spatially, I probe the temporality of state policies, disjunctive layers of state actions, and the positionality of state agents in order to show the contingent ways in which the selective management of poverty comes into being. Such a porous web of governance opens up a space for friction which is not entirely controlled by the state, as is evident in the minimal capacity of government officials to regulate rural migrants. Whereas studies of governmentality have tended to focus on the process of normalization, evincing more interest in how subjects are governed than in why (and how) governing fails (Dean 1992; Rose 1999), I prefer to draw attention to the "messy" processes and outcomes of state governance (cf. O'Malley, Weir, and Shearing 1997; Gupta 2001; Kohrman 2005; Kipnis 2007, 2008; Li 2007).

To return to the question of "governing," in this book I draw on Foucault's notion of governmentality not only as an analytic but also as a mode of a subject-making project in which new kinds of categorization and classification are undertaken through specific policies, programs, and campaigns. Of significance is that impoverished workers are not automatically reduced to the ahistorical population nor to being seen as self-regulating citizens. This book points to conflicting dialogues between impoverished workers and state agents, showing how the voices and actions of the governed, often elided in the discussion of "governing," inform and interfere with state governance to a great extent.

The Population, the Citizen, and the People

How are China's impoverished workers constructed and regulated when they are subject to state practices of governing poverty? Nikolas Rose defines governance as "any strategy, tactic, process, procedure or program for controlling, regulating, shaping, mastering or exercising authority over others in a nation, organization or locality" (Rose 1999: 15). Such an activity is, he argues, "both made possible by and constrained by what can be thought and what cannot be thought at any particular moment in our history" (1999: 8). Significantly, the rationale inherent in invoking "the people" is thinkable enough among many laid-off workers who expect recognition and acknowledgment for their contribution to national development. It is nevertheless questionable among many government officials and poverty researchers who need to render these workers "governable" for policy implementation or who believe that "the people" should be reborn as self-managing citizens equipped with high "quality" and a good education. Today these interlocutors of China's urban poverty mobilize new analytical categories such as "the population" (*renkou*) and "the citizen" (*gongmin*), whether they are conducting collaborative projects with international agencies or discussing whether or not laid-off workers are qualified to participate in the nation's continued development.

In this book I investigate these new categories of subjectivity, focusing on their problematic role in shaping notions of who the poor are and should be. Instead of naturalizing these categories as globally circulated discourses, I explore how they are understood and sought in their complex relationships to the localized form of subjectivity—"the people." In particular, I delve into the issue of how impoverished workers are often caught between the "self-sacrificing" principle of "the people" and the "self-managing" principle of "the citizen," as well as between the political stage of "the people" and the numerical table of "the population."

The question of "the population" begins with an anecdote. One day in July 2007, a laid-off worker, Zhou Yongming, visited the government office in Hadong. He was dissatisfied with a recent decision to exclude him from the minimum livelihood guarantee (*dibao*). He had been excluded, a street-level official told him, because he had begun to work in the factory again. Zhou retorted: "Don't you know how many times the factory stops running? I've not received even one yuan! Look at me without just repeating bullshit regulations. Shouldn't you serve the people? Isn't it ridiculous that we workers are dying in poverty after sacrificing our entire lives for the state? We sacrificed ourselves for the Party. We lived just as the Party wanted us to!"

Dibao has been the party-state's primary program for addressing urban poverty since the late 1990s. Like many other policies responding to the problem of unemployment, it arose out of the Chinese government's increasing concern that social instability would accompany massive layoffs and labor protests. Yet the historical origin of *dibao* is in striking contrast to its ahistorical design. That design is tied to the emergence of new rationales that normalize these former workers into "the population," that is, into numbers without history.

Like Zhou Yongming, however, "numbers" do not necessarily remain silent. They still speak out and make themselves heard in the actual process of governing. In this book I argue that the question of "the population" provides a window into the shifting politics of (post)socialism because the question, above all, pertains to the changing relationship between the nation-state and its subjects. I particularly explore the tensions that arise in the reconfiguration of this relationship by centering on those who are governed. In particular, what does it mean for those who were associated with "the people" to be newly incorporated into "the population"? How do they themselves understand the distinction between "Serve the People" and "Serve the Population"?

The distinction, to borrow Michel Foucault's terms, is that between "the sovereign-subject relationship" and "the government-population relationship" (2007). Foucault argues that, in contrast to the sovereign-subject relationship, the government-population relationship is no longer based on obedience or the refusal of obedience because the population is a datum on a series of variables.[13] In this sense, the shift from "Serve the People" to "Serve the Population" means that the direct negotiation or confrontation that workers experienced in their relationship to the party-state is being made invisible.[14] Visible performances between the party-state and impoverished workers become unnecessary because these workers are reduced to a series of variables and their face-to-face dialogues are replaced by the calculation of numbers.

This book shows how impoverished workers do not necessarily subject themselves to but continuously struggle with the new gazes and techniques directed toward them. The political platform of "the people" is not entirely replaced by the numerical table of "the population." Almost every day in the government office in Hadong, Zhou Yongming and many other residents work to restore what many scholars have criticized as a "sloppy" Maoist legacy. They are reluctant to be reduced to "the population." Instead they invoke "the people," trying to reclaim their historicity and political status under the socialism of the past while making their relationship to the party-state visible and palpable (see chapter 3).

In addition to "the population," this book also examines "the citizen" as a new object of government. Under Western theories of the social contract, the citizen is commonly understood to be a person who, as a member of a nation-state, has both rights and responsibilities. Citizens create a "civil society," in which they enjoy autonomous rights in return for their conforming to law or political authority. Many scholars, however, have questioned the conventional assumption that civil society is an autonomous and self-constituted realm that contrasts with the state. They have argued that the relationship between the state and civil society is mutually constitutive rather than antagonistic and that "civil society" as the opposite pole of "the state" does not actually function autonomously even in European countries (Gordon 1991; Comaroff and Comaroff 1999; Rocca 2002a; Ferguson 2006; Holston 2008).[15]

Not taking the development of "civil society" as the primary condition for grassroots movements, this book raises particular questions. For example, why and in what way has the language of "civil society" (*gongmin shehui*) or "citizenship" (*gongminquan*) become dominant in China's recent policy implementation and scholarly projects? How does the new discourse of citizen-making pertain to the management of poverty? And how do impoverished workers interpret and respond to the tension between "the people" and "the citizen"?

Currently in the PRC, the discourse of citizenship has emerged not only to describe an ideal type of political status but also as a governing rationale that pushes citizens to regulate their own conduct. As Ching Kwan Lee argues, legal activism based on "citizens' rights to legal justice" (*gongmin de hefaquanyi*) is preferred particularly by young migrant workers in the south, who never experienced the socialist work unit system (Lee 2007: 8–13, 27). In the northeast, however, the enduring voice of "the people"—more precisely the historically paternalistic relationship between the party-state and its people—makes workers reluctant to insist on their "rights" to receive protection from the government. There I found citizenship discourses predominating not so much when workers adopted law-based discourses to articulate their political demands as when they were encouraged—often forced—to ask themselves "what the good citizen should do" (cf. O'Neill 2010: 14).

This book ethnographically details the workings of the state's campaign of "community self-governance" to explore how government officials mobilize the techniques of citizen-making in sites of poverty management (see chapter 4). The invocation of "community" (*shequ*), as a new basic component of urban governance that has replaced the collapsed work unit, has raised awareness among many scholars. They have selectively embraced the idea of "community" as a valorized alternative for coping with the crisis of state sovereignty and proclaimed a "citizen" (*gongmin*) of the community to be an "advanced" and "educated" partner of the state, not an opponent to it.

What I witnessed during my two years' fieldwork in Hadong, however, is that the meaning of "voluntarism" and "empowerment" that the idea of "community" invokes was often reduced to the mere shifting of the state's workload to the local level. Various kinds of responsibilities that the government should take in institutional ways were loaded onto the shoulders of street-level cadres, mostly female laid-off workers. These workers were recruited as Community[16] cadres through the policy of "public posts" (*gongyixing gangwei*), a policy that the government introduced in hopes of reemploying large numbers of laid-off workers in their forties and fifties. One cadre said to me: "This policy shows how our socialist country still differs from other capitalist countries. It's a policy that the state introduced to rescue workers. It proves that our state did not abandon us and still respects our contribution to the country." Such conviction, however, has been dampened by the new rationale regarding how "the people" should be reborn as self-managing "citizens" who no longer depend on the state. Instead of presupposing the citizen as an idealized, autonomous subject, I suggest that we need to problematize the very autonomy that the citizen is encouraged—and often urged—to cultivate, as reflected in moral slogans like "empowerment" and "voluntarism."

CHAPTER 1

In Search of "the People"

On the morning of August 14, 2006, I headed to Hadong with a friend from the Harbin Institute of Technology. He and I got off the bus at Taiping Bridge and transferred to another bus to Hadong. As the bus reached a bridge across the Harbin East Railway, nothing could be seen for all the dust. Our bus was barely able to cross the bridge and then could not budge another inch. Trucks loaded with junk, buses headed toward nearby rural villages, and donkey carts with odds and ends of food were chaotically entangled. No traffic police could be seen. The impatient driver changed his route and abruptly entered a street market. The bus did not reach its stop until it had bumped against a fruit cart and torn down a tent, while the passengers endured curses from angry vendors.

What greeted me after this unexpected adventure was a contrast in dullness. Thirty to forty men were milling around a couple of billiard tables in the street at an entrance to the main road in Hadong. After passing a local market where many of stalls were vacant, my friend and I encountered a couple of grand but empty buildings. One had been the Cultural Palace of the Fenghuang factory, the other its reception hall. With their backs against those buildings, a cluster of retirees in Mao suits gathered like a flock of doves, chatting with one another. After we walked along narrow, winding paths, the residential compounds of the Fenghuang factory finally came into view. Old single-story houses (*pingfang*) were lined up in a row, while a few multistory

FIGURE 1.1.   Central street (*zhongyang dajie*) in Daoli (June 2005)

FIGURE 1.2.   Residential compound of the Fenghuang work unit (August 2006)

apartment buildings (*loufang*) were sparsely located. "I'm afraid that you had a great deal of difficulty coming here. This place is now no better than a shantytown [*pinminku*]. You should go to the central street [*zhongyang dajie*] to see the real Harbin," a Community cadre welcomed me on my first visit— half with pleasure and half with anxiety.

Harbin is the capital of Heilongjiang province in northeast China, and Hadong, literally translated as "east of Harbin," is part of the Daowai district of Harbin. The people of Hadong, however, are in Harbin but not of it. Their neighborhood is excluded from the topographical history of Harbin when government officials, journalists, and even scholars evoke the city's earlier life in the late nineteenth and early twentieth centuries. In their accounts, Harbin remains a polyglot place that advanced from a small fishing village to a "world-famous city overnight" (Meng 2000: 6). They rewrite the city's colonial history in terms of cultural diversity and cosmopolitan openness. The portrait of Harbin they attempt to reconstruct begins with the story of the railway. The Russians' construction of the Chinese Eastern Railway (1898–1903), and then the opening of the Songhua River port, dramatically transformed the remote village into an arena of competition among the former Soviet Union, Japan, China, and Western countries during the first half of the twentieth century. The influence of Russia declined after its defeat in the Russo-Japanese War (1904–1905), and thereafter several thousand nationals from thirty-three countries settled in Harbin. White Russians who had fled after the Russian Civil War (1918) and Jews who had escaped the Holocaust found a refuge there. Japanese who had settled in search of better lives and Koreans who had fled from Japanese colonial exploitation in their home country also sought a new life in the city (Lahusen 2001; Carter 2002).

The first three decades of the twentieth century—before the Japanese occupied Harbin in 1932—dominate the official "history" of Harbin, generating a wide array of attention to the "polyethnic" and "multicultural" city (Wolff 1999). In fact, the area covered by this "history" of Harbin in the late 1920s constitutes less than 30 percent of today's Harbin, and only about 1.4 percent if one adds to the city proper seven counties and three county-level cities in suburban Harbin. Foreigners lived in only two districts, Daoli and Nangang.[1] Yet the modern story of this limited area is now widely presented as the "history" of Harbin owing to its contribution to the city's reputation as a "cosmopolitan" hub, a reputation prized in most post-Mao cities. The central street in Daoli (figure 1.1), abounding with a variety of European-style buildings, has become a crucial stop on the urban pilgrimage on which government officials first guide visiting businesspeople from China and abroad. Some old Russian- and Western-style buildings were destroyed during the Cultural Revolution. Yet other "survivals," which stand out sparsely among rows of dreary concrete buildings in Nangang and Daoli, have become must-see spots for tourists. They represent the living present for those who desire Harbin's rebirth as a hub of international investment and development.

Hadong is representative of what the old historiography no longer represents: the working class, the factory, and dust. The specter of "the people" haunts this former workers' village. Men and women in Hadong frequently invoke "the days of Chairman Mao" as a time when, they say, they were greeted with social recognition and honor as the masters of the country. When I first arrived in Hadong, it had been more than three decades since Mao died and China's reform (*gaige kaifang*) started. Cultural Revolution posters were still sold in street markets. Mugs and certificates—old prizes from the Fenghuang factory—were displayed in many houses. Impoverished workers frequently invoked "the people" when they spoke of the past, when they chatted about newspaper articles—mostly reporting some embezzlement or corruption scandal involving government officials—or when they argued with local cadres over state policies.

This chapter focuses on such invocations of "the people" and "the days of Chairman Mao." These claims gain significance when Hadong residents mobilize their collective nostalgia for "Fenghuang," that is, the work unit which officially declared bankruptcy in December 2005 after a decade-long decline. When I speak of invoking "the people," I do not mean that impoverished (ex-)workers use terms such as "the people" (*renmin*), "working class" (*gongren jieji*), and "Serve the People" (*wei renmin fuwu*) in their everyday life, at every moment or in every thought. I mean that these workers frequently conjure up the *aura* attached to these terms when they narrate their histories of impoverishment or press for their right to governmental protection. Individual failure or fate is rarely a cause to which they attribute their poverty. Rather, these workers give to their impoverishment weight by linking it to the larger social transformations under which their status has shifted from "the people" to "the poor." Unwilling to become "the poor," they grasp at invocations of "the people" in response to the invisibility of their position and indifference to their history.

Beyond detailing specific ways in which invoking "the people" manifests itself, my discussion in this chapter probes the tensions embedded in the very claim. Not all workers were privileged as "the people" who deserved protection and recognition from the party-state. The production of "the people" has occurred unevenly along lines of male and female, state and non-state, and urban and rural relations. I thus trace the inherent multiplicity of "the people" while extending both the temporal and spatial terrains of Fenghuang and Hadong. To begin, I explore how gender inequality has been historically structured through the division of work sectors within the Fenghuang work unit. The enduring division between state-owned *gongchang* and collective-owned *gongsi* in Fenghuang reveals a gendered dimension to the people's "sacrifice." Next I examine the split within "the people" through the uneasy relationships that urban workers have forged with nearby peri-urban farmers (*cainong*) and newly arrived rural migrants. The historical rural-urban tension within "the people" looms large as these urbanites struggle to re-territorialize the increasingly blurred boundaries of urban and rural spaces in Hadong. All these issues will unfold differences, ambiguities, or contradictions that have been sedimented under the banner of "the people."

Before detailing how the claim of belonging to "the people" is invoked, questioned, and pluralized in Hadong, I want first to explain the topography of northeast China (*dongbei*), one of the places to which those who live in Hadong have a profound emotional attachment. On a territorial scale, northeast China encompasses Harbin; Harbin encompasses Hadong; yet Hadong and northeast China are locations that the new "history" of Harbin no longer encompasses. Rather than imagining each place as one in a graduated series, however, I prefer to detach them from a presumed succession of locales in order to establish how each one gains its own significance not on a regional scale but as an independent place-name[2] in the historiographies of those who try to attach their own affective causes to it. Thus, "northeast China" is represented here as a place-name through which my informants contemporize their past experiences of pride, honor, recognition, and membership in a wider society.

Northeast China: Mirror of the Socialist Working Class

In 2007 an article in the *Phoenix Weekly* (*Fenghuang Zhoukan*), a Hong Kong magazine, stirred up a heated controversy in China. The title of the article was "The Revitalization of the People of the Northeast Should Precede the Project of Revitalizing the Northeast" ("Zhenxing dongbei, xianzhenxing dongbeiren"). Not surprisingly, the article is full of biting satire, describing why "northeasterners" should be blamed for their own decline. It begins with the author's testimony: "I have lived away from my home, *dongbei* [the northeast], for so long. My friends often say that northeasterners are no good—they get angry easily and like a fight. Last month I finally visited home after a long absence. I was surprised that many small new shops stood in a row on the street. On that street, however, a fellow cursed and picked a fight as soon as he felt offended. . . . I witnessed the very scene that I thought I had wiped out of my memory. *Dongbei!* This is *dongbei!* I could not but deplore the fight scene. *Dongbei,* you have not changed a bit even though I left you more than a decade ago. Your appearance may have changed. Yet your barbarous talk and behavior have not changed at all."

The stage on which my work is set, northeast China (*dongbei*), is thus home to people who, according to the author of the article, are lazy, ignorant, unsophisticated, belligerent, and swaggering. His sarcasm was disturbing to those who remembered that the honorific title "eldest son of the republic" (*gongheguo de zhangzi*) was conferred on the very same northeasterners in Mao's era. Northeast China, including administratively the three north-eastern provinces of Heilongjiang, Jilin, and Liaoning, used to be a socialist heartland in the People's Republic of China. It was a staging area for the People's Liberation Army during the Civil War from 1945 to 1948 as well as an advance base during the Korean War from 1950 to 1953. In the first three decades following the PRC's founding, northeast China maintained its role as "the eldest son" of the republic by serving as the national base for China's heavy industry.

Before 1949, northeast China, often called Manchuria, never appeared at the center of mainstream Chinese histories. Despite being the homeland of the Manchus, who established the Qing dynasty (1644–1912), the region had remained a sparsely populated, "empty" land.[3] The Qing dynasty prohibited

FIGURE 1.3.   Map of northeast China (dotted area)

Chinese migration in order to preserve the Manchu way of life from the Han Chinese. The prohibition (*fengjin*) against migration was gradually relaxed because Chinese settlers became a valuable source of taxation revenue for the Manchu banner armies and their families in the northeast regions (Elliot 2001). The prohibition was officially relaxed in the wake of severe drought and famine in the late nineteenth century in northern China (Li and Shi 1987: 19–25).[4] From 1891 to 1942, about 25 million poverty-stricken Chinese people left for the "empty land" of the northeast (Gottschang and Lary 2000: 2).

The celebrated history of northeast China began with the building of the People's Republic. The teleological narrative of the rise from hardship to glory, from the migration history of poverty-stricken refugees to the pioneer history of new socialism, appears seamless when northeasterners passionately narrate their story. In March 1950 Mao Zedong visited Shenyang, the capital city of Liaoning province, and proposed building an industrial base in northeast China. He suggested that the region should be a primary focus for national development, providing industrial products to China's other regions (Gao 2004: 25). Forced industrial development during the period of Japanese occupation, the early completion of land reform, and the early end of the Civil War helped make the three northeastern provinces ready for industrial development (Duara 2003; C. K. Lee 2007; Hurst 2009). During the first Five-Year Plan (1953–1957), 46 out of 156 key projects for national development were implemented in the northeast. Equipped with industrial facilities, and proud of a rich and vast land with little population, northeast China embraced the influx of people from other regions even after the founding of the PRC. Early on the state undertook to accept a population influx from the collective migration (*jiti yimin*) from overly populated provinces such as Shandong, Hebei, and Henan. Voluntarily or not, a large number of workers, cadres, engineers, and intellectuals from other regions came to northeast China to contribute to socialist development (Li and Shi 1987: 176–78).

Nevertheless, the pioneer phase of Maoist socialism did not last long. Northeast China in general declined from a socialist industrial base to a moribund rustbelt amidst the market reform. Deng Xiaoping's "opening" market reforms transformed the militarized, self-sufficiency-oriented development processes that had once attracted socialist planners into liabilities (Hurst 2009: 41; Chung, Lai, and Joo 2009: 109). Because of its high concentration of state sectors, northeast China suffered tremendously under the drastic restructuring of state-owned enterprises (SOEs) initiated by then-premier Zhu Rongji in the mid-1990s. As increasingly inefficient SOEs became an enormous burden to the national budget, the central government allowed banks to permit more SOEs to go bankrupt and then sold them off to domestic or foreign buyers. The region experienced nearly a quarter of the 30 to 40 million layoffs suffered nationally by SOE workers.[5] This restructuring led to more than three thousand worker strikes and protests every year in the late 1990s and the early 2000s (Kernen and Rocca 2000; C. K. Lee 2003, 2007).

The impoverishment of northeast China becomes clear in comparison with the great prosperity of coastal areas in south China which have welcomed both foreign investment and the state's strategic supports since the late 1970s. According to official statistical data, GDP increased by 73 times in Jiangsu, 109 times in Zhejiang, and 120 times in Guangdong—all in China's southern regions—between 1978 and 2005.[6] In northeastern regions, in contrast, GDP increased by 35 times in Liaoning, 44 times in Jilin, and 32 times in Heilongjiang during the same period.[7] The geographical proximity to past socialist allies such as Russia and North Korea is no longer seen as an advantage; rather it is the subject of self-mockery among northeasterners when seen against the proximity of southern coastal regions to Taiwan, Hong Kong, and other Southeast Asian countries, which has stimulated their prosperity.[8] In 2003 Guangdong province in the south accounted for 14.62 percent ($7.8 billion) of foreign direct investment (FDI) flows, while Heilongjiang accounted for only 0.6 percent ($0.3 billion) (Siddharthan 2006: 3).

In this sense, old industrial bases in northeast China, as well as coastal areas in south China, are exemplary sites for what Aihwa Ong, in exploring the metamorphosis of governmental techniques within one nation-state, calls "graduated sovereignty" (1999, 2006), that is, a flexible management of sovereignty. By tracing how a particular form of governmentality has emerged in China as an adjustment to the dictates of global capital, she suggests that "the nature of state sovereignty must be rethought as a set of coexisting strategies of government within a single national space" (Ong 2006: 95). Economic Development Zones in south China have been set apart as exemplary sites where the *exception* to sovereign rule is invoked to create new economic possibilities. I find that northeast China—as the counterpart of coastal areas in south China—is another example of graduated sovereignty. But whereas those coastal areas attracted foreign investment early on with the support of central and local governments, industrial bases in northeast China were considered the last bastion of state socialism—all the more so owing to the high percentage of state-owned enterprises. One laid-off worker in Hadong said to me with a sigh: "Just after market reform, the state let southern folks step on the accelerator while making us [northeasterners] step on the brake.

They ran fast, but we walked slowly. But now people blame us for the slow growth of our region."

In all, I argue, northeast China is not merely a geographical locale. It is an emotion-laden place-name for many (ex-)workers whom I met in Hadong and elsewhere in northeast China. An affective connection arises when these workers discover a common destiny between their own position and that of the place to which they belong, specifically the radical shift from intrepid pioneers of socialist industry to backward dropouts from the market economy. In this sense, "northeasterners" (*dongbei ren*) is more than an expression of native-place identity. The simultaneous decline of China's working class and northeast China prompts me to explore, borrowing from Sherry B. Ortner, "the hidden life of *class*" (1998).[9] When public discourses mock northeastern-ers for their radical shift from being the "sons of the Republic" to ignorant dropouts, their hidden criticism is directed, albeit not always, toward socialist workers, all the more so because of the historical position of northeast China as an incubator of socialist industrialism. Thus the categories of *dongbei* and *dongbei ren,* though colored by ethnic and cultural styles, in fact implicate the working class as the problem. This is the reason why northeast China has become a place where the claim of representing "the people" is invoked and challenged, leading to the political critique of the category itself. Northeast-erners often highlight the *dongbei*'s sacrifice for and contribution to national development; yet their claim is questioned and contested by public accounts, as in the sarcastic critique in the *Phoenix Weekly.* In these accounts, *dongbei* is often constructed as an "asymmetric counter-concept" of a re-emerging China (Koselleck 1985: 160), that is, as a place of negation that should be eliminated for the sake of China's successful market-oriented development. Hadong is represented as the place of negation by its residents themselves as well as by outsiders.

Hadong: Stories of Decline

One evening in December 2006, three men in their fifties were drinking at a hole-in-the-wall bar in Hadong. All of them had been laid off by Fenghuang within the past year. The "mysterious" buyout policy (*maiduan*) of their work unit was the subject of their conversation.[10] One of them complained: "In the days of Chairman Mao, people always did things according to the rules [*zhade jiushi zhade*]. Who would dare to disobey orders from above? Now, units change central documents as they like. On paper, we workers were supposed to receive a lump sum representing 1,700 yuan for each year of service in Fenghuang. But we got only 1,500 yuan.[11] Damn it!"

"Things were not that way in Mao's era." This is one of the most common refrains that I heard from middle-aged laid-off workers and older retirees during my two-year stay in Hadong. Their nostalgic remarks usually began, "In the days of Chairman Mao..." Few were interested in discussing a time "*before* the days of Chairman Mao" because, as one retiree said, Fenghuang factory was not built until 1950. Early settlers remembered Hadong prior to the construction of the factory simply as a "wasteland" (*huangdi*), where nothing had ever existed. Another term, *pinminku* (shantytown), frequently appears in the city and district gazetteers tracing Hadong's past. These gazetteers state that Hadong had been a small rural village (*tun*) in 1898 when the construction of the Chinese Eastern Railway was launched. Later it became a refuge for poor urbanites who lost their homes to the flooding of the Songhua River and the construction of the nearby railway station in the early 1930s.[12] Not until 1938, after the Japanese occupation, was Hadong officially incorporated into the city of Harbin.[13] From then on, the area's reputation as a shantytown began to harden. For example, more than 50 percent of the morgues in Harbin were located around Hadong by the late 1930s. Where the residential communities surrounding the Fenghuang factory now stand, the Japanese had built a camp for reeducating Chinese political prisoners. Although the Japanese had also built small-scale factories around Hadong, it remained "Harbin, but not Harbin" in the memories of longtime residents.

The building of the Fenghuang work unit radically shifted the reputation of the place from a "shantytown" to a "workers' village." When the Korean War broke out in 1950, the Chinese government decided to move some of the factories in Liaoning province, which borders North Korea, to Heilongjiang province for safety. That year, military, machine, paper-making, textile, and rubber factories were moved to China's farthest north.[14] Fenghuang was one of these factories: originally located in Shenyang, in Liaoning province, the state-owned enterprise was resettled in northern areas of Hadong in October 1950. One factory was built on old facilities that the Japanese army had left behind; most factories were newly built with the support of Soviet technicians. Some workers were recruited from the nearby countryside in the early 1950s, while others were reassigned from a parent factory in Shenyang. After the factory was established, however, recruiting workers became stricter: only persons with a "good" class origin and "superior political thought" were allowed employment in the work unit directly under the control of the central government.

The onetime "wasteland" was gradually transformed into a workers' village as single-story houses, schools, and hospitals for workers and their families were built between the mid-1950s and the early 1960s. The number of workers, no more than five hundred in the early 1950s, had increased to ten thousand a decade later. Workers at Fenghuang were guaranteed the best package of welfare benefits of all the factories in the area. All employees received free medical care from the unit, and their families paid only 50 percent of the usual medical fee. Patients requiring surgery that was too difficult to be provided at the work-unit hospital were sent to downtown Harbin, with full coverage from the unit. During the Cultural Revolution, except in its early violent stage, Fenghuang received protection from the military owing to the sensitivity of its products. The work unit even established its own collective farm near Harbin to prevent some of the workers' children from being sent to the remote countryside for labor (*xiaxiang*). After returning to Harbin in the late 1970s and early 1980s, these nominally sent-down youths became Fenghuang workers by "inheriting" the positions of their parents (*dingti*). When the number of returnees among workers' children increased dramatically in the late 1970s, the work unit attempted to absorb them by building more workshops within the unit. Pride and honor spontaneously arose through the comparison with workers in other nearby factories.

"Who would have imagined that so much prosperous factory work would die out all of a sudden?" Although most residents said as much, the notice of Fenghuang's "death," in fact, did not befall them "all of a sudden": like a cancer, the death of the work unit came on slowly, over a long period of time—almost fifteen years—until finally the factory officially declared bankruptcy in December 2005. The end of the cold war and other related changes in the national and international situation made most of the products it initially manufactured insufficiently competitive. After the 1980s, Fenghuang desperately tried to recover its solvency by diversifying into bicycles, motorbikes, and other alloy products. Still, it couldn't stop the decline. From then on, desperate efforts to overcome hardship became a main theme running through the factory's newsletter (*Fenghuang ribao*). In 1990, for instance, the Fenghuang director in his New Year speech stated: "Last year was rigorous and painful.... Our factory was mercilessly drawn into a whirlpool of serious loss. Yet our workers never flinched, but did everything to overcome hardship, thus making our factory survive despite difficulties.... The New Year has come.... We should not pin our hopes on the state subsidy. Our survival and development are possible only when we face up to difficulties, elevate our spirit, endure more hardships, and contribute more to our factory."[15]

Nevertheless, workers' efforts to endure the hardships never paid off. For about fifteen years, Fenghuang workers were "off duty" (*xiagang*), which meant that they lost wages and other social benefits though they still belonged to the work unit. Wage arrears became common. Most workers were on a "long vacation" (*changjia*) without any work. Hospitals for workers and schools for their children kept running despite the bankruptcy of the unit. Yet they were so poorly managed that even impoverished workers were reluctant to use them. The fate of the Fenghuang Cultural Palace, which is now no better than a haunted house, dramatizes the death of the work unit more vividly than anything else because of its magnificent size as well as its central location in Hadong. It no longer features such events as the Fenghuang art festival and the Fenghuang revolutionary song contest, let alone plays and films. More and more, residents do not hesitate to call their own community *pinminku,* the old reputation of Hadong prior to 1949—as their work unit is no longer willing to assume responsibility for mountains of garbage and broken water pipes, not to mention the angry laid-off workers and retirees. "We can no longer see the fireworks from this neighborhood," a laid-off worker said regretfully while cooking on the eve of the Spring Festival in 2007. He explained: "The display of fireworks in Hadong was really a grand sight. Every Spring Festival, Fenghuang spent more than 100,000 yuan for fireworks and firecrackers. Every family gathered around the Cultural Palace to see the fireworks. How exciting it was! Yet our work unit, like the fireworks, vanished completely." His remarks sounded even sadder because the streets of Hadong were so quiet that night.

Given such circumstances, narratives of sacrifice and contribution loom enormously large in local residents' invocation of "the people." In their accounts, Fenghuang's success, which once filled them with pride and honor, would never have been achievable without their selfless efforts. Their narratives are both more mundane and more individual than many social scientists and activists often imagine when they bring up the term "resistance." On street corners, in markets, and in local government offices, grievances against the work unit, and even against the party-state, usually begin with, though are not limited to, the scrupulous tabulation of disadvantages each individual has faced.

For example, sixty-five-year-old Yang Shaojun, whom I met on a street corner in Hadong, spit out his grievances about Fenghuang by bringing up the "ridiculously small" wage that he had received in the past. "Workers' wages were no more than 20 to 30 yuan [a month] in the 1950s and 40 yuan in the 1960s. It was not until I had been working fifteen years in Fenghuang that my wage finally reached 50 yuan." Yang had started work in 1958. "Imagine if you had to raise six or seven children on only 50 yuan! How harsh it was! Instead of paying us higher wages, the directors of Fenghuang returned a large margin to the state. They were different from today's corrupt cadres. Nevertheless, we workers had no complaints at all. In the 1960s to 1970s, we workers were full of passion. I mean it! Pure and simple, we truly wanted to live like Lei Feng [a model soldier in the Maoist era]. Like Lei Feng, we wanted to sacrifice ourselves for others."

Starting with grievances about the "ridiculously small" wages in the past, the narratives of older retirees often end with grievances about their "ridiculously small" pensions. Sixty-eight-year-old Li Lisheng, who was sitting next to Yang Shaojun, said to me and other neighbors: "How is it reasonable that we workers receive only 600 yuan a month for a pension while young actors on TV make hundreds of thousands of yuan? Whose contribution is bigger? Do you know what 'pension' means? It means that we people have the right to live as compensation for our contribution to the state." Li's friend Du Chao retorted, "Who cares about our contribution these days? Even in Hadong, nobody cares about us. Yesterday a meeting for original CCP members in Fenghuang was held in the street office. In the meeting we retirees let loose with our anger. Isn't it deplorable that we don't have even a small center for our activities despite our great contribution to Fenghuang?" These narratives of contribution are also widespread among middle-aged laid-off workers who recall their sacrifice amidst the decline of Fenghuang. Fifty-two-year-old Yu Jianghua told me about her futile attempt to help Fenghuang survive: "Around the late 1980s, it already seemed that Fenghuang had no chance of recovery. It was common that wages went unpaid for several months. Some workers had already left the factory in search of a better chance for making money. Still, most workers decided to remain in Fenghuang and spurred production to the end. Yet what is the consequence of our selfless sacrifice?"[16]

In the narratives of Hadong residents, the protagonists of "selfless sacrifice" are sometimes referred to as *dongbei ren* (northeasterners). As I noted earlier, *dongbei* (northeast China) is not merely a geographical locale but an emotionally loaded name for many workers whom I met in Hadong. These workers are deeply attached to the place precisely because the decline of northeast China from a socialist industrial base to a moribund rustbelt parallels their own fall from "intrepid pioneer workers" of socialist industry to the "ignorant dropouts" of a market economy. "Northeast China was called 'the eldest son of the republic' [*gongheguo de zhangzi*]. Do you know what that means? Northeast China was the first area liberated by the Communist Party during the Civil War. Since then, we *dongbei ren* have devoted our resources to the state without compensation. What came to us after all these sacrifices? Total neglect! Total betrayal!"[17] Laid-off worker Zhang Luoyong spit out these words as he told me how his father, originally from Shandong province, had settled in northeast China. After contrasting the workers' selfless sacrifice with the state's blatant betrayal, Zhang concluded his remarks by highlighting the contribution of the former to national development. "Deng Xiaoping said that 'development is the solid truth' [*fazhan caishi yingdaoli*].[18] National development is good, isn't it? That's the very contribution that we *dongbei ren* have tirelessly made since 1949!" Unlike "proletarian dictatorship" or "revolution," "national development" continues to be a powerful signifier throughout the socialist regime. The "floating" nature of the signifier allows Zhang and many other workers to anchor their logic of contribution and sacrifice in China's current paradigm of development. Yet whose sacrifice? This simple question, which I now address by exploring the historical problem of gender in the Fenghuang work unit, baffles workers themselves, making their invocation of "the people" highly ambiguous.

Gendered Sacrifice

"Although I started work in 1958, I have never taken off the 'poor cap' [*kunnan maozi*][19] in my life." Seventy-one-year-old Yu Jixiang always began with her reference to a "poor cap" whenever she told me about her harsh life. In Yu's accounts, *gongsi,* a local term for the collectively owned work unit sector, and *gongchang,* a local term for the state sector in the work unit, were distinct from each other. "My family was always poor, even though I worked like a dog. In Fenghuang, the final work assigned to me [before retirement] was to make fried dough at an eating house in the *gongsi*. Unlike work in the *gongchang,* work in the *gongsi* was diverse and miscellaneous [*za*]. In winter I began work by having to melt ice stuck in a frying pan. It was extremely cold, but I couldn't put on many clothes. I couldn't because those clothes were so thick with oil. I couldn't separate them. How grubby my work was! There is no way of getting out of poverty. All my children as well as I have never had a formal job throughout life." Yu Jixiang was a retiree in Fenghuang. Yet she never forgot to add that she was from the *gongsi,* not the *gongchang,* whenever I asked her about her work in Fenghuang: "You don't know how big the difference between *gongchang* and *gongsi* was! In Fenghuang, people were not the same at all!"

To understand the difference between *gongchang* and *gongsi,* one must first understand the complicated nature of the state-owned enterprise in China. Prior to economic reform in the late 1970s, work units in China's cities were classified into three categories based on their primary functions: (1) government or party organizations (*dangzheng jiguan*), (2) enterprises (*qiye danwei*), and (3) institutions (*shiye danwei*) (Y. Wang 2004: 30). The *qiye danwei* were classified into state-owned enterprises (SOEs) and collective-owned enterprises (COEs). According to the classification, Fenghuang was an SOE; the central government was the ultimate authority for its operation. This does not mean, however, that all sectors in Fenghuang were directly supervised by the government. For around three decades, the Fenghuang work unit, like many other SOEs, built various workshops under its own authority, for political or economic reasons; these workshops mostly belonged to COEs, owned by a "collective," that is, by the workers of the enterprise.[20]

Thus the difference between *gongchang* and *gongsi* that Yu Jixiang and other residents in Hadong commonly referred to is analogous to that between SOEs and COEs in China's work unit system. Although it is widely said that the work unit system guaranteed welfare packages for all its workers, this was by no means true for workers in COEs, who had very limited access to the full range of those benefits that permanent workers in SOEs enjoyed (Dixon 1981; Walder 1984, 1986; Whyte and Parish 1984; Solinger 1995; Lü and Perry 1997; Wong 1998; Rocca 2002b). Furthermore, the distinction between SOEs and COEs was far from gender-neutral. I turn now to a discussion of how gender inequality has been historically structured through the division between *gongchang* and *gongsi* within the Fenghuang work unit.

The gendered division of labor was not uncommon in Maoist China, although it was ideologically denied (Wolf 1985; Honig and Hershatter 1988; Bian, Logan, and Shu 2000; Liu 2007). Particularly focusing on the work unit system, Jieyu Liu (2007) argues that specific working practices shaped and perpetuated gender inequality despite the socialist rhetoric of equality. The perpetuation of gender inequality was not so much a matter of predetermined logic within a work unit as it was produced at the intersection of China's broader socioeconomic fluctuations and preexisting cultural constructions of gender relations. Let me illustrate this point through the evolution of the *gongsi*, the collectively owned sector in Fenghuang.

In the institutional history of Fenghuang, there were three important moments in the transformation of the *gongsi*. First, it began with the "family enterprise" (*jiashu chang*) during the Great Leap Forward, when the party-state undertook a radical project to transform China into a modern communist society. In 1958 the Women's Federation, a mass organization that arguably represents the rights and interests of women under the CCP, put up banners reading "No Loafers in the Home" (*jiali wuxianren*). It organized a campaign to urge women to get out of the home and participate in the People's Commune. Naturally, workers who entered family enterprises through this campaign were all women. When Fenghuang recruited workers in the early 1950s, these women had not entered the factory because they needed to care for their children.[21] In the late 1950s, when these women were forced to work outside the home, only temporary, hard work awaited them.

Yu Jixiang grumbled: "During that time [the Great Leap Forward], I was told that housewives like me should work outside. In the family enterprise, I spent most of my time pulling a cart, picking up scrap metal which *gongchang* workers dumped, and welding it into worthless iron." Despite their having to work outside the home, rearing children remained solely the women's responsibility. Seventy-four-year-old Sun Jiemin recalled: "Loafing at home was unthinkable in those days. I went to work, leaving my five children at a day care center. To give them breast milk, I had to visit the center several times a day." When, however, the Great Leap Forward ended in failure, followed by economic havoc, most female workers in the family enterprises were called upon to return home. Sun Jiemin continued: "You must know how difficult life was right after the Great Leap Forward. The family enterprise stopped production. Women were forced to go back home to share the hardship of the state."

Then, during the Cultural Revolution, these "laid-off" female workers were once again encouraged to work outside the home in the "5/7 factories" (*wuqi gongchang*), which arose out of Mao's "May 7 Directive" (*wuqi zhishi*) in 1966.[22] Wang Xin, a former director in Fenghuang (*gongchang*), recalled: "Chairman Mao said that female comrades should be able to do what male comrades did. He stressed that women should contribute to socialism by organizing their own work rather than loafing at home. His words led to the building of 5/7 factories everywhere in China. In Fenghuang, around 260 women, who had been 'laid off' after the Great Leap Forward, returned to do factory work." After the family enterprise, the 5/7 factory became the second form of *gongsi*. In the 5/7 factory, about 95 percent of workers were women. The work of the 5/7 factory was considered as "dirty and trifling" as that of the previous family enterprises. The factory was expected to deal with all sorts of work that could not be covered in *gongchang,* for example, spinning thread, making tofu, baking bricks, varnishing over lacquer, and so on. Not surprisingly, gendered metaphors loomed large in the distinction between *gongchang* and the 5/7 factory, that is, the distinction between "men's jobs" and "women's jobs," and thus men's "single and superior" work and women's "clumsy and inferior" work.

The third moment in the development of *gongsi* occurred in the late 1970s, when "sent-down" youths, who had been sent to the countryside during the Cultural Revolution, surged back into the cities and a crisis in urban employment became widespread. How to arrange work for these large numbers of youths was of great concern to the Chinese government.

In general, the government laid out three schemes to solve the crisis: first, encouraging workers to retire early so that their children could inherit their position (*dingti*); second, dividing up the work and assigning a portion to each individual (*fenpian baogan*); and third, sending contract and temporary workers, most of whom were the holders of rural household permits, back to the countryside (Xiao 2006: 45).

The building of *gongsi* fell under the second scheme. In 1979 the Fenghuang work unit expanded the scale of the 5/7 factory and renamed it the Fenghuang Service Corporation (*Fenghuang fuwu gongsi*).[23] Along with the influx of sent-down youths, *gongsi* accepted many young male workers in their twenties for the first time. Nevertheless, the percentage of women among workers remained much higher in *gongsi* than in *gongchang*. Unlike *gongchang*, the *gongsi* was a collective-owned enterprise which never offered a lifetime guarantee of employment. Most older workers in *gongchang* opted to give their positions to their sons rather than their daughters when they decided to retire early for the sake of their children. Forty-six-year-old Wang Haijie, who had entered the *gongsi* during that time, told me: "In Fenghuang, my father worked in the *gongchang* while my mother worked in a *gongsi*. This pattern was very common in Hadong. Because my father had not yet reached the age for early retirement, my younger brother first went to the *gongsi*, inheriting my mother's position. Then he later moved to the *gongchang* when my father was old enough to retire. I envied my brother, but I understood my parents anyway." The family of Yu Jixiang, whom I introduced earlier, also followed this pattern. Yu's eldest son had inherited his father's job in the *gongchang*.[24] Back from the countryside, Yu's other son "had no choice but to enter the *gongsi*," Yu said. Yu finally retired in 1983 in order to pass her job at the *gongsi* to her daughter. In all, a *gongsi* was a less popular option for older workers who wanted to leave their position to their children; these workers tried, if possible, to bequeath their or their spouse's position at a *gongchang* to "the most significant" child, in most cases meaning the eldest son.

The transformation of *gongsi* shows that the gender division of labor in Fenghuang—the male-centered *gongchang* versus the female-centered *gongsi*—was not a consequence of any predetermined labor qualifications. Rather, it was a consequence of mutual interrelations between much larger events in China's socialist history (the Great Leap Forward, the Cultural Revolution, and the massive return of sent-down youths) and cultural discourses and/or practices of gender (such as preferring a son to a daughter, assuming the rearing of children to be "female" work, or distinguishing "male" work from "female" work).

Not surprisingly, all (ex-)workers in *gongsi* express resentment at how *gongchang* and *gongsi* have differed from each other. For example, one informant told me: "Workers in the *gongchang* left the factory at a scheduled time. Yet the closing hour was meaningless for us [in the *gongsi*]. If somebody suddenly called that a frozen pipe had burst, we had to run to fix it. But no extra money was given to us." Another said: "In the *gongsi* my daughter got burned because of an accident in a gas tank. She managed to get reimbursement for 80 percent of the charges for her operation. Unlike at the *gongchang,* however, no wages were provided while she was in the hospital. My daughter's feet are still so swollen that she can't find any shoes that fit her." Another informant complained: "Work in the *gongchang* was much easier than in the *gongsi*. Nevertheless, they [workers in the *gongchang*] frequently applied for sick leave. They received wages even on sick leave. The *gongchang* had its own hospital. Nothing in the *gongsi!* When I was extremely sick, I had to buy my medicine myself." A woman related: "My husband received 200 yuan when he retired from the *gongchang* in the mid-1980s. Yet I got nothing from the *gongsi*.[25] Now I get 380 yuan for my pension while other retirees from the *gongchang* receive at least 600 to 700 yuan. My husband is dead. He should've lived and I should've died for the family!"[26]

The difference between *gongchang* and *gongsi* haunts impoverished workers even now through the differential stipulations in unemployment policies. When Fenghuang officially declared bankruptcy in December 2005, the *gongchang* employed around ten thousand workers, while the *gongsi* employed around five thousand. That year the "buyout" system was applied only to regular workers (*zhengshi gong*) in the *gongchang.* These workers received a lump sum representing 1,570 yuan for each year of service.[27] Excluded from the buyout policy, contract workers (*hetong gong*) in the *gongchang* received a monthly unemployment allowance (*shiyejin*) for two years.[28] Still, neither the buyout payment nor the unemployment allowance was given to either regular or contract workers in the *gongsi*. These workers from the collective-owned enterprise were excluded from a variety of actions planned by the Harbin government to alleviate the unemployment problem amidst the bankruptcy of Fenghuang.

"Fenghuang is just like a big family." Wang Haijie, a laid-off worker from the *gongsi,* compared her own family with the "Fenghuang family": "A husband is to the *gongchang* what a wife is to the *gongsi*. This situation is very common in Hadong." I asked her, "What if it were the other way around?" She answered: "Well, the opposite case would lead to endless quarrels between husband and wife. For family peace, it is better that the husband has a job superior to his wife's." With her answer, Wang Haijie showed a keen awareness of the hierarchy between "formal and primary" work in the *gongchang* and "informal and secondary" work in the *gongsi*. The cultural notion of a "normal" family, however, kept her from viewing this hierarchy as part of a problematic gender inequality. The difference between *gongchang* and *gongsi* shows us a gendered dimension of the people's "sacrifice"; this difference accordingly disrupts the homogeneity of "the people" which is often elided in the narratives of "selfless sacrifice."

In the next section, I introduce another factor that illustrates the inherent multiplicity of "the people": the enduring rural-urban divide. As we shall see, urban workers in Hadong are remapping their space both geographically and demographically while excluding peri-urban farmers and rural migrants from the category of "the people" that they invoke.

The Split within "the People"

One day in September 2006 I asked Community cadres to introduce to me former directors of Fenghuang. One cadre quickly came up with the name Li Mei: "The husband of Li Mei's second aunt used to be a workshop director at Fenghuang. You should first meet Li Mei's family. But you won't be able to find her house. Let me ask her to take you with her." I wondered why she had said that. Although only one month had passed since I came to Hadong, I was confident that I knew the residential compounds of the Fenghuang work unit. Li Mei's house was not in the compounds, however. Following her, I passed long streets in the compounds and finally found myself face-to-face with small mounds covered with mud and dumped garbage. As we climbed one of the mounds, large fields of vegetables suddenly came into view. Passing the fields, Li Mei and I entered a muddy, winding path along which small gray houses were jumbled against one another. Chickens, pigs, and even goats wandered everywhere along the path. In contrast to the residential compound of Fenghuang, here all the shacks were scattered in a disorganized way. Li Mei said: "This is not the neighborhood of Fenghuang workers. This is where peri-urban farmers [*cainong*][29] lived, although rural migrants have overwhelmed this area now."

In northern Hadong, the lands of peri-urban farmers lie adjacent to the residential compounds of the Fenghuang factory. About one hundred peri-urban farmers in Hadong had officially belonged to the "Third Production Team of the Shengli Production Brigade"—a rural collective unit—until part of their land was expropriated for the construction of a sewage disposal plant in 1996, and they received urban household permits (*hukou*). Although these peasants had been incorporated into the new urban administrative system, about fifty people still farmed their contract land as members of the "Shengli Peri-urban Farmers' Association" (*caishe;* hereafter Shengli). The extent of cultivatable lands had decreased in the wake of rapid urbanization. Some members had not yet received land even though they qualified simply by having reached the age of eighteen. Other members had decided to find any other work (*dagong*) in the city rather than farming.

Although in most cases peri-urban farmers have been better off than peasants in the countryside, their proximity to the city has led them to highlight their misfortunes by comparing themselves with urban workers rather than with rural peasants. Luo Bing, a retired member of Shengli, told me: "I graduated from elementary school just when the Cultural Revolution started. The school was a mess. There was no exam for further schooling. What could I do? I had no choice but to work in Shengli." Luo began there in 1966. She continued: "Urban workers in Fenghuang had regular work hours. But we peasants woke up at two a.m. and worked until eight or nine p.m. in the summer. We got nothing equivalent to a regular wage." As of October 2006, retired members of Shengli received monthly payments of 230 yuan as a supplementary living allowance, a remarkably low figure in comparison with the 500 to 700 yuan provided to Fenghuang factory retirees as a pension. "Can you believe it?" Shengli members often complained to me. "Two hundred and thirty yuan is even less than the poorest people receive as relief from the government."[30]

Since the farmers received urban household permits in the mid-1990s, the area they occupy has been under the jurisdiction of the same local government that administers urban workers in Hadong. Like urban workers, these peri-urban farmers in Shengli have qualified for a variety of welfare benefits given only to urban *hukou* holders. A former peri-urban farmer has even become a Community director in northern Hadong.[31] Nevertheless, most peri-urban farmers in Shengli are *in* Hadong but not *of* it. Just as Hadong is excluded from the topography of Harbin, so is Shengli excluded from that of Hadong. The worker-peasant alliance, which the socialist regime once emphasized under the umbrella of "the people," was never actually achieved (see chapters 5 and 6). Hadong remains purely an honorable workers' village when urban workers in Fenghuang narrate the history of their place. "The people" that these workers invoke never include peri-urban farmers, or "peasants," in their words. Only in the nostalgic accounts of urban workers or in their laments over Hadong's decline do these peri-urban farmers appear. One laid-off worker said to me: "You don't know how many girls in Shengli desperately dreamed of marrying urban workers from Fenghuang. Workers and peasants were fundamentally different. We workers were lifted up by the state. Peasants? Their life was always bitter." Urban workers like him still call the Community cadre in Hadong who used to be a peri-urban farmer a "peasant" to highlight her "inferior" background. Coming out of the Community office, an old retiree from Fenghuang muttered to me sarcastically: "Everyone is equal in this country. See? A peasant is now a commander in chief of this neighborhood and shouting at workers!"

Yet there is another group that confounds urban workers' invocation of "the people" more formidably than even peri-urban farmers do: newly arrived rural migrants. "Hadong has no hope any longer. See? This place is full of peasants. They are *everywhere*." This lament is one I heard frequently from urban workers during my stay in Hadong. Whereas peri-urban farmers have lived in close proximity to but still apart from urban workers, rural migrants, whose origins are extremely diverse, are "permeating everywhere," as one retiree from Fenghuang told me mournfully. In chapter 6 I examine at greater length how the historically layered urban-rural tension has been felt among urban laid-off workers and rural migrants and how the tension has defined the different ways in which both groups experience exclusion and also respond to it. Yet here it is important to mention the dynamics of the local political economy: how rural migrants have in fact helped forestall the collapse of Hadong by entering into tenant-landlord relationships with urbanites. These migrants have nevertheless become a primary target of the urbanites' blame for Hadong's "territorial stigmatization" (Wacquant 2008).

In Hadong, the arrival of rural migrants coincided with the beginning of the breakdown of the Fenghuang work unit. The influx, which had started in the mid-1980s, began to explode during the late 1990s. The number of rural migrants remains a mystery, however. Most urban residents whom I met insisted that the number of migrants was almost equal to that of the urban population. According to official data from the Street Office, in 2008 the urban population (*changzhu renkou*) numbered 36,000, while the floating population (*liudong renkou*) was about 22,000. Yet the latter figure decreases to 9,240 if we put together all the data that cadres collected for the implementation of the one-child policy in eleven Communities under the administration of the street office. Furthermore, data from the police survey in Hadong put the "registered" floating population at only 1,312. Government officials attributed the differences in numbers to the great flexibility—and thus uncontrollability—of the rural migrant population. According to one official, the predominance of the urban population in statistical data was related to the redevelopment that was expected to occur in the near future. Although the government's previously announced plan to build a road in this area had not been reconfirmed by official sources, young urban residents who had moved to other areas were still keeping their *hukou* in Hadong, expecting future compensation. Not surprisingly, rural migrants have filled the empty spaces that these urban residents left while keeping them in their names. With its main road linking Hadong to downtown Harbin as well as to the highway running east to nearby rural areas, Hadong has become an ideal locale for rural migrants.

These rural migrants and urban workers are routinely connected as "tenants" and "homeowners," respectively. It is important to note that many of China's impoverished workers are de facto homeowners regardless of their material hardships. In a state-owned work unit like Fenghuang, urban workers paid an extremely low rent for their housing, which was allocated by their unit. Most of them purchased their house at a greatly discounted price in the mid-1990s during the housing reform (see chapter 2). It was not easy for them, however, to sell their dilapidated house and move to a better one because the market value of their housing was too low. Instead, impoverished urbanites compensated for their meager income by renting a portion of their home to incoming rural migrants. So did peri-urban farmers, although the rent on their houses (80 to 150 yuan per month) was lower than for those of urban workers (100 to 200 yuan per month). And rents in Hadong were extremely low in comparison to those in downtown Harbin, which usually ranged from 600 to 800 yuan (as of 2007). Nevertheless, this regular income was extremely important for many urban laid-off workers, retirees, and peri-urban farmers who no longer had regular wages, who needed to supplement their meager pensions to support their unemployed children, or whose land has already been expropriated.

Given the reality that rural migrants contribute to lessening the misery of local residents by becoming their tenants, it is ironic that these migrants are blamed for the ghettoization of Hadong. It is important to remember that the social and ecological suffering commonly experienced by residents is first and foremost related to the breakdown of Fenghuang. After Fenghuang declared bankruptcy, a factory from a nearby city took over control of the facility. The new factory has continued to use the name Fenghuang, changing the full name from the Fenghuang Work Unit to the Fenghuang Company, signaling that the factory no longer plays a parental role toward its workers and their families. Above all, the Fenghuang Company no longer considers Hadong a residential compound for its workers, for which it should assume responsibility. The new managers have insisted that they are no longer accountable for workers' residences because the compound has become "privatized." They emphasize that many workers in the Fenghuang work unit had already purchased their houses. In contrast, the local government has blamed the Fenghuang Company for ignoring the ghettoization of Hadong, pointing out that in the past, not the government but the work unit always assumed responsibility for the maintenance of workers' residential compounds. While higher-level government officials and factory managers are busy shifting responsibility onto each other, street-level cadres, urban workers, and even peri-urban farmers have increasingly blamed rural migrants for the crisis affecting Hadong's public amenities: dirty public toilets, muddy roads, mountains of garbage, broken water pipes, and rising crime rates.

The split within "the people" has become palpable in Hadong. "Peasants," who had in ideological terms constituted one of the primary classes constituting "the people," along with urban workers, are now excluded when workers invoke "the people." In his well-known *Report on an Investigation of the Peasant Movement in Hunan,* Mao Zedong (1927) refuted Party members' concerns that the peasants' struggle against the landlords was too violent. He wrote: "If your revolutionary viewpoint is firmly established and if you have been to the villages and looked around, you will undoubtedly feel thrilled as never before. Countless thousands of the enslaved—the peasants—are striking down the enemies who battened on their flesh. What the peasants are doing is absolutely right, what they are doing is fine!" (1965: 27). Although Mao considered the violence of the peasants an expression of their progressiveness and a new direction for the Chinese revolution, the term "peasants" (*nongmin*) has in fact persisted as a derogatory cultural category, implying backwardness (see Cohen 1993: 27). Urban workers call rural migrants *nongmin* to highlight their perceived ignorance. Even peri-urban farmers, who are denigrated as *nongmin* by urban workers, attempt to distinguish themselves from rural migrants by calling them "real" *nongmin* while emphasizing that they themselves are, unlike rural migrants, urban *hukou* holders. More important, as I show in chapter 5, *nongmin* has become a self-disparaging expression by which most rural migrants identify themselves collectively. Their persistent use of the term "peasants" affirms their "otherness" in their uneven relationships with urbanites.

On November 18, 2006, a People's Congress election was held. Community cadres were busy putting up election posters and banners. The radio was turned up to capture the attention of residents, who hurried by on their way to work, most without turning to look at the election display, let alone stopping to cast their ballots. One laid-off urban woman poured out her grievances when a cadre asked her to vote: "What's the election for? I have never seen a candidate listed here. Who the hell represents the people? No show like this was necessary in the past. In those days, the Party served the people wholeheartedly." Sun Yufen, a rural migrant woman, was returning home after making her rounds of the neighborhood collecting pieces of old metal from a nearby rail yard. Community cadres did not call out to Sun, nor did she greet them. Sun was not interested in the Community cadres nor they in her. Sun Yufen was not eligible to vote since she was a rural migrant without an urban household registration. "What's the election for?" Sun later asked the same question that the urban woman had. Yet Sun's question came from a different context. Whereas the urban woman criticized the Party for ignoring "the people," Sun Yufen criticized urbanites for ignoring and exploiting peasants: "It is peasants who pour the cement when urbanites build their apartments. Urbanites do nothing other than supervision. Here they take our money [in rent] and still ignore us. They are no better than landlords [*dizhu*], aren't they? What is the People's Congress for when land-lords are reappearing?"

We have seen the mundane ways in which impoverished residents in Hadong invoke their claim of belonging to "the people." The Fenghuang work unit is a vessel for their collective nostalgia for the Maoist days, when the residents' membership in the largest state-owned enterprise in Hadong brought them great honor and filled them with pride. Responding to the inherent ambivalence in their "master" status, impoverished workers have highlighted their contribution to and sacrifice for Fenghuang. Still, this claim fails to unite these workers under the banner of "the people." As I have shown, their invocation of "the people" is riddled with tensions.

Two primary aspects of these tensions, as we have seen, are the experiences of those in the Fenghuang work unit, and the relationship between Fenghuang workers and newly arrived rural migrants as well as peri-urban farmers in Hadong. I demonstrated the multiplicity of "the people" within the work unit, especially the way gender inequality has been historically structured through the division of work sectors. The gendered formation of the *gongchang-gongsi* distinction in Fenghuang—that is, the male-centered *gongchang* versus the female-centered *gongsi*—was not the result of any pre-determined labor needs but a consequence of mutual interrelations between much larger events in China's socialist history and cultural discourses and practices surrounding gender in China.

We have also seen the rural-urban tension embedded in the claim of belonging to "the people" beyond the work unit, especially the ways in which peri-urban farmers as well as newly arrived rural migrants have disrupted the image of "an honorable workers' village," as urban workers have fashioned Hadong in their invocation of "the people." I extended Hadong both spatially and demographically by contrasting the Fenghuang work unit with the compounds of peri-urban farmers adjacent to it and by examining the uneven relationships that Fenghuang workers are building with rural migrants who have begun to settle in Hadong. Impoverished workers' claim of being "the people" turns out to be exclusionary, for one can see how these workers have shut out their former counterparts, the "peasants" who once constituted a primary class of "the people" along with them.

In this chapter I have introduced the processes of impoverishment experienced by urban workers in Hadong in terms of their invocation of the socialist past. Yet the fact must not be ignored that these workers, living in one of the most rapidly growing countries in the world today, are attached to the new market economy as passionately as they are to the socialism of the past. In the next chapter I examine further the meaning of impoverishment by drawing attention to the coincidental encounter between the evocation of "the people" and the current consumer fever under market triumphalism. The crazed pursuit of a new home is a perfect example of this encounter.

CHAPTER 2

Gambling on a New Home

One day in July 2007, fifty-four-year-old Chen Yuhua suggested that I visit a model home for a new apartment complex near Hadong. To help stabilize its financial situation, a nearby state-owned farm had decided to put up six of these apartment buildings in cooperation with a private real estate company. Located on the outskirts of the city, the new apartments had a purchase price of 2,400 yuan per square meter, which seemed reasonable compared to housing prices in downtown Harbin. Although this apartment complex targeted middle- and low-incomes buyers, it was named Elegance Life Garden. "Garden" (*yuan*) is a word commonly used in the names of newly constructed luxury neighborhoods (Zhang 2008: 28). Chen Yuhua and I walked alongside a long wall bearing an advertisement for Elegance Life Garden. "We are creating a brand-new model home with classical elegance," read the advertisement, showing a picture in which a few people, who looked white, were walking along idly, and a couple of luxurious cars drove by colorful apartment buildings with grassy lawns and gardens. This picture was a striking contrast to the real Hadong just across the street, a vista of old shacks and dirty roads crowded with discarded tires, rotten vegetables, and shabbily dressed people.

When Chen Yuhua and I finally arrived at the model home, it was already bustling with masses of curious people who had come to look around or to seek more information from salespersons. Very excited, Chen Yuhua took me to see a diorama of the apartment complex, which was displayed in the model home. She pointed at a small apartment, measuring forty square meters (about 130 square feet), the second-smallest size. Chen Yuhua said to me: "This is the apartment I want to buy. Like me, most of the people who come here seem to be interested in an apartment with small square footage. Yet they are badly located among the buildings. Look at the building I picked. It is next to a boiler room. It must be pretty noisy. But I need to buy a new home now. I'm afraid I won't have another chance if I give up now. The housing prices in Harbin keep skyrocketing every year."

I had known for a long time how Chen Yuhua dreamed of purchasing a new house. Given the fact that this complex included some very small apartments, her wish did not seem to be entirely unrealistic. But it did not seem to be entirely reasonable either. Chen Yuhua was one of the urban laid-off workers stuck in Hadong. After the factory where she had worked became insolvent in the early 1990s, she passed through various temporary jobs with meager wages of 300 to 400 yuan a month. Although she became a Community cadre in charge of collecting garbage in 2001 (see chapter 4), she had only recently begun to receive stable wages from the government. Her husband had also been laid off when the Fenghuang work unit declared bankruptcy. Although he had recently received a lump-sum

FIGURE 2.1.   Chen Yuhua points at an apartment she wishes to purchase (July 2007)

payment according to the buyout policy (*maiduan*), it was supposed to go toward paying the premium on his future pension and clearing the family's debts, which had increased since his wages had been paid only rarely for a decade. The situation of other Hadong residents who visited the model home was no different from Chen's. After being laid off from or "voluntarily" leaving their decrepit work units, most of these residents were eking out a living as, variously, a motorbike driver, a nanny, a guard, a repairman, a vendor, and so forth. The job insecurity that they commonly experienced made me doubt whether they would be able to pay off any kind of mortgage steadily over ten to twenty years. The real estate company advertised that the proposed construction of Elegance Life Garden would be a great benefit to low-income families. Yet the company neglected the fact that amidst the massive restructuring of the socialist work unit system, these low-income families in post-Mao China had lost their sources of stable income for paying off a mortgage on a long-term basis.

My doubts foreshadowed reality. A few weeks later I found that neither Chen Yuhua nor other Hadong residents had succeeded in purchasing new housing. Some had failed to demonstrate to a bank that they would be capable of making a lump-sum down payment on time or of paying off a fixed mortgage over a longer period. Others, including Chen Yuhua, had to give up their dream when the purchase price of the new apartment suddenly jumped from 2,400 yuan to 2,900 yuan per square meter. The soaring housing prices were simply beyond their control. What intrigued me, however, was that such stories of failure never dampened their aspirations for a new home. While in Hadong, I always heard numerous discussions about purchasing a house or rumors about who had bought or was going to buy one. Envy of someone who had succeeded in buying, self-deprecation at being unable to buy, and the will to own were woven together into powerful narratives of desire for new housing.

In this chapter I further examine the ambiguous location of "the people" by probing the dream among many laid-off workers in Hadong of purchasing a new home. How have these workers come to shape their aspirations for new commercial housing despite their de facto inability to afford it? Here I seek my answer with an eye to the unexpected encounter between the myth of "equal" poverty that China's working classes shared as "the people" and the recent casino-style quest for wealth, which Jean Comaroff and John L. Comaroff (2000) view as the manifestation of neoliberal capitalism. As David Harvey (2005) puts it, China's economic reform in the late 1970s "accidentally" coincided with the turn to neoliberal solutions in North America and much of western Europe. Disorganized, dispersed means of making money, which were viewed as a transitional phase in the new regimes of accumulation in many Western countries (Harvey 1990: 121–24), have become the norm in China's fast-growing market economy: from flexible layoffs in labor markets and the rapid growth of "informal economies" to high-risk dealings in stocks and real estate in consumer markets. Market pioneers have even added a nationalistic dimension to their quest for wealth, frequently quoting Deng Xiaoping's famous argument that some people's "getting rich first" (*xianfu lun*) is necessary for China's development.[1]

In this chapter I argue that impoverished workers' aspirations for the seemingly impossible dream of wealth are informed by the intersection of their socialist past and the current neoliberal fever of consumerism. Having grown up in "equal" poverty during the Mao period, many residents of Hadong shared life experiences with the newly rich until those past social equalities shifted radically into the grim inequalities of the present. Memories of this shared past prompt endless talk about the sudden wealth of old comrades, spurring workers' dreams of "catching up." The purchase of new housing has become the very manifestation of their aspirations amidst China's escalating real estate values. Gambling their savings on new housing, impoverished workers experience social suffering not because they are excluded from such high-risk market activities but because they participate in these activities passionately, regardless of their material conditions.

To advance these arguments, I critically engage Pierre Bourdieu's discussion of the cultural reproduction of class boundaries (1984, 2005). In his analysis of the French housing market in the 1980s, Bourdieu illustrates how the suffering of the petit bourgeoisie results from an entire set of economic and social conditions produced by the state's housing policy. For instance, the French state, through forms of financial assistance such as loans, tax exemptions, and cheap credit targeted toward homeownership, has induced housing seekers to believe that ownership is the best "choice" for them. But they are eventually trapped by housing policies and advertisements that measure them "against their aspirations rather than their possibilities," leaving them with "no option but to cope with the consequences of their decisions" (Bourdieu 2005: 185).

Bourdieu's argument is compelling in that he shows how the act of buying a house is not a mechanical consequence of necessity corresponding to the supply-demand curve but rather the social and cultural construction of economic dispositions through a wide array of state interventions. One's economic disposition—especially "taste," as he puts it—contributes to defining one's demand. In Bourdieu's discussion, however, one's taste remains closely tied to one's material conditions even though that taste is partly shaped by the mechanisms of the housing market. Participation in the play of this market is confined to members of the petit bourgeois classes who have accumulated a certain amount of economic capital. Here the participation of the working classes is unthinkable because, in Bourdieu's logic, these classes' "habitus," which has been internalized throughout the course of their lives, does not allow them to have the same taste as the petit bourgeoisie. In French society, he argues, the taste for necessity and the principle of conformity—"Don't bite off more than you can chew!"—determine the choice of the working classes, a choice that includes "the renunciation of symbolic profits that are in any case inaccessible" (Bourdieu 1984: 379).

A shared habitus, however, does not necessarily imply a shared preference for a certain cultural lifestyle (Ferguson 1999: 278–79). Instead of identifying shared cultural practices as indicative of a particular class, my ethnography of the "nonconformist" pursuit of better housing among the poor brings to light more dynamic processes through which class subjectivity is constructed. And people's class subjectivity is, as Sylvia Yanagisako puts it, "formed in relation to both their past social trajectories and their present location" (2002: 100). In this chapter I thus navigate the historical trajectories of urban workers in Hadong in order to discover how these workers, not willing to restrict their choices only to necessity, have come to pursue a seemingly impossible dream beyond their economic status. To repeat, in the Maoist era, China's urban workers had been not only the ideological representatives of the socialist regime but also its main beneficiaries. Rather than internalizing their status as the poor, these workers are inclined to highlight how they shared a common past with those who now do not hesitate to call themselves "the middle classes" (*zhongchan jieceng*) while living in luxurious newly built villas. The "odd" taste of Chen Yuhua and other poor urbanites in Hadong is not understandable unless one juxtaposes their present condition with their past social trajectory.

I juxtapose workers' ordinary narratives about class subjectivity with extraordinary acts in which they "gamble" their savings to purchase housing. I first analyze the fluctuating housing conditions that these workers face in Hadong and provide an overview of the shifts in China's housing policy under market reform. I then turn to ethnographic accounts of how these workers narrate and cultivate their class-specific subjectivity amidst the dramatic social mobility experienced by many in China in the past several decades. Such accounts bring to light the historical contexts in which these workers refuse to admit class differences and invoke their expectations of "catching up." Next I show how these workers' aspirations for upward mobility are manifested through their speculative pursuit of better housing, with grave consequences. Finally, I turn to a government housing policy focused on "affordability" and its hidden assumption that the poor do not deserve to "choose" better housing. The "nonconformist" taste in housing among Hadong's poor leads them to contest governmental actions constructing demands and desires deemed appropriate for low-income households.

The Shifting Housing Context

Much as in other cities in China, Harbin is always under construction. This is particularly true in the summer because the land freezes over during a bitterly cold winter. Bus routes are always changing to avoid construction sites. Some buildings are rising while others are being brutally bulldozed. If we restrict our view to residential buildings, in most cases commercial housing (*shangpin fang*) is going up, and public housing (*yuan gongyou zhufang*) is disappearing.

Public housing used to be the predominant form of housing in China's cities during the Mao period. After the founding of the People's Republic of China in 1949, the ownership of private property was forbidden. Urban residents lived either in large housing compounds that work units built and maintained for their workers or in mixed neighborhoods that the municipal housing bureau provided for households without a work unit. Only a small amount of owner-occupied private housing—known as "self-built housing" (*zijian zhufang*)—dating from before 1949 was retained, and no new private housing was built (Logan, Fang, and Zhang 2009: 917). Given the fact that the sale of public housing was impossible, residents commonly viewed housing as one of the welfare benefits distributed by their work units or the local government. The low rent, however, was insufficient even for covering the cost of maintenance, let alone the initial investment (Zhou 2006: 280). Inequality in the provision of housing was related not to price but to access, owing to the critical shortage.[2] The allocation of housing was always a source of contention since it was considered the most significant of all the welfare benefits that workers received from their work units.[3]

After China's market-oriented reform, however, the government gradually took steps toward the privatization of housing. Because privatization was in fact an ideological reversal in this socialist country, the government attempted to justify the sale of public housing by emphasizing that it would create economic benefits such as solving the housing shortage and improving housing quality (Zhang 1999). Starting in 1979, urban residents were encouraged to purchase their existing homes, at greatly discounted prices; individual purchasers were asked to pay only one third to two thirds of the total housing cost, and the remainder was paid by their work units (Zhang 1999: 595). This did not mean the immediate privatization of property rights. Even through the mid-1990s, the question whether urban residents would have more than use rights remained uncertain (Davis 2003: 185). Despite some complex changes in ownership, however, many became de facto homeowners before the full-fledged commercialization of urban housing got under way (Bian et al. 1997; Zhang 1999; J. Lee 2000; Oi 2003; Zhou 2006). The discounted sale of public housing continued until the late 1990s, when the State Council decided to terminate welfare allocation of housing throughout the country (Davis 2006: 286).

During the late 1990s, the demand for urban housing soared amidst the nation's fast-growing economy and rapid urbanization processes. More important, this was also the period when urban work units, which had played a role as de facto housing owners and managers, began to face the full pressure of massive restructuring, including the dismantling of the "iron rice pot" (see introduction). Numerous urban workers lost their "lifetime" job just as they gained their own housing.

Furthermore, the housing that these workers gained never provided them with a "lifetime" guarantee either. First, the residential compounds of the working classes began to deteriorate once the work units that had managed them declared bankruptcy or were sold to private companies. Second, these decaying villages were increasingly exposed to the threat of demolition (*chaiqian*) as the real estate development craze began to sweep China's cities. In her work on the struggle over property rights in China, Li Zhang (2004) discusses how the abuse of property law, which remains "murky," led to a sharp increase in the construction of commercial housing. Even though the right to private property was written into the Constitution in 2004, property law in China has not changed the system of land tenure by which the state owns all the land in the city. The state policy, however, subsequently allowed the *transfer* of land use rights, thus opening a space where entrepreneurs, government officials, work unit cadres, and foreign investors could amass enormous wealth through the arbitrary transfer of such rights (Zhang 2004, 2010; Hsing 2010). Low-income families in old decaying neighborhoods have been increasingly pushed into the outskirts of the cities without proper compensation or adequate legal protection.

Located on the eastern periphery of Harbin, Hadong was one of the neighborhoods where an eviction notice from real estate developers or government officials—a "death sentence," in the words of one resident— would soon be delivered to impoverished urban workers. Mountains of refuse and waste on the streets made it clear why the residents themselves stigmatized their own community. Few proudly remarked that Hadong had been one of several residential compounds (*jiashuqu*) of the Fenghuang work unit.

One day in June 2007 I was having lunch with Chen Yuhua in her home. A neighbor who had joined us said to Chen, indicating her old washing machine, "It's time to dump that antique, isn't it?" Chen Yuhua explained to me what she meant: "My aunt gave me her old washing machine when she moved to a new house. But the machine remains a useless antique. Twenty years ago the Fenghuang work unit promised that it would build sewer lines for residents. Now the factory no longer exists. Everything is over! I'm so sick and tired of living in this shantytown. I'm tired of going to the nasty public toilet at night. I'm tired of burning coal in the winter. Fenghuang no longer provides coal to its residents. How expensive it is these days! To save coal, I have my daughter Yang Yang stay at her aunt's when winter comes. If Yang Yang comes home for a visit," she said, "I attach a plank to a bed in my room. Three of us [Chen Yuhua, her husband, and Yang Yang] sleep together instead of burning coal for Yang Yang's room. Even in summer, Yang Yang goes to her aunt's if she has to work late. It's been awhile since streetlamps

FIGURE 2.2. Chen Yuhua cooking in her kitchen–living room (August 2006)

here worked properly. How dangerous this place is! I'm sick of everything here. Whenever I enter my neighborhood and open the door of my house, I feel as if something is pressing down on my chest."

Like Chen Yuhua, most residents in Hadong no longer develop a sense of place, meaning "both a shared objective position and the subjective sentiment of having a 'place of our own'" (Wacquant 2008: 7). Initially planned as a residential area for qualified workers, and carefully managed by the work unit, this run-down neighborhood on the urban periphery contrasts with those in many Latin American and other Asian countries where large numbers of rural migrants have constructed illegal communities with their own hands and developed "a sphere of independence" against state violence (Holston 2008: 238; cf. Paley 2001; Goldstein 2004; Cho 2005). With one voice, residents in Hadong said to me, "Without Fenghuang, there'd be no Hadong" (*meiyou fenghuang, meiyou, hadong*). In other words, these residents have identified the collapse of the work unit with that of their home.

Such historical conditions explain why most residents of Hadong were not very agitated about widespread rumors that their neighborhood would be demolished in the near future. Hearing of the government's plan for building a new road, these residents have accepted the disappearance of their neighborhood as an eventuality that cannot be avoided. For those who are no longer attached to their neighborhood, what is at stake is not to protect their place against the threat of eviction but to prepare themselves for a better exit. As I noted earlier, however, most residents of Hadong barely manage to subsist on meager pensions, temporary work, or other governmental supports. To put it bluntly, they will never be prepared for a better exit. Though not officially, local government representatives whom I interviewed in December 2007 told me that residents of Hadong would receive as compensation 2,000 yuan (for original housing) and 1,500 yuan (for newly built housing) per square meter in case of eviction. Such compensation is extremely meager if one recalls that the average price of housing in Harbin was 3,688 yuan per square meter at that time.[4] One resident said to me with resignation, "If we are thrown out of here, we have no place to go but the countryside." During my fieldwork, however, I saw no residents prepare for going to the countryside. What I witnessed instead were abundant rumors, promises, grumbles, gestures, and actions relating to the aspiration for new, better housing. In order to understand such eruptive discourses of aspiration, I next analyze how local residents ordinarily narrate their life trajectories and compare them with those of others. This reveals the historically informed ways in which these workers cultivate their class subjectivity in their everyday lives.

Expectations of "Catching Up"

One day in March 2007 I was chatting with forty-seven-year-old Li Hong at her house in Hadong. Li Hong was a laid-off worker in Fenghuang. I had first met her when I, with a local government official, had visited recipients of the minimum livelihood guarantee (*dibao*), a governmental scheme for assisting the urban poor since the late 1990s (see chapter 3). Suffering from a chronic heart disease for a decade, she was all skin and bones. Since then I had frequently visited her house. Her illness prevented her from finding any temporary work, and her self-consciousness about her skeletal appearance often kept her from leaving her small, dark room. That day her twenty-two-year-old daughter, Sun Meimei, returned home after finishing her part-time job at KFC. With tremendous excitement Meimei showed us a photo album that she had had made recently. It was common for young women of her age to get made up and dressed like a fashion model and have their picture taken. I was amazed by her beauty, the fancy outfits, and the high quality of every photo. Yet I was also surprised that Meimei spent 100 yuan having the album made. Her mother was laid off. Her father remained at the Fenghuang Company but with meager wages of 500 to 600 yuan a month. A college (*dazhuan*) senior majoring in art education, Meimei earned only 4.1 yuan per hour at KFC. Although she complemented her living expenses by selling her artwork once in awhile, her tuition mostly came from a generous cousin in southern China. Given these dire circumstances, spending 100 yuan for such an album seemed a lavish style of consumption. What surprised me more was Li Hong's warm response to the album. Rather than scolding her daughter for spending too much money, Li Hong gazed happily at the lovely outfits in the album and exclaimed: "How beautiful my daughter is! Who in my generation would have imagined this kind of album? We had almost nothing to choose from in a store. My daughter's life shouldn't be the same as mine. Look at these pictures. They're so fancy!"

Mostly laid off in their forties and fifties, China's impoverished workers like Li Hong, and like Chen Yuhua, whom I mentioned earlier, are often called the "forty–fifty unit." These workers were born and grew up during a period of natural disasters that occurred immediately after the Great Leap Forward in the late 1950s, and then found themselves on the threshold of the turmoil of the Cultural Revolution (1966–1976). Many of them—more than 17 million students—gave up their schooling and went to the countryside in order to "learn from the peasants" through the "sent-down" movement (*xiaxiang*), which in fact was aimed at alleviating the problem of soaring unemployment in the cities (Meisner 1999: 528). Most returned to the cities from the late 1970s onward, and finding a job became increasingly difficult. With the enterprise restructuring since the mid-1990s, this generation, especially female workers, was the first to be laid off on the pretext of their lack of skills and education (Honig and Hershatter 1988; Yang 1999; Cook and Jolly 2000). This situation was exacerbated by the fact that the children of these laid-off workers were mostly in senior high school or college. These children—in most cases only one for each family—constituted the first generation under China's one-child policy. Their working-class parents had lost the material means to support them at the very time when these children were expected to receive a great deal of attention and care as the "only hope" for their family (Fong 2004). Given the tortuous ways in which these workers' personal biographies are intertwined with the history of the socialist regime, Eva Hung and Stephen Chiu call the "forty–fifty unit" the "lost generation," observing that "their real (and perceived) cumulative disadvantages over their life course have contributed to their strong sense of having been 'abandoned' by the society and 'lost' in the market transition" (2003: 231; cf. Pan 2002: 91).

Such stories of the "lost generation" are powerful and widespread; they are frequently repeated among other generations as well as by the "forty–fifty unit." I would emphasize, however, that the stories of the latter end up being more varied than the "lost generation" metaphor suggests. It is important to remember that this generation commonly suffered from the turmoil of the Cultural Revolution and the series of other political campaigns during the Maoist era. Yet it is also important to remember that another kind of turmoil, the nation's market reform, radically diversified the life trajectories of that generation. Deng Xiaoping's "opening" market reform, starting in the late 1970s, brought as much opportunity as frustration to the entire nation. Specifically, during the first two decades of the reform, when laws and policies for regulating the reckless accumulation of capital had not yet been developed, savvy "pioneers" seized golden opportunities to amass wealth through numerous licit and illicit means. Leaving their ailing work units and "jumping into the sea" (*xiahai*) much earlier than others, these market pioneers profited immensely by utilizing the gap between state-controlled prices and market-regulated ones, mobilizing gray-market resources based on their previous social and political positions, and plunging into the market economy in activities ranging from real estate transactions through personal connections (*guanxi*) to government officials to simply selling clothes, purses, or drugs on the street. In other words, the initial phase of China's market reform created greatly different paths among urban workers, who were commonly celebrated as most representative of "the people" under the socialist regime and were then abandoned when the nation became preoccupied with market-oriented development.

My continuing conversation with Li Hong showed her keen awareness of the different paths her generation has taken. As I expressed an interest in her photos, Sun Meimei delightedly brought out other photos taken with her college friends. When I was looking at a picture in which she and some friends were posed with their arms around one another's shoulders in front of the famous Commemoration Tower of Victory over the Flood in Harbin, Meimei pointed at a friend with a chubby face and said to me: "Juntao is the most popular one of us. He's been to Hong Kong and even Macao! His house in a new economy development district (*kaifaqu*) is over a hundred square meters! His laptop, CD player, and whatever are all Sony's! Juntao's father drives a Mercedes-Benz! He sometimes comes to pick his son up..." Before Meimei could finish expressing her envy of Juntao, Li Hong interrupted, saying to me: "Can you believe that his father used to be a worker in a small recycling plant? I remember his work unit, although it doesn't exist anymore. In Harbin it was one of the last places to which people wanted to be assigned. Their job was to collect all the dirty, stinky clothes from here and there. They even picked up the clothes of the dead. I don't know exactly how Juntao's father got rich," she said. "But rumor has it that he left his factory much earlier than others and started selling leather jackets in partnership with a distant cousin in southern China. Wait a minute...Someone also said that he had sold health products made in Hong Kong. Who the hell knows where those products came from? No one can be rich without the guts to deceive others!"

Later, I learned that Chen Yuhua, the laid-off woman who had taken me to see the new model home, had worked in the same work unit as Juntao's father. She had only a vague memory of him because he had left the work unit very early, in the mid-1980s. Yet the story of his success opened the floodgates to a torrent of remarks about Chen Yuhua's tortuous life. She told me: "I graduated from middle school in 1971. Policy had become more relaxed in those days. I decided not to go to the countryside. But people from my father's work unit kept coming to me to persuade me to go. I caught a severe cold in the nick of time, and a doctor issued a certificate stating that I had pneumonia. Thanks to the certificate, I was able to avoid going to the countryside and instead received a job allocation in the city!"

Chen Yuhua continued: "At the time I thought that I was pretty lucky. But my luck ran out when I was assigned to the recycling plant. How dirty my work was! It was before I even got married." I asked her when she got married. "It was in 1980," said Chen. "I wish I had married well! It's no use having regrets. Marriage gave me more bad luck. I never wanted to find a husband in my poor collective-owned factory. I was tall and pretty enough to be introduced to a man from a state-owned factory. That's how I met my husband. At that time I had also been introduced to a short guy studying at Jilin University. I simply ignored him. A college diploma," she explained, "was nothing compared to the work pass [*gongzuozheng*] from the state-owned factory. But look at how things went. My husband in Fenghuang ended up being laid off and hanging around in search of any kind of temporary work. On the other hand, that short guy is a professor now. Who imagined that intellectuals [*zhishi fenzi*] would make so much money![5] I should have left my work unit early, like Wang Zhen [Jintao's father]. You don't know how many old school friends of mine left their work units early and grabbed a great opportunity for getting rich."

What intrigues me most in the reflections of Li Hong, Sun Meimei, and Chen Yuhua is how they *refuse* to admit class differences. These working-class women do not seem to perceive "the gaps between the cultural practices and preferences of the different classes" which Bourdieu found manifest in French society in the late twentieth century (1984: 381). Making a luxurious photo album while working at KFC for meager wages, as Sun Meimei did, does not follow the "principle of conformity," which Bourdieu saw as the only explicit norm of popular taste (380). Li Hong and Chen Yuhua view the emerging middle classes not as people whose lifestyles are completely beyond their reach but as those they could have caught up with if they had only been more fortunate or seized an opportunity. In other words, in the case of the "forty–fifty unit," it is important to remember that impoverished workers stuck in rundown neighborhoods (like Li Hong and Chen Yuhua) and the newly rich living in extravagant villas (like Wang Zhen) shared many life experiences under the socialist regime. Beneath the umbrella of "the people," both parties commonly withstood political turbulence and had to cultivate frugality in their lives owing to the scarcity of goods. Impoverished workers in Hadong talked endlessly about how their old classmates or friends with whom they once lived and worked together in the countryside as "sent-down" youth have tasted sudden wealth by seizing and cleverly using new opportunities offered by the initial economic reform. Thus, these workers' awareness of the growing gap between them and their old companions who have become rich is intensified by their memories of how they were once all *equal*.

Such a refusal of distinct class boundaries on the part of middle-aged working-class individuals can also be understood through the widespread uneasiness of the newly rich. In her analysis of the new Chinese middle class, Li Zhang asks why the newly rich are so preoccupied with consumption. New residents of the upscale neighborhoods tend, according to her, to be lumped into one of two categories: *zuo shengyi de* (businesspeople) and *da laoban* (big bosses). Among them, asking how they generate their income is a social taboo because they took advantage of the emerging private market before the competition intensified and often did and still do business outside the bounds of the law and official rules (2008: 30, 37). Under such circumstances, argues Zhang, consumption becomes important in cultivating and performing their sense of being "middle class." To be considered "middle class," for example, they must seek leisure-class services such as hair styling, manicures, massages, and so on. They must also send their children to the United States and elsewhere for education. In other words, they desperately need to display evidence of a distinctive lifestyle, one that corresponds to their "middle-class" status. In China's fast-growing, fast-shifting cities, the class boundaries that people recognize and experience in their daily lives are accordingly not fixed but more elastic, volatile, and uncertain.

It is under these circumstances that the will to "catch up" emerges among impoverished urban workers. Their narratives of frustration ("I was not lucky" or "I missed a chance") and of hope ("if I am lucky" or "if given the chance") in fact reveal how inextricably intertwined the two emotions are. Finishing her remarks on her tortuous life trajectory, Chen Yuhua said to me: "My life right now is over. I'm old enough now. I spent my whole life working my fingers to the bone. But I still can't buy a new house without an enormous mortgage. How exhausting! My whole life has been in vain [*yibeizi guang fendou*]!" Nevertheless, Chen Yuhua is one among many Hadong residents who never stop thinking of and talking about the possibility of acquiring new housing. Like others, she dwells incessantly on stories of her friends, her friends' friends, and the friends of her friends' friends who succeeded in purchasing new housing.

Her expectations of "catching up" are prompted further by the unique history that urban workers had as a privileged class under the socialist regime. Whereas most ghetto residents in the United States or slum dwellers in India have been mired in poverty throughout their lives (Appadurai 2004; Wacquant 2008), impoverished workers in China's shantytowns were once "the people," serving as both ideological representatives and the main beneficiaries of the socialist regime. The socialist work unit system, despite its hierarchical differences, guaranteed its workers a variety of perquisites. When unprecedented market-driven reforms abruptly turned many of these workers into China's "new urban poor," the Chinese government began to develop a spate of welfare policies directed at them, for instance, the reemployment project, pension and medical insurance reforms, the minimum livelihood guarantee, unemployment allowances, housing subsidies, tax breaks, micro-financing, and so on (see chapter 3). Above all, the government has attempted to secure housing for workers by ordering every work unit to sell public housing under its supervision to urban workers at greatly discounted prices. By the end of the 1990s, the homeownership rate in urban China had increased sharply, from about 30 percent in 1995 to more than 70 percent in 2000 (Zhou 2006: 279).

Thus the gaping economic polarization in post-Mao China does not necessarily lead impoverished workers to accept downward mobility as their fate. Encouraged by the memories they share with the newly rich, and by the aforementioned state policies directed toward them, these workers ceaselessly assert their desire, will, and intention to catch up with others' success. The purchase of new housing has become one of the primary means toward this end. In the next section I show how China's real estate bubble in the early years of the twenty-first century has raised aspirations as well as frustrations even among impoverished workers. To realize their aspirations, these workers anxiously wager what little they have, with serious consequences.

The Speculating Poor

On a late afternoon in March 2007, I met Cao Guiying on the street on my way to the local government office. A bruise next to her nose caught my eye. I could guess what had happened to her. Yet I did not want to ask questions on the street, where elderly retirees chat idly. After asking her to say hi for me to her daughter Li Mei, I went on my way. When I arrived at the local government office, I realized that Cao Guiying had just stopped by to ask the government to help her son Li Qiang with his school expenses. Community cadres were already busy gossiping about the bruise on her face. My guess was right. A cadre who lives near Cao Guiying was telling the others how she was brutally beaten by her drunken husband the night before: "How scary he is! Once he's drunk, nobody can stop him. He even swings around a kitchen knife at his wife and Li Mei." I asked if he had always beaten her during their marriage. "Yes," the cadre responded, "but he has become more violent since his wife lost all their money while running a money-lending business. Cao worked like hell and made some money. One day, she gave it all to someone. The guy promised that he would make high interest payments on it every month. But he suddenly died after she got only one month's interest. His wife was gone. Only his six-year-old daughter was at home when Cao finally found his house. You cannot force a six-year-old girl to pay money back. Stupid Cao had no official contract with him. Her family was completely ruined! Her husband mentions her mistake whenever he beats her savagely. How pitiful she is!"

A few days after seeing her on the street, I visited Cao's home. As usual, I was watching TV with Li Mei when Cao Guiying came home from the factory. I noticed burns on her hands. "What happened to you?" I asked instinctively. Cao replied: "It's no use of putting on several pairs of gloves because I have to touch liquid chemicals every day. Yet my condition is better than others'. Their skin is already stripped off. We are working twelve-hour shifts. We need to keep producing plastic bottles while eating lunch and breathing in poisonous gas. My lungs and stomach are collapsing." With a sigh she continued: "I worked like crazy to buy a new house. I had a dream that my family would live together in a better house. You know that my son rarely comes home. He stays at his cousin's while going to school. He hates his dad. He hates this shack. But he's a good son. He studies very hard. I wish I hadn't stupidly lost all my money."

During another conversation, however, I found that her aspirations for a new home went beyond the lovely dream of a reuniting her family. Two stories had inspired Cao Guiying to gamble her savings. One had to do with a co-worker of her husband's, a Korean Chinese (*chaoxianzu*) who returned in glory after working in South Korea and purchased a new apartment in downtown Harbin. Cao was struck by his success because the man's family of four had been so destitute that they had lived off her family for some time. The other story that intrigued Cao concerned a friend of Li Mei's whose family was said to have made a fortune when they sold a house for nearly twice what they had paid for it only a couple of years earlier. Sighing deeply, Cao Guiying said to me: "I was anxious when I lent all my money to the guy who died. Everybody said that Hadong would soon be gone, demolished. The housing prices in Harbin were skyrocketing. People who had purchased a house earlier made a lot of money when housing prices went up. They were coining money while loafing at home. It seemed that everybody made it, except for my family."

Cao's story of misfortune was one of many I heard in Hadong—stories about people who went bankrupt because they dabbled in stocks, money lending, pyramid schemes (*chuanxiao*), and so on. Their gambling ruined not only themselves but also their friends and families who lent them a good chunk of money. And their reckless attempt to make a fortune, as shown in Cao's story, was deeply entangled with their aspiration for a new home. It is intriguing to compare their perspective with that of those who advo-cate affordable housing. Scholars and activists have long insisted that access to secure housing is one of the most basic human rights. They have thus opposed any speculative activities that treat a house as a mere capital good for economic investment. It is in this context that Bourdieu argues that "the purchase of a house, being connected with the family as household, and with its permanence over time, which it presupposes and also aims to guarantee, is both an economic investment...and a social one, in so far as it contains within it a wager on the future or, more exactly, a biological and social *reproductive project*" (2005: 21).

What interests me is how Bourdieu's "reproductive project" describes the seemingly speculative risks that impoverished workers take in the hope of purchasing a new house for their family. China's average housing prices have risen continuously from 1,948 yuan in 2000 to 2,549 yuan in 2004 (Zhang, Weng, and Zhou 2007: 302). In the first eleven months of 2009, average housing prices reached 4,600 yuan per square meter, up 27.8 percent from the same period in 2008.[6] News about housing price hikes, which appeared every day in the mass media,[7] dismays not only white-collar professionals but also working-class parents, who fear leaving their children in poverty. Cao's husband once told me: "In the days of Chairman Mao, housing was not a big deal. Workers received housing from their work units, while peasants built their own housing. Who would've imagined that young college graduates would be committing suicide because they can't afford to buy a house? These days, no house, no marriage. I'm afraid that my son can't afford to marry." Workers' worries about their children's future evolve into an urgent mission to buy *now*, as they face fears of a real estate bubble. Significantly, it is not only fear but also expectation that spurs their rush to buy. As Cao Guiying said: "Once I succeed in buying a house, its value will rise continuously. The house will become my pension until I leave it to my son."

The flexibility, uncertainty, and unpredictability that overwhelmed the neoliberal market economy have produced enormously tragic events, as witnessed in the recent subprime mortgage crises. Housing prices underwent a steep decline in the United States, and soaring stock markets suddenly took a nosedive around the globe. Nevertheless, China's booming economy made even poor people like Cao Guiying view the very uncertainty in the housing market not as a bad omen but as an opportunity for chasing a fortune. In their minds, housing as subsistence and housing as investment are not entirely distinguishable. A new house is considered an ever-renewable resource for family survival, the value of which will continuously increase along with real estate price hikes. Many residents of Hadong desperately assemble a down payment by using the lump sum they received through the buyout policy at Fenghuang, gambling their savings on stocks or through money lending, and even squeezing the meager pensions of their elderly parents. Or at least they do so until most of them, like Cao Guiying, experience deep disappointment even before they get as far as a real estate company.

One might wonder why governmental affordable housing policies are not visible in the housing stories of these impoverished workers. After spurring fears of a real estate bubble, the Chinese government put an emphasis on affordability, implementing various programs in recent years. Yet for whom does this "affordability" matter? What if the "affordability" is not interpreted as an ideologically correct assertion of the right to a residence but criticized as legitimizing the residential hierarchy in which only the rich are seen as deserving better housing? In the next section I revisit the story of Chen Yuhua and explore the problematic responses among the poor to the state's housing policies. Their refusal to admit class differences is revealed in their preferences in housing as well as in their decision to purchase housing, and in their complex responses to the government's affordable housing program.

Beyond "Affordability"

I have discussed the shifting condition of urban housing in China and have shown how the privatization of housing and the real estate craze have trapped many laid-off workers in a dangerous position despite their new status as homeowners. It is in this context that the Chinese government has advanced policies for supporting secure homeownership. These policies primarily include the Housing Provident Fund (*zhufang gongjijin,* hereafter HPF) and the Affordable Housing Program (*jingji shiyong fang,* hereafter AHP). Starting in the mid-1990s, the HPF is a compulsory housing savings plan under which both the work unit and the individual contribute to a common account. It can be used for a variety of homeowning purposes, including outright purchase, down payment, or monthly mortgage expenses (J. Lee 2000; Duda, Zhang, and Dong 2005; Davis 2006). Literally translated as "economical and comfortable housing," the AHP, started in 1997–98, particularly targets low-income households. Real estate companies are encouraged to build complexes of relatively small, affordable apartments in exchange for subsidies such as a reduction in development costs and fees paid to the local government (Duda, Zhang, and Dong 2005).

Both the HPF and the AHP are intended to "smooth the transition from state to individual housing ownership" (Asian Development Bank 2009). They are aimed at reinforcing affordability in housing while protecting urban residents from the threat of speculation. Nevertheless, these policies were discussed less widely than I expected in Hadong. The unpopularity of the HPF was understandable: most laid-off, unemployed, and temporarily employed workers in Hadong no longer belonged to the work units that would have made them eligible for the HPF. As many scholars have argued, the scheme "ended up advantaging employees in the financially and economically most viable enterprises and within this group, privileged employees with a high level of employment stability" (Tomba 2004: 17–18; cf. J. Lee 2000). Residents' lukewarm response to the AHP was puzzling, however, given that the policy focused exclusively on low-income households.

In July 2007 I ran into Chen Yuhua and her neighbor Yang Kun in front of the local government office. Chen looked very anxious. She had received information from an insider that the state-owned farm, which had allocated its land for the construction of the Elegance Life Garden complex, was offering its employees the privilege of choosing their desired apartment location in advance. She asked me to go with her to the model home once again to check out the information. At that moment I was staring at a notice in the government office. Its title was "How to Apply for the Affordable Housing Program." The qualification criteria for the AHP were as follows: (1) applicants had to be the holders of a valid Harbin residence permit (*hukou*); (2) the per capita annual disposable income of their household (as of 2006) had to be less than 7,045.5 yuan; and (3) the per capita area of the existing living space for their household had to be under 11.68 square meters (about thirty-eight square feet). If applicants who qualified under these criteria were chosen by lottery, the Harbin government would subsidize their purchase of housing (within designated districts) by paying them 30,000 yuan. I asked Chen Yuhua, "Aren't you interested in applying for the AHP?" She answered without hesitation: "It's corrupt and not suitable. And the apartment complexes provided by the affordable housing program are located in even more peripheral areas than Hadong." Yang Kun added: "It's good anyway if you're chosen for the affordable housing. The price of affordable housing increases, too. You can sell it when its price goes up."

In fact, Chen's judgment that the affordable housing program is "corrupt and not suitable" looms large in scholarly and public criticisms of that scheme. Scholars have argued that the AHP remains out of reach for many low-income households. Not only are the qualification criteria for the AHP not strictly monitored, but also the annual income threshold is high enough for even upper-middle-income households to be eligible for the scheme (Tomba 2004; Duda, Zhang, and Dong 2005). In Harbin, the income threshold of 7,045.5 yuan for the AHP was lower than the per capita annual disposable income (11,230 yuan) in the city in 2006. Yet it was much higher than the minimum cost of living that year of 3,120 yuan (260 × 12).

In addition, it was widely thought that no one would win the lottery without personal connections (*guanxi*). Incomplete screening processes made even the housing available under the AHP a likely target for speculation. Chen Yuhua's remarks, however, pointed to more than just the loopholes and errors that emerged in the process of enacting the AHP. It was not simply because affordable housing was "out of reach" that she showed little interest. It was also because the new housing available under the program was usually in unfavorable locations, "even more peripheral than Hadong." Her neighbor's remarks were perplexing too in that she viewed affordable housing not as a means of subsistence but as a means of investment.

Significantly, the affordable housing program constructs rather than merely reflects the demand of low-income households. Although the context differs, Bourdieu's critique of housing policy in French society makes perfect sense in this case: "In effect, the state—and those who are able to impose their views through it—contributes very substantially to producing the state of the housing market, doing this largely through all the forms of regulation and financial assistance aimed at *promoting particular ways of bringing tastes to fruition* in terms of housing" (2005: 15–16; emphasis added). Yet what Bourdieu elides in his critique is that those for whom the policy was put into effect are not necessarily slaves to these "particular ways" of imposing certain tastes on them. Chen Yuhua and Yang Kun are low-income women who reject the policy assumption that it is acceptable for low-income households to live on the periphery of town or to obtain housing only for subsistence. Like Li Hong, who willingly overlooked her daughter's overspending, they do not conform to the presumed lifestyle of the working classes. Maintaining the historically informed expectation of "catching up," they sometimes refuse to abide by the expectations of others about what the working classes are like.

Chen Yuhua's refusal to conform to the demand constructed by the state never helped her realize her wish, however. The economic condition of Chen's family was in fact much better than that of Cao Guiying, whom I introduced earlier. Chen's daughter Yang Yang was working in a state-owned enterprise. She was willing to use on behalf of her family the Housing Provident Fund that her factory sets aside for its permanent workers. As I noted earlier, no HPF was available for most impoverished workers who had left their work units. It was no wonder that Chen said with pride: "The Housing Provident Fund is calculated on the basis of the number of years workers served. As you know, not every work unit runs the fund. My daughter has that privilege because her work unit is strong and it belongs to the state [*guojia de dongxi*]. Under the regulations, my daughter can loan 96,000 yuan.

I will use that money for a down payment and then pay around 500 yuan in monthly payments for twenty years. I've also found that my distant cousin knows an employee in the real estate company. He will help me choose my favorite location in the apartments." Despite all these efforts, however, she had to give up her plan when the purchase price of the new apartments suddenly jumped from 2,400 yuan to 2,900 yuan per square meter, as I mentioned earlier. Neither welfare assistance nor the personal connections that she cultivated could solve her problem. The skyrocketing housing price was simply beyond her control. Although her economic situation made her relatively better off than others in Hadong, Chen, unlike veteran speculators, was not prepared for the market violence associated with a real estate bubble.

In this chapter I have delved into the experiential contradictions of urban poverty by exploring how the impoverished workers' invocation of "the people" in Hadong ironically resonates with the current market economy. In the previous chapter, the claim of belonging to "the people" was shown to be these workers' way of seeking social recognition and honor as the former masters of the country. In this chapter we see how that same claim is used to evoke the nostalgic myth of "equal" poverty under socialism, filling impoverished workers with the desire to "catch up" and spurring their refusal to be treated as "the poor." In both cases the invocation of "the people" contributes to making impoverished workers unwilling to become "the poor."

I have focused here on the housing ordeal with which urban workers must grapple. I have explored their intrepid attempts to purchase new commercial housing despite their inability to afford it. The working-class subjectivity that unfolds in their choices of housing as well as in their everyday lives is not limited by necessity. Their "nonconformist" pursuit of better housing is informed in part by their memories of the socialist past, when these workers shared many life experiences with those who have since become newly rich, before past social equalities gave way to the present daunting inequalities. Stories of colleagues who left the work unit system early and thus were able to achieve great wealth must not be ignored. It is in this context that these workers' aspirations are not "impossible" but rather hover in the space of "maybe,"[8] as they repeat stories of how people who lived and worked alongside them not long ago have now become wealthy. Their seemingly reckless pursuit of fortune appears realizable against a backdrop of flexible neoliberal markets and China's escalating real estate values. In rejecting the affordable housing program, these workers again refuse to conform to expectations about what the poor are and should be, expectations constructed by policymakers that do not reflect reality.

As I have shown, however, the "nonconformist" subjectivity often produces tragic ramifications. These impoverished workers experience social suffering not because they are completely excluded from a wider society but because they are ceaselessly lured into gambling their destiny on China's historical contingencies. They are no better than transient gamblers at a roulette table in a casino that is run by veteran speculators, gamblers who anxiously bet a small amount of money (that is in fact big money for them) until they lose it all and quit at a loss. Hopes and frustrations are inextricably intertwined in their effort to alter their destiny, to the point where they are reluctant to leave the table despite their recurring losses.

Before closing this chapter, I want to revisit Chen Yuhua's story to emphasize how "chasing a fortune" has become not a one-time bet but a crucial part of the life of the poor. When I returned to Harbin in February 2008, I was surprised to learn that Chen Yuhua had moved to a new apartment. She was anxiously waiting for me at a bus stop in Hadong to bring me to her new home. "I was looking forward to your coming back. You won't believe what happened while you were absent!" Chen and I took a bus toward downtown Harbin and got off after passing five stops. A large apartment complex came into view. Though not as luxurious as one of the upscale gated condominium complexes for the newly rich, her apartment complex was even larger than Elegance Life Garden, where she had failed to purchase an apartment, and even closer to downtown Harbin. Very excited, she began to show me her living room, bedroom, kitchen, bathroom, and balcony, one by one. "Wenying, did you bring your camera?" she asked. "Take whatever pictures you want. Isn't this new house great? I still can't believe I got this place. Look at this. I finally made it!"

Interestingly, Chen Yuhua had "made it" thanks to her daughter Yang Yang's "successful" marriage. Throughout my fieldwork, I was aware how preoccupied Chen was with whom Yang Yang would marry. She was upset because her daughter ignored a graduate student and an army doctor to whom a marriage broker had introduced her and persisted in dating a less educated boyfriend. Chen and her husband finally allowed Yang Yang to marry the boyfriend, however, because "his parents are very rich." Chen told me that his mother was so shocked to see her "shack" in Hadong that she immediately gave her some money so that her family could "get out of" it.

In Hadong, Chen Yuhua's case still remains an exception, although most residents rarely abandon their dream of "catching up" and their hope of winning a fortune as they plunge into the speculative market economy. In the next two chapters I explore further the situation of those who are stuck in Hadong, focusing on their encounters with governmental efforts to impose new modes of subjectivity on them.

CHAPTER 3

On the Border between
"the People" and "the Population"

The Guangming street office *(jiedao banshichu)* in Hadong holds a meeting every Monday. Primary officials in the street office as well as local cadres from eleven Communities *(shequ)* under the authority of the office participate in the event. The meeting is the final destination, the place where any instructions from the central government reach the street level of administration, having passed through each level of government in the province, the city, and the district of the city. On the last Monday in October 2006, the main purpose of the meeting was to prepare for an upcoming inspection from the District Bureau of Labor and Social Security *(laodong yu shehui baozhang)*. Song Xiaowei, who had been put in charge of "labor and social security" in the street office, began by announcing the basic target numbers, established the previous January, that every Community was to reach before the inspection. Song's announcement was thus a reminder to Community cadres to continue working toward these numbers until the higher-level government officials visited Hadong. She listed the target figures one by one:

1. Number of persons provided with new jobs by each Community: one hundred
2. Number of new jobs created by each Community: seventy-five
3. Number of registered unemployed persons: sixty-eight

4. The rate of registered unemployment: 4.5 percent
5. Number of laid-off or unemployed persons who were reemployed: seventy-five
6. Number of reemployed persons (in item 5) in their forties to fifties: twenty-five
7. Number of laid-off or unemployed persons receiving job training: seventy
8. Number of persons (in item 7) who were reemployed: forty-five
9. Number of persons receiving job training relating to self-employment *(chuangye)*: fifteen
10. Number of persons (in item 9) undertaking self-employment: nine
11. Number of persons provided with "public posts" *(gongyixing gangwei)* by each Community: six
12. Number of persons (in item 11) in their forties to fifties: four
13. Number of persons who left for other provinces or foreign countries in search of work: twenty
14. Number of persons provided with micro-credit *(xiaoe danbao)* by each Community: five
15. Number of times that residents were introduced to job opportunities by each Community: eighty

After enumerating all the target numbers, Song Xiaowei explained how these numbers would be adjusted up or down according to the scale of each Community. Community cadres busily took down everything that Song announced. Some of them were grumbling in a whisper about how unrealistic the target numbers were. Yet the usual acquiescence was more noticeable than complaints. The announcement of target figures is a routine performance in which many bureaucrats have participated throughout the socialist period. It is a technical process whereby they opt to create a new "reality" that fits in with any scheme prescribed by a higher authority. This time, however, the new "reality" that Community cadres were being pressed to "achieve" included not merely the numbers that would evidence the successful outcome of job training, reemployment, and community service. It also included a new mode of subjectivity that techniques such as categorization and numerization imposed on urban laid-off workers with their remarkable claim to certainty. To receive protection under the umbrella of the government, impoverished workers were expected to enter "an intelligible field" (Rose 1999: 33), where they were technically positioned, counted, and diagnosed according to particular criteria that they had little leverage to influence.

At the meeting, however, one laid-off worker broke into this very intelligible field. Half drunk, he beat a security guard who tried to stop him from entering the meeting hall, then loudly shouted at the officials: "Whatever you say is bullshit. It's useless! You should help me. I don't even have rice to feed my child!" The room was suddenly in an uproar. Some Community cadres laughed at him, saying, "How can you still drink and smoke if you don't even have any rice?" or "How can you think only about sucking money from the government? Go out and find work!" The man retorted angrily: "I quit smoking. Bullshit! Nobody looked down on us workers in the past!" The uproar continued until a security guard forced him to leave and the deputy director of the street office shouted at the local cadres to quiet down.

Individuals need to be known to be governed. To be known, they need to be constituted as a unified and particular grouping (see Cruikshank 1999; Dean 1999). "The population" is a collective form of grouping that renders focused research, measurement, and intervention possible. It is one of the most essential forms of subject making for the operation of what Timothy Mitchell (2002) calls "techno-politics," that is, a mechanism for simplifying the complicated world into statistics and diagrams. As anthropologists have long shown in their research on development projects, however, there is an inexorable gap between the simplified mapping of the population and the unmappable actualities of human lives (Ferguson 1994; Gupta 2001; Li 2007). The drunken laid-off worker at the government meeting invaded the intelligible field where he existed only as numbers. He refused to be converted into part of an ahistorical, indexical population, instead invoking the socialist past when "workers" received recognition from a wider society. What does it mean for those who were associated with "the people" to be newly incorporated into "the population"? How do they themselves understand and respond to the distinction between "Serve the People" and "Serve the Population"?

In this chapter I examine the tension embedded in governing China's urban poverty with an eye to the new problematics of "the population" and its complex encounters with much older invocations of "the people." To govern, as Michel Foucault succinctly notes, means to act on the actions of subjects who retain the capacity to act otherwise (Foucault 1982: 220). To govern poverty, in this sense, means to render the poor manageable, imbuing them with new modes of subjectivity. In contemporary China, this normative task is fraught with an enormous degree of contestation between the poor and government officials because many of today's urban poor are unwilling to abandon the title that the party-state once bestowed on them as urban workers: "masters of the country." Becoming normalized into calculated variables dramatically transforms the relationship that these workers once had with the party-state.

In this chapter I delve into this contestation over the management of urban poverty by focusing on the actual workings of the minimum livelihood guarantee (*zuidi shenghuo baozhang zhidu*), colloquially known as *dibao*. Since the late 1990s, *dibao* has been the party-state's primary policy for dealing with urban poverty. The Chinese government has proclaimed *dibao* to be the most large-scale, comprehensive, and scientific antipoverty scheme in the history of the PRC. In doing so, the government has distinguished *dibao* from the old Maoist scheme of social relief (*shehui jiuji*), which had targeted an extremely small number of people outside the work unit system. I find the *dibao* policy intriguing because of the odd encounter between a specific group that it targets and a specific rationale that it newly enforces. As I show, the policy has emerged in tandem with the sudden increase in laid-off urban workers, not the poor in general; nevertheless, it has introduced a new rationale which holds that poverty should be measured and calculated in numerical tables, in which these laid-off workers are reduced to numbers along with other poor people.

I argue that the practices of *dibao* oscillate between two modes of reasoning, or "governmentality" in Foucault's term (1991), that is, between being on the political stage of "the people" and being in the numerical table of "the population." As I noted in the introduction, figuring the poor as "the people" grew out of the PRC's ideological (and deeply Maoist) "Serve the People" doctrine, representing a conviction that gives both voice and leverage to these workers. It highlights intimate (and often paternalistic) relationships between the party-state and its people, revealing the leading role of the state in dealing with the impoverishment of former representatives of socialism. In contrast, figuring these workers as "the population" illuminates new kinds of programmatic attempts to convert them into "numbers" without history. These efforts not only assert the universality of poverty but also dissipate the historicity of urban workers and their political status by resituating them among the poor in general. The logic of "the people" is not entirely displaced by the logic of "the population" but rather dovetails with it, as I show through my analyses of the origin of *dibao,* the tensions among government officials at different levels, and above all the resistance of impoverished local residents, who have reacted to the new scheme by invoking the socialist claim that they are "the people" and conjuring up the specter of popular violence, much as urban workers did during the Mao period. Their reaction, however, has ended up unintentionally reinforcing the precariousness of their position. Pressured street-level officials have relied on the old socialist category of labor as the local yardstick for *dibao*, thus excluding many laid-off workers from the scheme. Accordingly, I show how governance in contemporary China is performed through the complex relationships between a governing body and its subjects; that is, it is performed neither merely through the construction of the subjects as a governable group nor merely through their resistance to the apparatus. Only the actual practices and processes of governing reveal how it is eventually "effected" (Ferguson 1994: 13).

The four parts of this chapter lay out the workings of *dibao* in Hadong and in China more generally. I first briefly lay out how China's *dibao* policy for addressing urban poverty was originally directed not toward the poor in general but toward a specific group of the poor: urban laid-off workers. I then analyze the process by which these former workers have been recategorized from the working class to the poor population under the *dibao* scheme. Next I discuss what it is exactly that troubles the applicants for and recipients of *dibao*, delving into the dissonance between the discourses they inhabit and the discourses within which the *dibao* scheme operates. Finally, I examine how local residents in Hadong troubled by the workings of *dibao* challenge it with the socialist claim that they are "the people" and show how this resistance produces the unintended outcome of excluding many of them from the scheme.

The Birth of *Dibao*

In July 2005 Lin Yan and I visited a shantytown in west Harbin where most residents were laid-off railroad workers. Lin Yan is a sociology professor whose specialty is urban poverty. To give me a better sense of "the urban poor" in China, she introduced me to some residents with whom her students had conducted interviews on the subject of urban poverty. Lin Yan and I first met Zhou Bing. A former railroad worker, Zhou Bing was unable to speak since suffering a cerebral hemorrhage. He was accompanied by his wife, Xu Yang, who sold hairpins and hats on the street after she had been forced to retire early from her work unit. The family could barely survive on Xu Yang's small income, the pension of Zhou Bing's mother, and *dibao* from the government. Lin Yan began to ask questions about the family's income, debt, housing, furniture, and so on. This routine interview suddenly became a passionate conversation as soon as Lin Yan and Xu Yang realized that they had lived in neighboring villages as "sent-down" youth during the Cultural Revolution. Reminiscing about those days, they recalled memories of their life in the countryside and by contrast the perilous "adventure" of their return to Harbin. Both had been naïve revolutionary youth who aspired to memorize Mao's works and had willingly accepted labor in the countryside. Yet this common past seemed to amplify the present disparity between them. With a car and a vacation villa, Lin Yan did not hesitate to call herself one of China's emerging middle class. In contrast, Xu Yang's present situation was even more difficult than in the "bad old days." Even a road linking her neighborhood to a main road with a bus stop had disappeared, owing to widespread redevelopment nearby, leaving her family virtually in isolation.

Dibao came into being amidst the social unrest of the 1990s, which saw the transformation of the near-equality of the past into the present grim inequality between people like Lin Yan and Xu Yang in the wake of sweeping actions taken by the state, including the widespread selling off of many state-owned enterprises and the accompanying downsizing of the state workforce. Although *dibao* originated in Shanghai in 1993, by the late 1990s it had become the foremost national urban antipoverty scheme (for details, see Tang, Sha, and Ren 2003: 20–25; Solinger 2010: 257–59). Urgent pronouncements from the central government had a great impact on the rapid implementation of *dibao*. In one instance the State Council officially announced the "Bulletin for Establishing the Minimum Living Standard Scheme for Urban Dwellers throughout the Country" (hereafter "Bulletin") in February 1997 and the "Regulations Regarding the Minimum Living Standard Scheme for Urban Residents" (hereafter "Regulations") in September 1999. The total number of people eligible to receive *dibao* dramatically increased nationwide from 0.85 million in 1996 to 2.66 million in 1999 and 23.3 million in 2008.[1]

Significantly, the explosion in the size of the *dibao* population does not necessarily indicate a sudden increase in the number of urban poor in general; rather, it indicates the sudden expansion of a specific category of poor people, that is, urban laid-off workers. Despite the persistence of the chronically disadvantaged urban poor (see introduction), not until the massive layoffs in the late 1990s did the *dibao* scheme gain its full-fledged form. The 1997 "Bulletin" defined *dibao* recipients as "city [village] residents holding nonagricultural residence permits whose per capita family income falls below the minimum living standard line," followed by the specification of three categories of eligibility: (1) residents with no source of livelihood, no ability to work, and no one who could be legally designated as responsible for their support; (2) residents who were collecting or had exhausted their unemployment insurance, who had not yet found new employment, and whose per capita family income fell below the minimum living standard; and

(3) employed workers or laid-off workers collecting a salary, minimum wage, or basic living expense payments, or retired workers collecting a pension whose per capita family income still fell below the minimum living standard.[2] The first category was the main target for social relief in the Mao period; the two others, which mirror the state's critical attention to urban laid-off workers and other "dropouts" from the market transition, were added more recently to the governmental scheme.

This attention is manifest in the remarkable change in the *dibao* budget in the early 2000s, when increasing labor unrest caused by massive layoffs was considered one of the greatest threats to social stability (Perry and Selden 2003; Solinger 2008). The total budget rose dramatically from 2.2 billion yuan in 2000 to 4.2 billion yuan in 2001 and 10.9 billion yuan in 2002 (ZM 2007). Explaining the background behind the sudden increase, a poverty researcher at the Chinese Academy of Social Sciences told me: "As for the financial support for the *dibao* budget in 2001 and 2002, nobody can deny that political concern was given a significant weight. At that time, high-level government officials worked in an environment in which it was assumed that the problem of unemployment and layoffs could be—and should be—solved within a few months. They were highly anxious about social instability in the city."

Nevertheless, the historical origin of *dibao* is in striking contrast to its ahistorical design. That design is tied to the emergence of new rationales that normalize these former workers into "the population" instead of acknowledging their historical contribution as socialist workers, as some of my informants argued.

From "the Working Class" to "the Poor Population"

My thinking about the concept of "the population" borrows much from Michel Foucault. He sees "the population" as associated with "bio-power," that is, "the set of mechanisms through which the basic biological features of the human species became the object of a political strategy" (Foucault 2007: 1). In his account, "the population" refers not to a series of individuals but to bodies as a *species,* "imbued with the mechanics of life and serving as the basis of the biological processes: propagation, births and morality, the level of health, life expectancy and longevity, with all the conditions that can cause these to vary" (Foucault 1978: 139). Thus the attempt to govern people as "the population" is deployed not around the multiplicity of individuals but around the calculated management of large, not-yet-differentiated groups through classification and numericization (see Legg 2005).

In China, the attempt to govern the poor as "the population" was made by many state officials and intellectuals during the late Qing and the Republican period, the late nineteenth century and the early twentieth century; these officials and intellectuals were trained to study globally circulated grammars of governing as one of the state-building projects. The construction of the socialist regime in 1949, however, made it both unacceptable and unnecessary to regulate and classify the poor as a specific population. In cities, the Maoist ideal of egalitarianism gained its material form through the realization of nearly full employment for urban residents despite the recurring crisis of insufficient job assignment. Social relief (*shehui jiuji*) was of little importance because it was directed toward an extremely small number of people who had "fallen through the cracks" of the welfare system (Tang, Sha, and Ren 2003: 28). Furthermore, the Maoist narrative of equal poverty made it impossible to perceive a specific category of "the poor" in a thinkable form. Most residents of Hadong who lived through the Mao period viewed the term *pinmin* (poor people) and the term *laobaixing* (common people) as mutually interchangeable. Recipients of social aid were given specific names, such as "relief family" (*jiujihu*) in the parlance of the national government, or "difficult family" (*kunnanhu*) or "especially difficult family" (*tekunhu*) in the parlance of the work unit. Yet residents paid little attention to these names, not only because the number of recipients and the amount of funds were extremely limited, but also because there was felt to be little distinction between the living standard of recipients and that of other workers.

In contrast, the post-Mao policy for addressing urban poverty has created a new regime in which individual poverty has developed into a social "problem" and "the urban poor" have become a target population in policy implementation as well as in scholarly projects. That is to say, poverty has become "the object of new problematization" (Escobar 1995: 24), which means that it has been reborn as a knowable and manageable form for governmental programming. Under this regime, urban laid-off workers have become a primary target of the policy in convergence with their invocation of the privilege accorded to "the people," who should be protected. What it means to belong to "the people," however, has been transformed under this new regime. Becoming the recipients of *dibao* has meant becoming the poor population (*pinkun renkou*)— no longer political subjects but a particular "species" to be regulated for the sake of social stability. In contrast with social relief in Mao's era, *dibao* is a scheme for governing impoverished laid-off workers as "the poor population" in post-reform China. This new way of being impoverished is expressed in four ways.

First, *dibao* has displaced the historical universality of being poor in the sense that the targeted population is reduced to a series of empirical variables.

The most important variable that determines who receives *dibao* is income—whether a family's per capita income falls below the level of the local minimum living standard ("Regulations," Article 2). The extent of a recipient's disability or illness is a supplemental consideration. According to this policy, it does not matter whether one is a former outsider who did not belong to any work unit or a laid-off worker whose memories are replete with socialist contribution and idealistic sacrifice. Instead, it is the numbers that matter in determining whether or not one is qualified for *dibao* and how much one may receive; specifically, the factors used in the calculation are total income, the degree of disability or disease, the number of children, and the size of one's present housing.[3] This scheme thus introduces a new rationale which holds that poverty can be calculated.

Second, *dibao* has not only reduced impoverished laid-off workers to numbers but also advanced the idea of "the deserving poor," those who follow the state's policies and maintain a frugal lifestyle. The Harbin government enforces a specific local regulation stating that even a family with an income below the poverty line is not qualified for *dibao* if the family (1) has failed to pay a fine (*shehui fuyangfei*) after violating the family planning policy; (2) includes drug, gambling, or alcohol addicts; (3) includes a child whose school was selected at the parents' own expense (*zifei*)[4] or who attended a private kindergarten; (4) includes a student who selected a college or a major with higher-than-average tuition expenses;[5] (5) lives in housing that is more than twice as commodious per person as the local average; (6) has renovated or redecorated their housing within the preceding two years; (7) owns nonessential possessions such as a car, motorbike, air conditioner, or high-quality decorations; (8) has purchased within the past year new electronic goods such as a television set, refrigerator, or audio equipment totaling more than 1,000 yuan; (9) shows a propensity to consume which exceeds that of typical *dibao* recipients; or (10) invests in stocks.[6] This regulation allows officials to stipulate what *dibao* recipients should and should not do while distinguishing acceptable desires from improper ones. According to the regulation, *dibao* recipients do not deserve to provide their child with a better education, pursue a lifestyle beyond the bounds of necessity, or benefit from any lucky break, such as a stock investment. As Lisa Rofel points out, public narratives of desire are suffused with the theme of power—the power "to differentiate among those deemed appropriate subjects of these imaginations and those cast as inappropriate" (2007: 24). As for the poor, their desire to consume as well as their capacity to consume is called into question. Though stipulated differently from place to place, such local restrictions are widespread across other cities in China.

Third, *dibao* has done away with face-to-face, often theatrical perfor-mances of need while highlighting regularization and standardization as pri-mary techniques for governing the poor population. Policies related to *dibao* have been enacted in contrast to the paternalism of the Mao era, when local government or work unit cadres often visited workers from poor families and opened their hearts to them. The Chinese elite and professional classes have typically welcomed *dibao* insofar as it has led to a shift away from a simple, moralistic, and non-professional form of relief toward a more institutional, comprehensive, and scientific form of assistance. Power over life, or what Foucault calls "bio-power" (1978: 140–45), has been exercised along with extensive care regarding the *dibao* recipients' health, education, and housing. The following list shows the types of supplementary assistance available for *dibao* recipients in Harbin in July 2007:[7]

Medical assistance

- Provides recipients with annual medical expenses from 50 yuan to 120 yuan after classifying them into five grades according to the ability to work, income, and degree of disability
- Basic medical relief: supplements the fee for a checkup (100 percent exemption), medical advice (50 percent exemption), medical exami-nation (10 percent exemption for less than 100 yuan and 20 percent for over 100 yuan), and hospitalization (15 percent exemption)
- Medical relief for serious disease: (1) limited to patients whose disease is included in the governmental list of serious illnesses; (2) in the case of the "three no's *(sanwu),* provides 40 percent of the total medical expenses for that year (up to 8,000 yuan); (3) in the case of other recipients, provides 30 percent of the total medical expenses for the year (up to 5,000 yuan)

Supplementary monetary assistance for old age and disability

- Provides an old person who lives alone with 60 yuan (for those sixty to sixty-nine years old) or 80 yuan (for those over seventy) per month
- Provides the disabled with 60 yuan per month

Supplementary monetary assistance for children

- Provides 10 yuan to a one-child family until the child turns eighteen
- Provides 60 yuan to a family with a student (from elementary school to senior high school)
- Provides some tuition (1,500 yuan in 2006) to a family with a child who has entered college

Housing assistance

- Guarantees low-rent housing for a family whose per capita housing area is less than 10 square meters (grading the priority order according to age and the degree of disability)
- Guarantees compensation up to 70,000 yuan in the case of housing dismantlement (since 2007)[8]

Other assistance

- Provides heating expenses (40 yuan monthly for six months)
- Provides relief supplies such as rice, cooking oil, and winter clothes during the holiday season

With individuals carefully numericized and classified, however, this care has made the emotional connection between the giver and the recipient less important. What John and Jean Comaroff (2006) call "the fetishism of the law" is intensified along with the state's preoccupation with strictness and fairness: the human touch is denied and even regarded to be dangerous. Under the slogan "Doing Administration According to the Law" (*yifa banshi, yifa xing-zheng*), the Harbin government has built in numerous regulations for increasing transparency where government officials deal with *dibao*.

Finally, *dibao* has both induced and been induced by the emergence of knowledge that aims to eliminate poverty as a social danger while making it "compatible with a market economy" (Tang, Sha, and Ren 2003: 55). Several studies of *dibao* have been deeply influenced by the discourses of international agencies. Intellectuals have learned globally circulated "scientific" methods from organizations such as the United Nations, the World Bank, and the Asian Development Bank (Guan 1999; Li 2000; Lu and Montes 2002; Tang, Sha, and Ren 2003). In their accounts, the crisis of employment and pensions has been resituated into "internationally common" narratives from which even the word "socialism" has been eradicated. These narratives no longer acknowledge that in China the term "unemployment" was truly unfamiliar to most urbanites and that pensions were considered fair compensation for workers' extremely low income under the socialist regime.

Nevertheless, this new form of poverty knowledge for regulating the urban poor in terms of "the population" does not make Chinese scholars entirely aloof technicians. These scholars have sought to become masters of justice, believing that scientific expert knowledge can not only cure the problem of poverty but also rescue China from the havoc of the socialist past. They believe that they can "serve the people" better by applying scientific methods to solving social problems. For example, Lin Yan, the sociology professor whom I introduced earlier in this chapter, persists in what she calls the socialist sense of responsibility even when her "scientific" efforts reduce laid-off workers to ahistorical numbers. Lin Yan speaks often of the sufferings of her old friends, who spent their youth in the countryside with her and are now experiencing harsh impoverishment owing to massive layoffs. Her intellectual mission includes reporting problematic cases of *dibao* to the local government, although these activities are filtered through her "expert" position in relation to "the poor."

Tracing the history of poverty knowledge in the United States, Alice O'Connor argues that poverty research becomes an inescapably political act owing to the disparity of status and interest between researcher and subject. "An Educated elite," she writes, "categorizes, stigmatizes, and even neutralizes the poor and disadvantaged through analysis that obscures the political nature of social and economic inequality" (2001: 12). It is important to note, however, that in China, both "educated elites" and "the poor" still share common memories of poverty under socialism despite recent upheavals that have distanced them from each other. Although the *dibao* policy is embellished with "scientific" and "objective" language that obscures the socialist past, especially the history of class struggle, its architects and researchers are no less familiar with the political stage on which "the people" live than with the empirical tables demarcating attributes of "the population." This tension inevitably boils over when street-level cadres and poor residents face each other directly. In the next two sections of this chapter I return to Hadong to show how the normalization of "the people" into a "population" is at stake in the implementation of *dibao*. Despite the transformation of governance, the "numbers" still speak out and make themselves heard on the streets of Hadong.

"Poverty Is Flexible!"

How has *dibao* been perceived by the people on whom it is enacted? What does it actually mean to the impoverished workers that *dibao* has introduced a new way of seeing poverty as an ahistorical and calculable condition? How is it significant for them that they are considered to be no longer the working class but the poor population? Under the new plan for addressing urban poverty, the historicity of workers has disappeared; the qualification for being "the poor" has been newly imposed; the human face of the giver and the recipient have become invisible; and poverty knowledge has been produced as a way to model the poor. Yet do the impoverished workers themselves take these changes as seriously as scholars do? Barbara Cruikshank argues that defining and regulating the poor constitute the first condition for governmental intervention: "To motivate 'the poor' to help themselves, they had to be known; however, the truth of the poor could not be told before the poor were isolated as a group" (1999: 76). Although her argument insightfully points to the production of truth-power for making the poor a governable group, it draws little attention to how the poor themselves view this production.

In Hadong, I found that what troubles the recipients of *dibao* most is a new form of governance called "dynamic management" (*dongtai guanli*). If poverty can be calculated, it can also be considered flexible. All government officials whom I met strongly emphasized that *dibao* is not a permanently guaranteed benefit for a particular family because the income of recipients is always changing. When I asked how *dibao* differs from the previous system of social relief, a former officer of the Civil Affairs Bureau in Heilongjiang province stressed the useful role that *dibao* has played in the new economy: "The purpose of *dibao* is to help you so that you can become accustomed to the market economy. Under the market economy, it is not unusual to be frequently unemployed or reemployed. One day you are laid off from a factory and become a recipient of *dibao*. But you graduate from *dibao* if you find another job. You can even be the boss of a company after graduation!"

The dynamic management of poverty, a key to *dibao,* is based on the rationalization that one's poverty is temporary and that one's economic circumstances are bound to improve after a difficult period—that indeed one should expect such ups and downs throughout one's life. Nevertheless, contradictions arise from the inexorable gap between the great flexibility in a person's life that the *dibao* plan presumes and the relatively long duration of poverty in a person's actual life. Let me illustrate this point through the case of the Li Mei family in Hadong.

I first met twenty-four-year-old Li Mei in September 2006. Her family had been recipients of *dibao* since 2004. With little work to do, Li Mei's father had been on a "long vacation" (*changjia*) from the Fenghuang factory—an involuntary rest of almost ten years as a result of the factory's downslide. Li Mei's mother, Cao Guiying (see chapter 2), periodically alternated jobs. From spring to autumn she grew vegetables, as a peri-urban farmer. In winter she worked twelve hours a day at a nearby small plastics factory. Li Mei had ended her schooling ten years earlier owing to hypersensitive asthma. She sometimes sold the vegetables that her mother grew or worked part-time as a cashier in a nearby Internet café, although her asthma prevented her from doing these jobs for long. Most of the income that Li Mei and her parents earned was spent on educating Li Mei's younger brother, who was preparing for the college entrance exam. In 2006 the Li family received a monthly total of 160 yuan for *dibao* from the Harbin government: 100 yuan after deducting 700 yuan (the family's total income as calculated by the government) from 800 yuan (200 yuan [the poverty line] × 4 [the number of persons in the family]) and an additional 60 yuan for supplementary school, heating, and medical expenses.

In January 2007, however, the Li family was suddenly excluded from *dibao* when the government entered a cycle of reemphasizing its policy of "dynamic management." A Community cadre explained to me: "Li Mei's father began to go to the Fenghuang factory again. He receives more than 500 yuan now. Li Mei is over eighteen [the official working age]. The presumed income[9] should have been applied to her much earlier, though I know she is sick." Despite the increased income from Li Mei's father's employment, the Li family's poverty continued unabated since they were now excluded from *dibao*. Li Mei's father did not always receive "more than 500 yuan" because the ailing factory operated irregularly. According to the calculation of the presumed income standard, Li Mei was expected to work; yet her asthma prevented her from holding a steady job. To make matters worse, Li Mei's brother needed more money to pay for special classes to prepare for the college entrance exam. Li Mei's mother often burned her hands while working in a factory filled with poisonous air. Vomiting was a regular part of her day, for she was not permitted to step away from the assembly line where she was assisting in the manufacture of plastic buckets, not even to eat a meal. In the early morning, Li Mei sold vegetables at the street market in Hadong. Back home, she would watch TV or sometimes go to the hospital to get an IV infusion. Her alcoholic father went to work every day, returning at lunch to fill his stomach with a glass of grain alcohol (*baijiu*) and a steamed bun. All of them worked, but they were still poverty-stricken. What was "flexible" was not their impoverished life but rather the governmental techniques for regulating it. The flexibility of poverty prescribed by the government is contradicted by the relative persistence of poverty experienced by local residents.

Another reason why the principle of "dynamic management" is considered problematic is related to the "encompassing" nature of *dibao*. Unlike the previous system of social relief, the *dibao* plan provides extensive assistance, which encompasses a variety of support for housing, education, medical care, and even heating expenses, as detailed above. This is why local residents consider *dibao* a sort of "gift collection." Yet what if the "gift collection" disappears all of sudden because they are excluded from *dibao*? Gao Shan was one of the *dibao* recipients who were anxious about being "expelled" from the plan in the near future. When I interviewed her in October 2006, Gao's family received 240 yuan, after the government deducted 360 yuan (Gao's monthly income) from a total of 600 (200 yuan [the poverty line] ×3 [the number of persons in the family]). In addition, Gao Shan received 30 yuan per quarter for a medical expense supplement and 60 yuan per month as a school expense supplement for her younger daughter. To supplement their heating expenses, the Harbin government also provided her family with 40 yuan per month. More important, Gao Shan's elder daughter received 1,500 yuan when she entered college in early 2006. Once Gao's family was excluded from *dibao,* all those benefits would soon disappear. "Once the government deletes my name from the *dibao* list, everything will be changed. It's not just about a monthly stipend," Gao Shan told me anxiously. Yet the *dibao* program's principle of "dynamic management" forces on poor people like her the belief not only that poverty is flexible but also that managing one's own poverty is flexible.

The Calculating Machine

Although the assumed flexibility of poverty management is problematic, local residents cannot easily identify their increasing grievances over *dibao* because of the dissonance between the discourses they inhabit and the discourses within which the *dibao* scheme operates. Such dissonance is unavoidable because *dibao* serves as a "calculating machine."[10] It is a machine whose enormously scrupulous but enigmatic calculation of family income ends up restraining local residents from intervening in the workings of the program even when they feel it is not producing fair results. Residents cannot usually understand the official jargon used to operate this machine. It is impervious to poor people's own descriptions of their poverty, which include unaffordable school expenses, dilapidated housing, ailing bodies, even starvation. For instance, the conversation between a government official, Song Xiaomei, and a retiree, Wang Ailin, which occurred in a district government in Harbin in October 2006 shows how the calculating machine creates an inability to communicate between the two:

> WANG AILIN: Why don't you give some money to my family? My husband can't even walk now. My house is gone, too.
>
> SONG XIAOMEI: What's gone is gone. Your house has nothing to do with *dibao.*
>
> WANG: Who cares if the government doesn't care when my house is gone?

SONG: Look at this document. It shows exactly who qualifies for the *dibao* benefits. Your family is not eligible for *dibao* because the total income of you and your daughter is more than 600 yuan. I'm sure that you already heard from the street office.

WANG: My husband is completely paralyzed. I have little money to take care of him. I can't afford to send him to a hospital.

This calculating machine baffles not only ordinary residents but also street-level government officials—especially Community cadres. As I show in the next chapter, most of the Community cadres in Hadong are middle-aged laid-off female workers who barely managed to achieve their position through the government's reemployment policies. In virtually every public meeting I attended about *dibao,* officials from the street office would criticize Community cadres who, facing as many economic difficulties as their local residents, described their neighbors' poverty using locally familiar language. In January 2007 Yu Jianhua, who had recently been put in charge of *dibao* in the Hadong street office, notified Community cadres that the income guidelines for informal work, which were formerly understood as existing in name only and were rarely if ever consulted let alone applied in particular situations, should henceforth be strictly enforced in the calculation of income. She admonished them: "If people have no evidence of wages, you should refer to the table of income guidelines.[11] You should memorize every detail of this table!" Failing to appreciate Yu Jianhua's emphatic tone, a Community cadre, Dai Honghua, began to relate the story of one needy woman: "One of our residents has two children, each of whom has a disease. Since her husband passed away, she has barely survived on rag picking." Yu Jianhua responded with obvious irritation: "Did you hear what I told you so far? Do you know how high the income from rag picking is [as listed in the table]? It is 800 to 2,500 yuan! No one can change this standard. The state determined it!" Dai Honghua then grumbled to herself: "Eight hundred to 2,500 yuan! Unbelievable!"

Local residents who are dissatisfied with a decision to deny, reduce, or diminish their benefits often visit the Community office, the street office, and even the district government to plead their desperate case. Officials attempt to silence their pleas by explaining how the government fairly calculated the degree of their poverty according to law and policy. By naturalizing a particular rationale based on calculations as incontestable and authoritative, government officials have reduced local grievances to useless utterances. Residents remain nothing but "the object of information, never a subject in communication," to borrow from Foucault (1977: 200).

One *dibao* recipient, Sun Hong, said to me: "How can the payment of *dibao* be so different? Since the breakdown of the Fenghuang factory, we all have had the same difficulties. Why does my neighbor get 200 yuan for *dibao* while I get only 120? Cadres use inscrutable words whenever I ask." Given her past experience in the work unit, where individual difficulties were addressed by way of face-to-face relationships between cadres and workers, the application of *dibao* as a calculating machine is strange indeed. In Foucault's terms, the calculating machine pivots no longer on the "sovereign-subject relationship" but on the "government-population relationship" (see 2007: 65–76), replacing face-to-face dialogues with numerical calculations. Such a shift in fact loosens the bond connecting local residents like Sun Hong to the party-state through the play of enigmatic numbers. If the calculating machine prevents the poor from having their voices heard, what other path is there for them? How do the poor break through the calculating machine? Familiar Maoist narratives about "the people" have reemerged in an attempt to overcome this predicament.

Fear of "the People"

The dissonance between the discourses that the poor inhabit and the discourses within which the *dibao* scheme operates has crippled conversation between government officials and local residents. As conversation has been made impossible, angry residents have begun to attack the morality of Community cadres. Grumbling over *dibao* has grown into uncontrolled rumors about officials' corruption: "*Dibao* is given to those who make big money by secretly working outside"; "X got *dibao* because she got along with a Community cadre"; "I couldn't become a recipient because I had no one to help me within the government." Whether they are true or not, all these rumors create a serious burden for Community cadres. Although the *dibao* plan emphasizes regularization and standardization through the strict enforcement of law, the socialist principle that relief should be provided under the supervision of the masses of the people (*renmin qunzhong*) has not been entirely abandoned. A retired worker, Jiang Jun, stressed how important the judgment of the people was during the Maoist era in designating his family an "especially difficult family" in his factory. "Back then," he told me, "the work unit posted a notice about the situation of my family. It detailed that I had six children and that my father had cancer. Everyone had a right to determine whether my situation was correct or not. Never did I dare to lie, because any lie would cut my wages and could even cause me to be expelled from the unit permanently. In those days, you were criticized for having capitalist thought even if you raised only one chicken. How frightening the eyes of the people were!"

Under the *dibao* plan, this system of peer supervision within the work unit has survived in the form of the "public notice" (*zhangbang gongbu*).[12] The government's use of the public notice shows that the calculating machine of *dibao* has not made a complete break with the logic of "the people" in its operations. Article 9 of the "Regulations" notes, "As for any recipients who will receive the minimum livelihood guarantee, the government agency for screening and managing it should publicly post the information regarding any *dibao* applicants in order to allow the general public to judge the eligibility of the applicants." The public notice is precisely the means by which the masses are afforded the right to oversee the government's decision making and to report any problems with the distribution of *dibao*. Community cadres are required to post a notice in public gathering places in their neighborhood in which recipients' names, the amount of money they will receive, and the reason why they will receive *dibao* are described in detail; the notice must remain posted for at least seven days prior to a final decision. By inviting public scrutiny of each decision, government officials allow residents to determine whether their neighbors are "actually poor" or not. Officials are then required to reexamine the situation of any applicants whose eligibility is cast into doubt by their neighbors.

This public notice has been a source of anxiety among local cadres, who fear that the comments of residents may leave them vulnerable to criticism from their higher-ups, who are preoccupied with social stability, and eventually endanger their position through disciplinary action taken by the government if any wrongdoing were to be discovered in policy implementation. The public notice portion of the *dibao* application process was the subject of a meeting in the street office on December 18, 2006. Yu Jianhua began by complaining that some Community cadres had neglected to put up a public notice about the *dibao* applicants: "Don't you know how important the public notice is? You should definitely put up a poster. If the people disagree with an eligibility determination, there is nothing you can do about it. What if any trouble arises because you didn't? The public notice is not a thing you should be afraid of!" The oldest Community cadre, Xu Ying, protested: "You know that one of my residents cannot move at all. Totally paralyzed, he has no means of livelihood. Should I withdraw his qualification because of negative opinions from the masses?" Yu Jianhua strongly refuted this, however. "I know that you're talking about Liao. Of course I admit that his life is difficult. But how can he be a recipient without the signatures of his neighbors? The *dibao* money belongs to the Communist Party. It cannot be given to whomever you want. You should keep in mind that when you try to help someone, another four or five people in a similar situation are waiting their turn. They could raise a rebellion [*zaofan*]!"

"Rebel" was one of the most frequently used terms during the Cultural Revolution. In that period the antagonism between the rebel faction and the conservative faction was as widespread among workers as it was among Red Guard students. In the common usage, the rebel faction consisted of underprivileged groups targeting the radical overthrow of Chinese society, while the conservative faction included better-off groups supporting the political status quo (Rosen 1982; Unger 1982). This antagonism, however, was not necessarily ideological but had a more mundane basis (Perry and Li 1997: 64). Within the same school, factory, or even family in Hadong, two opposing groups emerged time and again during the Cultural Revolution—at odds over such matters as whether the group would support the governor of Heilongjiang province, whether they would defend the director of the Fenghuang factory, or whose faction constituted the real admirers of Chairman Mao. The word "rebel" was widely used to refer to anyone who challenged authority regardless of current factional struggles. Jiang Jun commented to me while criticizing corrupt officials in recent years: "During the Maoist period, cadres never dared to embezzle even 100 yuan. Who would have dared to practice corruption when the people would've stared at you? The people would rebel against you! 'We the people' would put up a 'big character' wall poster [*dazibao*] and level public criticism at you!" What Jiang Jun was addressing was not so much a statement of fact as, to borrow from Ching Kwan Lee, "the shared vision of the history" (2000: 228) in terms of which his critique of current officials could be legitimized.

Although both the wall poster and widespread public criticism common during the Cultural Revolution have disappeared, the word "rebel" still haunts low-level government officials and Community cadres despite (or because of) strict law enforcement against breaches of the *dibao* regulations. If any trouble occurs in the process of authorizing a *dibao* recipient—for example, if a resident visits the district or city government to complain about an unfair screening process in her or his neighborhood—these local officials may find themselves deposed, not directly by the people but through sanctions from higher government officials, whose primary concern is social stability. This is the context in which the *dibao* bureau of the district government set this goal for 2008: "Make the ratio of flawless selection of *dibao* recipients reach 100 percent and keep the rate of *dibao*-related complaints to the authorities [*shangfang*] below 3 percent."[13]

One day in June 2007, to avoid any trouble caused by the public notice system, Community cadre Lin Liping went to a "cooperative" neighbor to seek a signature for a *dibao* applicant. According to the "Regulations," at least two neighbors were supposed to judge the applicant's eligibility. The name of the *dibao* applicant was Jie Min, a forty-seven-year-old woman whose husband suffered from cerebral palsy. Lin Liping asked Jie Min not to tell anybody that she had applied for *dibao*. This was not because there were any real flaws in Jie Min's qualification but because Lin Liping was afraid that people would make up "idle gossip." I accompanied Lin Liping when she went to see Wang Guifen, the neighbor who was willing to sign for Jie Min. Wang Guifen used to be a teacher in the Fenghuang elementary school, and she was suffering from cerebral palsy like Jie Min's husband.

> LIN LIPING (ASKING WANG GUIFEN FOR HER SIGNATURE): Community cadres like me merely conduct household inspection [*ruhu diaocha*]. District officials will visit soon and ask you again whether Jie Min is qualified for *dibao* or not.
>
> WANG GUIFEN: Don't worry about it. I know well that Jie Min's family is in a miserable condition.
>
> WANG'S HUSBAND: Jie Min's child goes to school. He's still young.
>
> LIN LIPING (TO WANG GUIFEN): The reason I especially ask you to sign is because you're a reasonable person. You understand such circumstances better than anyone else does. Other residents make up false stories. They argue with me and keep asking why some folks are recipients and others aren't.
>
> WANG GUIFEN: Look at this neighborhood. Honestly, every family here deserves *dibao*.
>
> LIN LIPING: I know what you mean. People are all poor here. That's why there are too many gossips in this neighborhood. Anyway, you only have to sign this form. *Dibao* is extremely strict now. One's *dibao* goes away if a neighbor makes even a single call to the government and says that the family is not poor enough for *dibao*. Our community had some people who were left out of *dibao* for that reason.

On our way back to the Community office, Lin Liping began to complain about *dibao:* "It is too hard to determine who are poor. No problem if you're totally disabled and unable to work. But everyone begins to make a fuss about *dibao* if you're sick but still young. What would I do?"

During my fieldwork, I rarely saw local residents express their grievances about *dibao* through organized action. Still, many residents displeased, embarrassed, and even threatened local officials while visiting them individually or in small groups. For example, a drunken laid-off worker made an abrupt appearance at a meeting in the street office and shouted: "Are you really serving the people? The truth is that you do not serve the people [*Wei renmin fuwu*]. You serve the money [*Wei renminbi fuwu*]!" A middle-aged man whose *dibao* application was not accepted made a threatening retort to a Community director when she said that she was not responsible for the final decision: "If that is the case, what should I do? Shall I go to Hu Jintao [China's president] or Wen Jiabao [China's prime minister] about this?" Not being able to choke back his anger, he shouted on the street, "There are too many cadres who would have been dragged off to public rallies if they had worked in the era of Chairman Mao!" This citizen, and others like him, are not "rebels" in any familiar sense of the term; collective memories related to "rebellion," however, have cultivated a tension between local officials and residents. Therefore, because *dibao* is considered a breeding ground for anger and fear rather than the "final safety net," calculated management based on the level of income has become problematic. Any low-level official might ask: How can I best protect my position by soothing residents' complaints about *dibao?* The answer is found in the return to "labor" as the actual yardstick for determining who should be qualified for *dibao*.

The Recurring Claim of Labor

Fervor for work was the first and foremost proletarian ethic in socialist China (see Dixon 1981: 12; Rofel 1999: 122). Most adults in Hadong are still familiar with songs like "Labor Is Most Honorable" (*Laodong zui guangrong*) or a slogan like "You Don't Eat If You Don't Work" (*Bulaodongzhe budeshi*). The status of labor was elevated in many "work competitions" (*laodong jingsai*) organized by work units. These competitions—within a work unit or among work units— were widely used as a means to boost productivity. As many retirees in Hadong remembered, winning such competitions was considered a great honor, often helping one improve one's political status or gain promotion to a leadership position within the work unit as a cadre. The value of labor was highlighted among youth as well as workers. Throughout the socialist regime, the party-state made systematic efforts to instill *wu'ai* (five loves) among schoolchildren in the form of *"wu'ai* education." Love for labor (*ailaodong*) was one of the "five loves": "love for the motherland, love for the people, love for labor, love for science, and the cherishing of public property."[14] In short, labor was seen not merely as a means of production but as "a pedagogical tool" (Jeffery 2002: 331) through which workers would be reborn as "deserving" people qualified for building socialism.

In post-Mao China, the powerful link between labor and morality has persisted, although the meaning that it imposes on urban workers has radically shifted. Once celebrated as "the laboring people" (*laodong renmin*), urban workers are now accused of a lack of labor consciousness if they should become impoverished and dependent on government support. Mockery of those who "eat on *dibao*" (*chi dibao*) without actively searching for a new job runs throughout media accounts. Terms like "*dibao* sluggards" (*dibao lanhan*) or "*dibao*niks" (*dibao zu*) are frequently used in the media to denigrate "lazy" people who are supposedly satisfied with *dibao* and thus reluctant to look for work.[15] The *dibao* policy is considered to be flawed because its relatively comprehensive care has allegedly ended up making "getting a job" no better than "eating on *dibao*" (*jiuye buru chi dibao*).[16] These media accounts often end with remarks that highlight labor values in socialism: "'You don't eat if you don't work' should continue to serve as a guideline for China's social security system";[17] "We should stand on our own feet inspired by socialist values that honor hard work and dismiss laziness as a disgrace."[18]

The irony today is that people who are stigmatized as being "lazy" or "unwilling to work" have often been told that their labor is no longer wanted under the market economy. Nevertheless, such public censure of "dependency" is often, ironically, reproduced and rearticulated by the poor themselves, who are familiar with the socialist rhetoric of "loving labor." In Hadong an older retiree whose application for *dibao* had been rejected gave vent to her grievances, asking Community cadres: "Do you really think it makes sense that I'm not qualified for *dibao* while young folks eat on *dibao* [*chi dibao*]? Don't you know the socialist principle of *anlao fenpei* [distribution according to labor]? How are young folks who still can labor eating away the state's money without finding work?"

It is no wonder that, encountering widespread criticism by the poor themselves, as well as from the media, local government officials gradually began to emphasize labor as the yardstick for determining who should be qualified for *dibao*. The "ability to work" (*laodong nengli*) has been considered more acceptable by both local officials and residents than the official criterion—income—for receiving *dibao*. Local officials have applied the presumed income standard more strictly to people of working age (up to forty-five for women and fifty-five for men), often dissuading these individuals from applying for *dibao* by saying, "*Dibao* is not for those who can still work."

What is the consequence of transforming the actual criterion for *dibao* from income to an "ability to work"? The ironic outcome is that the very workers for whom *dibao* was designed have become the first to be denied

Table 3.1   Numbers of the overall population (with urban household permit) and *dibao*
recipients in Hadong, 1997–2006

	OVERALL POPULATION		DIBAO RECIPIENTS	
YEAR	**HOUSEHOLDS**	**PERSONS**	**HOUSEHOLDS**	**PERSONS**
1997	3,589	13,720	21	43
1998	3,989	13,068	23	46
1999	4,961	14,896	25	53
2000	5,320	15,328	44	90
2001	5,869	15,585	1,150	2,875
2002	6,118	16,359	1,130	2,825
2003	6,805	18,015	920	2,300
2004	6,028	17,260	845	2,112
2005	7,011	18,155	825	2,060
2006	8,509	20,615	796	1,990

Source: Internal materials, Guangming street office.

access to the plan. It has become rare for *dibao* to be granted to those who
are of working age unless they are disabled or gravely ill. Table 3.1 shows
how the number of *dibao* recipients in Hadong has changed since the policy
was first put in place in Harbin in 1997. The number dramatically increased
in 2001, when full implementation of the policy began, and plunged after
2002. The number of *dibao* households continued to decrease from 920 in
2003 to 796 in 2006, and those who were expelled from the plan mostly
came from the households of relatively young laid-off workers, although
local officials explained this exclusion as "the natural consequence of
dynamic management."

In this chapter I have demonstrated how local resistance against governmental
attempts to deal with poverty ironically reinforces the precarious state of the
poor. The new policy for addressing urban poverty is a kind of calculating
machine which has introduced new rationales of governance by erasing the
historicity of the poor and making poverty compatible with the "ebbs and
flows" of the market economy. The attempts by the poor to communicate
with this puzzling machine have ended up excluding many of them from its
protection. In other words, China's new management of urban poverty has
been created not through the mechanical construction of the poor as "the
poor population" but through complex relationships among the poor and
government officials at different levels.

Before closing this chapter, I want to address one important question:
If *dibao* was created to protect a particular group of the poor—urban
laid-off workers—whose lack of income presents a serious threat to social
stability but has instead ended up excluding many of them from the plan,

how should the state manage this paradox? How can the state prevent the excluded group from becoming a danger to social stability? Given such circumstances, the old ad hoc style of assistance based on face-to-face inter-actions and visible performances of poverty remains one of the techniques for managing the problem, although it has been widely criticized as an "unscientific" and "sloppy" Maoist legacy (Hong 2004: 64–78). As in Mao's era, the practice of "theaterization" increases the visibility of both laid-off workers and the party-state by attaching them to face-to-face relation-ships based on paternalism. Unlike in Mao's era, however, this performative practice addresses the concerns of these workers insofar as they are one of several "vulnerable groups" (*ruoshi qunti*)—the state's new term for them. This term strips these workers of the political power they once possessed as "the people." Despite the reduction of the poor to members of a category, the practice of theaterization has not fully disappeared, although local resi-dents rarely welcome the "improvised" form of assistance, which makes no promise of further protection for them. Let me conclude this chapter with one anecdote that reveals how this practice is being continued as the inevitable supplement to the government program of *dibao*.

In the fall of 2006 a man in his late forties killed himself in Hadong. After having been laid off from the Fenghuang factory, he had become an alcoholic and ended up divorced from his wife. His sixteen-year-old daughter headed to the street office after her father's death. In tears, she said to a government official, "My dad hanged himself because the government excluded him from *dibao*." Yet the official stressed: "Not all the poor are qualified for *dibao*. *Dibao* is a policy that has its own regulations."

Although local government officials first defended their decisions as "unbiased," the situation became complicated when the story of the man's suicide spread and finally caught the ear of municipal government officials. Upon hearing of the situation a week after it happened, the top director of *dibao* in Harbin immediately visited the local government. Enraged, he ordered that the case be processed on an emergency basis. His visit, fol-lowed by several phone calls from other senior officials, led to a sudden turnabout on the part of the local administration. Legality was no longer an issue. Apart from making cash donations, government officials in Hadong bought clothes for the daughter of the dead man and even underwrote her father's funeral by taking up a collection out of their own pockets. An official in the street office announced the "end" of this incident in a weekly meeting with Community cadres, saying: "Everyone knows how we have made great efforts to settle this matter. Senior leaders also rewarded us for our service. . . . She [the daughter of the dead man] expressed a deep gratitude for our efforts. I told her grandfather that we helped her only out of sympathy and that the government would not take further action related to this incident. Despite this emergency, you should keep in mind that our administration of *dibao* must be based on law and policy." Such "emergencies" have in fact become normal as the practice of "theaterization" is called upon in order to mediate any problems that *dibao* does not fully address.

CHAPTER 4

The Will to Survive

Mountains of refuse and waste are among the most troublesome problems in Hadong. Without drainpipes, residents usually throw the filthy water used for washing and cooking, in addition to urine and all kinds of solid waste, outside their houses. Although every street has a few small containers for wastewater and one large dustbin for solid waste, not all residents use them; it is not easy to haul garbage to a dustbin several blocks from their houses when temperatures fall below zero. In addition, the dustbin is usually jammed full because disposal trucks rarely visit this neighborhood on the urban periphery, although they are scheduled to do so. In summer, seldom does any of the solid garbage dry out because it is drenched by heavy rains. Once winter comes, all garbage, including coal ash, freezes, creating black mountains on every street corner. When the frozen garbage begins to melt in late April and early May—the period of "the patriotic cleaning campaign" (*aiguo weisheng yundong*)—the whole village becomes a "sewage disposal plant," in the words of one resident.

Hadong's garbage problem mirrors a double dilemma in that the total amount of garbage has increased significantly since the economic reform encouraged consumerism, while the work unit system, in which each work unit took charge of its residential compound, has collapsed in the midst of that same reform. Although the Fenghuang work unit in Hadong officially went bankrupt only a few years before my visit, its decline, which included a deterioration of the former workers' village, had started about fifteen years earlier. No improvement, large or small, had been made since the mud-walled houses built for workers in 1955 were remodeled as brick houses in 1978. In addition, little support from the government had been given to this urban periphery, where single-story houses would soon be demolished to make way for the spreading urban redevelopment.

Every morning, Community cadres appeared in the streets of Hadong with besoms and shovels in an effort to maintain the status quo in this soon-to-be-extinct place. These cadres, the lowest-level government officials, performed wide-ranging routine duties in urban administration. Interestingly, most of them were former factory workers—mostly female—who had experienced layoffs at various times and barely managed to find work through the state's reemployment policies. Except for a few young employees in recent years, most of the Community cadres had lived in Hadong as long as their neighbors and faced the same economic difficulties.

Forty-six-year-old Jiang Yun was one of these cadres. On a late afternoon in November 2006, Jiang Yun and I were on our way back from a weekly meeting at the street office. Jiang was depressed because a higher-level official in the meeting had publicly blamed her Community for neglecting the cleanup of garbage in its area. "If you aren't willing to work hard, resign

FIGURE 4.1. Garbage cleanup among Community cadres (April 2007)

right now!" This was what she had heard from street office director Li Yuming. Her depression intensified when she encountered angry residents on the streets: "The dustbin is already full. How are you using the cleaning fee we have paid? Do you expect us to live with all this garbage?" Jiang Yun grumbled in response: "Why are you shouting at me? Did I order the disposal truck not to come here?" Her words were interrupted by the familiar retort from a resident: "If that is the case, to whom should I complain? Shall I go to Hu Jintao [China's president] about this?"

In the midst of this noisy disturbance, I could not take my eyes off a magazine that Jiang Yun was holding in her right hand. It was the monthly journal, titled *Community* [*Shequ*], that she was forced to purchase from the street office. The front cover displayed a picture of some middle-class residents in a newly built gated community who had volunteered to explain to their neighbors how to use the recycling bins in their neighborhood. I took in the contrast between this run-down district of Hadong and the elegant middle-class neighborhood on the magazine cover, the contrast between frowns and smiles, reluctance and willingness, discord and partnership, and above all, rotten vegetables piled in the street and orderly recycling bins. Against the backdrop of the party-state's "building community" (*shequ jianshe*) campaign, the one setting was commonly criticized as a remnant of the past that ought to disappear while the other was praised as the future that should follow. Still, in contrast to the futuristic image of volunteering citizens on the cover of the magazine, the polemical scene in Hadong was the vivid reality that I had routinely witnessed. It was the scene that Community cadres and local residents of the decaying neighborhood performed painfully under the banner of "building community."

In this chapter I examine the ways in which "community" is practiced as a new mode of governing poverty in China's cities, in particular, how urban laid-off workers who have come to serve as Community cadres are forced to refashion themselves as self-motivating citizen volunteers under the party-state's campaign of building community.

Such compulsion may seem odd if one recalls how much attention the spirit of voluntarism and empowerment has received from scholars who view community as a new form of neoliberal governance. For instance, Barbara Cruikshank discusses the emergence of the "will to empower" in her analysis of antipoverty movements in the United States. Typical of what she calls "the liberal arts of conduct," the will to empower has become a "technology of citizenship," that is, "a method for constituting citizens out of subjects and maximizing their political participation" (1999: 67). "Community" has received singular attention from social activists, as well as from government officials, as a crucial site in which the poor are defined and motivated to cultivate the will to empower themselves.

This logic of empowerment has also raised awareness among many contemporary Chinese scholars in the wake of the party-state's "building community" campaign. Although it did not become a national policy until 2000, experiments started in various cities in the 1990s, when the reformulation of urban space became an urgent issue for the state amidst the breakdown of both the household registration system and the urban work unit system (Bray 2006: 531, 536). Replacing the work unit, the "community" (*shequ*) has emerged as a "new basic unit of urban governance" (Bray 2006: 530). The campaign has led many scholars to rethink the changing face of the relationship between the state and citizens in China.[1] They have selectively embraced the idea of "community" as a valorized alternative for coping with the crisis of state sovereignty in the midst of the nation's pro-market restructuring. Focusing on participation and voluntarism, these scholars have commonly interpreted the official term "community self-governance" (*shequ zizhi*) as self-governance *through* community.

Approximately fifteen years after the "building community" slogan swept China's cities, however, what I witnessed during the process of garbage cleanup in Hadong was not voluntary participation among residents in general but the compulsory labor of the lowest-level state officials, the Community cadres. The "community self-governance" of the cadres had become an expression not so much of "the will to empower" (Cruikshank 1999) as of the will to survive. Ironically, these cadres had attached themselves to the old Maoist doctrine of self-reliance when they became the vanguard of the "neoliberal" movement that views community as "a solution to problems of government" (Rose 1999: 170). How had this happened? What does their vulnerable status tell us about the ways in which poverty is managed in China's cities?

By delving into the fragile position of Community cadres, I examine how the specter of "the people" permeates governmental intervention through "community." In the decaying urban periphery, state governance through "community" has served two contradictory missions. One is to prompt laid-off workers to govern themselves through voluntary participation in their community—not to depend on the work unit or the government. The other is to rescue these laid-off workers by helping them gain reemployment in the state sector. Most Community cadres in Hadong managed to win their jobs with the government through the policy of "the public post" (*gongyixing gangwei*), which privileges urban laid-off workers. In one sense the Chinese state "did not abandon the people," as one cadre often tried to assure me. Nevertheless, governmental protection has accompanied the reconfiguration of "the people" as the historical tension embedded in the concept runs through the management of community. Historical gender and family problematics among "the people," combined with the tension between "the people" as a class and "the people" as a nation, have led to a situation in which the state "protects" mostly female, uneducated cadres in highly hierarchical ways while exploiting their liminal position in the state apparatus.

In what follows I detail the practices and processes that have engendered the vulnerability of Community cadres in Hadong. "Self-governance," rather than being a technique for mobilizing citizens as willing partners of the state, has become an unavoidable necessity for Community cadres' own survival through the convergence of two different practices. One is the local historical practice of marginalizing the Community, and the Residential Committee as its predecessor, in favor of a paternalistic work unit. The other is the state's practice of positioning the Community as simultaneously in and outside the state bureaucracy while casting doubt on the capabilities of Community cadres. Before delving into these practices, however, I want first to introduce governmental accounts of "community" in China, which have produced mixed discourses. When I argue that "self-governance" has become an expression not so much of the will to empower as of the will to survive, I do not mean that the party-state's grand plan to bid farewell to the people's "dependency" under socialism and to imbue citizens with a new self-mobilizing subjectivity has been blemished by local modifications. As Tania Li argues, more often plans of intervention per se are pulled together from an existing repertoire through bricolage (2007: 6).

Governance through Community: Ambiguous Missions

Recent attention to "community" around the globe is deeply intertwined with growing concerns about the place of the state amidst processes of neoliberalization. Against the political analytics structured by binaries between state and civil society, and between sovereignty and autonomy, Nikolas Rose and Peter Miller argue that modern forms of exercising power over national territories should be examined not through the monolithic entity of "the state" but through "government." They write: "Government is the historically constituted matrix within which are articulated all those dreams, schemes, strategies, and maneuvers of authorities that seek to shape the beliefs and conduct of others in desired directions by acting upon their will, their circumstances or their environment"

(Rose and Miller 1992: 175). According to Rose (1999), "community," or more precisely "government *through* community," has become characteristic of the liberal problematics of government. Citizens are mobilized to govern themselves, and community is re-created as a willing partner of the state, not in opposition to it. When the idea of community becomes a valorized alternative, the state is "no longer... required to answer all society's needs for order, security, health and productivity" (Rose 1999: 174).

Many scholars have selectively adopted Rose's insights when they analyze the increasing prevalence of discourses of "community" and "self-governance" outside North Atlantic countries, where the strong governance of the state apparatus is more palpable. They have noted that "community," as a new mode of governance, draws fresh awareness even in non-liberal settings. Yet they also argue that governmental concern with "community" constitutes a new device of control that does not necessarily reduce the presence of the state regardless of seemingly reduced state machinery (Sharma 2006; Song 2009).

China's acknowledgment of "government *through* community" brings to light not the retreat of state practices but their remapping, in which state authority is buttressed even though the state's former responsibilities are dispersed (see Ong and Zhang 2008; Sigley 2006; Hoffman 2010). Indeed from the outset, the idea of community has been institutionally configured by the state's urban administrative apparatus (Bray 2006: 546). In 2000 the Ministry of Civil Affairs issued a document titled "Views of the 'Ministry of Civil Affairs' on Promoting Urban Community Building throughout the Nation."[2] The document defines "community" as "a social group formed by people who live within a range of a certain region. The current range of community indicates an area under the jurisdiction of the [former] Residents' Committee [*jumin weiyuanhui*], the scale of which has been restructured since the reform of the urban administration." The Residents' Committee (RC) was officially referred to as "a mass organization of self-governance at the grassroots level,"[3] that is, outside the state bureaucracy. The RC, however, was in fact the lowest level of urban administrative unit in the PRC. Its cadres were given official responsibility to (1) promulgate state laws and policies; (2) educate residents about their legal rights and duties; (3) implement public services for residents; (4) mediate local disputes; (5) help the government implement its programs, such as public hygiene, the one-child policy, social relief, and youth education; and (6) transmit the residents' opinions to the government.[4] After the initiation of the building community campaign, the RC was officially renamed the Community Residents' Committee (*shequ jumin weiyuanhui*), simply abbreviated as the Community (*shequ*). The *shequ* is larger in scale than the RC because in some cases two or three RCs were merged into one Community. The duties of this new body are not entirely different from those of the RC; the duties of the former continue, while the administrative duties of local cadres have been extended to include dealing with urgent issues such as the minimum livelihood guarantee (*dibao*) and job training for laid-off workers. Government documents make it clear that the term "community" indicates both the lowest-level unit of urban administration and the neighborhood it covers. That is to say, "community" is not voluntarily formed by autonomous individual subjects, a concept deeply rooted in the Western imagination, but institutionally planned by state apparatuses.

What intrigues me in the remapping of state practices through community is the coexistence of conflicting missions directed toward it. One contradiction is found in the regrouping of the state bureaucracy. The Chinese state promoted the creation of "a smaller government and a bigger society" (*xiaozhengfu dashehui*) as the official goal of building community (Pan 2002). As I show in detail through the case of Hadong, however, the government has actually grown "bigger" as small groups of unpaid volunteers in the former RC have been turned in increasing numbers into Community cadres whose paycheck comes directly from government channels. The other contradiction is found in the membership of this Community. Never assuming an equal partnership between the government and the citizen, official documents on "community self-governance" are mostly preoccupied with developmentalist ideas that raise the standard of "culture and education" of community participants.[5] Such an emphasis on professionalism contradicts another governmental decision to recruit less well educated laid-off workers as Community cadres after some technical training (Shi 2006a). Because the idea of "community" emerged at the very moment when the urban work unit system began to collapse, the security-driven mission to incorporate urban workers under the umbrella of community has been as crucial as the emphasis on professionalism.

In all, the party-state's visionary scheme for building community pivots on an oxymoron, the bigger government that aims at a smaller government, as well as the professional efforts led by nonprofessional laid-off workers. In Hadong, Community cadres were at the core of these conflicting missions, for they were laid-off workers newly incorporated into state bureaucracy with the primary mission of building community. No longer mere messengers of guidelines handed down from above, these cadres were required by the government to "implement daily management efforts regarding *community* service, *community* health, *community* culture, *community* environment, and *community* security" as well as to "guide and organize *community* residents to build a civilized *community* and civilized family" (Shi 2006a: 89, emphasis added). Various kinds of responsibilities that the higher levels of government should be taking have been shifted onto these cadres' shoulders. In the next section I turn to Hadong to explore how this burden that Community cadres carry is normalized not only by local residents but also by the cadres themselves.

"The Parents Are Gone": From the Work Unit to the Community

As I showed in chapter 1, Fenghuang was not merely a factory but a "work unit" (*danwei*), which had an all-encompassing impact on every aspect of the lives of its workers and their families. By merging life and labor, the work unit system guaranteed its workers complete perquisites: secure jobs, affordable housing, medical care, subsidies, retirement pensions, and so on. To understand the fragile position of Community cadres and the ambivalent status of "community," one first needs to trace the historically asymmetrical relationship between the work unit and the Residential Committee.

The Work Unit: The Image of a "True Parent"

"Fenghuang did not stop taking care of workers even when it faced difficulties," retired cadre Feng Shizheng emphasized as he showed me a report from the Congress of Workers and Staff (*zhigong daibiao dahui*) in February 1987. He kept it as if it were a precious object to commemorate the first meeting that he had attended after being promoted to workshop director. The report included the welfare fund expenditures in the work unit during the previous year:

1. Expenses for medicine: 519,000 yuan
2. Expenses for day nurseries, preschools, and cafeterias: 51,000 yuan
3. Medical care expenses: 63,000 yuan
4. Poverty relief expenses: 25,000 yuan
5. Expenses for bathing and haircutting: 35,700 yuan
6. Subsidies for meat: 333,000 yuan
7. Subsidies for food and other necessities(except meat): 473,000 yuan
8. Expenses for books and periodicals for intellectuals, bonuses for developing science and technology (*keji lütie*), and bonuses for cadres: 66,000 yuan
9. Subsidies for one-child families (*dusheng zinü*): 52,000 yuan

10. Subsidies for women workers' sanitary napkins: 22,000 yuan
11. Subsidies for autumn vegetables eaten in winter (Chinese cabbage, potatoes, green onions, and radishes): 19,000 yuan[6]

Feng Shizheng proudly said to me: "Fenghuang was not a mere company as it is today. It was like a big family. In the family, parents take care of children. Even if they are very poor, they never give up raising their children. That's what Fenghuang did for its workers."

The metaphor of the work unit as "family," however, is in fact ambiguous and limited. As Dorinne K. Kondo (1990) illuminates through her ethnography of a Japanese company, the metaphor of "family" elides inherent hierarchies among workers as well as between workers and managers. The beneficiaries of the aforementioned welfare fund were not Fenghuang workers in general but only workers in the state sector (*gongchang*). As noted in chapter 1, the hierarchy in the work sector also resonated with gender inequality. Nevertheless, the feeling of present loss imbues the nostalgia expressed by many workers with a sense of certainty about the past. Nostalgia, as Lisa Rofel argues, is "a utopian gesture" that "searches for certitude in the face of the potential multivocality of meaning" (1999: 136). In the failure of workers to remember, or in their willingly ignoring, those tensions and fissures, their nostalgia for the Mao era reflects a desire to recapture the image of the "true parent" from their former work unit.

The image of the work unit as a parent still prevails among older retirees in Hadong. Seventy-four-year-old Wang Shaojun stressed to me how Fenghuang had had a reputation as an "honorable father," as he put it. "You might not know how proud we workers were of Fenghuang," he told me. "In the early 1950s, when I entered Fenghuang, there were a bunch of technicians from the USSR. Central government leaders such as Zhou Enlai and Zhu De visited our factory during that time. I saw them with my own eyes! Do you know why Fenghuang didn't go bankrupt until later [than other factories]? It's because our factory belonged neither to Harbin [city] nor to Heilongjiang [province]. It was directly under the control of the central government." This meant that it could not—and should not—close of its own accord. In the 1960s and 1970s, some young people got to enter a good work unit by paying money. Yet this was impossible in Fenghuang. It wasn't easy even if you contacted a provincial-level cadre."

Sixty-one-year-old Li Yaping remembered Fenghuang as a kind of "devoted mother." Li was assigned to Fenghuang after being discharged from military service in 1971. He recounted: "I had a family of eight, including old, sick parents. Fenghuang took pity on my situation and assigned me housing of thirty square meters. Chosen as an 'especially difficult family' [*tekun hu*], my family also received 30 yuan per quarter from Fenghuang for a few years. I still worship Chairman Mao. During that time, 'Serve the People' was not an empty promise at all. Cadres in Fenghuang took care of workers from the bottom of their hearts. They came to visit our family several times after my father had surgery." Similar praise came from seventy-two-year-old Zhang Yujian: "In the Mao era, Fenghuang rescued whoever was mentally retarded or starving to death. Cadres were true 'leaders' [*ling-dao*], though they are now often called 'bosses' [*laoban*]."

This image of a "true parent" was a strong theme running through the *Fenghuang Newsletter* even while the work unit was breaking down, from the late 1980s onward. For example, a letter from a retiree in a 1990 newsletter reads: "At present, our factory faces the hardest times since its establishment. I deeply appreciate Fenghuang for making the pension for thirty thousand retirees a top priority despite its difficulties. Isn't this the very expression of how the Party takes care of old workers? Some people take it for granted that the factory gives us a pension. They are wrong. How can we take it for granted in these severe circumstances, when numerous factories in Harbin cannot pay their workers a salary?"[7] I was somewhat cynical about the dramatic tone of this letter, but ex-workers who read it with me were not. For these workers, the exaggerated narrative acquired a kind of sincerity because its referent no longer existed.

The Residential Committee: "A Gossiping Place for Grannies"

What was the place of the Residential Committee during the time when the work unit was considered a "true parent"? Hadong had had fifteen RCs under the authority of the Guangming street office before they were reorganized into eleven Communities during the community building campaign in the early 1990s. As the lowest level of the state apparatus, the RC, like the work unit, intervened in the lives of local residents on matters ranging from public hygiene to the settling of local disputes and the care of families in need of relief (*jiuji hu*). The RC, however, and even the street office, its immediate superior, was far from being considered a counterpart of the work unit when local residents recalled what their lives were like during the Mao era. Wang Shaojun, Li Yaping, and Zhang Yujian, all of whom spoke highly of the work unit, seemed to have no interest in the RC when I brought it up. "The Residential Committee? It was where grannies merely conveyed the words of the state to the masses when they had nothing to do after retirement. They were not paid for their work," one informant told me. "The work unit did almost everything for workers. The grannies did not have much work to do. They were busy spreading gossip," said another.

In their narratives, the peripheral status of the RC parallels its "feminine" status. We can see this illustrated in the case of seventy-four-year-old Xu Ying, the eldest cadre in Hadong. One early November morning in 2006 I visited the Jiangbei Community office to see its director, Xu Ying. I wanted to hear about her experiences in the RC before it was reorganized as the Community. Her Community office, once a day nursery run by the Fenghuang work unit, had neither a boiler nor access to a water supply, although the temperature was near freezing. The atmosphere in the office was extremely serious. Xu Ying was chairing a meeting on an upcoming election for the People's Congress. She was reading government documents aloud while four other cadres listened to her quietly. This earnest atmosphere was quite different from what I had experienced in other Communities. "The young cadres of today tend not to take their work seriously," said Xu Ying, finally turning her attention to me after finishing the one-hour meeting. "In the past, we old cadres in the RC had a strong sense of responsibility. Putting off work was unthinkable."

Xu Ying retired early from the Fenghuang work unit in 1980 in order to turn her position over to her second son (*jieban*), who had returned to

FIGURE 4.2. Xu Ying (left) in her Community office (November 2006)

Harbin after spending six years in the countryside (*xiaxiang*). That year Xu Ying became an RC cadre on the recommendation of the Fenghuang trade union. "I was only forty-four at that time," she told me. "In addition, people rarely found a junior-middle school graduate in this neighborhood." I asked, "Among all retirees from Fenghuang?" Xu Ying answered "yes," although she specified "female" this time. "Until the mid-1990s, the street office selected RC cadres among female retirees from the Fenghuang work unit. I was hesitant at first because I wanted to take a rest. But some cadres in the trade union and the street office kept asking me to serve this neighborhood. 'You have little work to do.' That's what they kept telling me." I asked why cadres were selected only among women. "I don't know," Xu Ying answered in a puzzled tone. "This job is not what men usually do. It was quite unimportant. No men would take on such work without a salary."

Xu Ying began to describe her "unimportant" work in terms full of sincerity. "There was no special work to do when I first became the RC cadre," she said. "Deng Xiaoping declared the economic reform in the late 1970s. Yet it was not until the mid-1980s that we felt some sense of that reform. During that time, we cadres didn't even have a separate office. My home was my office. If I discovered any people suffering from economic difficulties, I contacted the trade union so that the work unit could protect them. If they had no work unit, I contacted the street office so that they could be selected as a 'relief family.'" She continued: "I myself took care of poor families, especially when the Spring Festival [Chinese New Year] was coming. I made sure that these families had enough oil for cooking or coal for a fire. Public security was also an important matter. Around the late 1970s, when the Cultural Revolution was nearly over, our neighborhood was crowded with jobless youths [*daiye qingnian*]. Without work, they loafed on the streets and even committed crimes. They hampered social stability. We cadres had to manage them. Also, I had to intervene in family disputes sometimes. I knew every situation in more than five hundred families in my neighborhood. A neighbor, Mr. Wang, was notorious for beating his wife." Xu Ying went on describing her work for a very long time, but she concluded her reminiscences quite simply: "My work was not that different from taking care of children at home. Anyway, it was quite miscellaneous and trivial [*za*]."

I was intrigued by the way Xu Ying narrated her recollections. Her interpretation was at odds with the sentiment of local cadres, who considered her a "true socialist woman." To them she was representative of "*funü*," a national female subject targeted by socialist mobilization (Barlow 1994a: 269; 1994b: 345). Yet the most disciplined among the cadres in Hadong, Xu Ying enumerated her past work seriously, in great detail, but then ended up calling it *za*.

Although *za* literally means sundry or miscellaneous, Xu Ying used the term negatively, implying that the miscellaneous things she dealt with were of little value.

Stevan Harrell has asserted that Maoist socialism tore down a traditional moral distinction in China that had separated female and male into "inner" and "outer" spheres: "China moved from a vision of a gendered division of labor, where some tasks were appropriate for women and others for men, to ideological denial of the gendered division of labor" (Harrell 2000: 74; see also Ebrey 1984; Mann 2000). This gendered division of labor was, according to his argument, radically denied in Mao's era because the role of the family diminished alongside the state's control over individual lives and its mobilization of production outside the household.

Nevertheless, the peripheral position of the RC reveals how deeply embedded the gendered division of labor was in local social practices despite the ideological denial of its existence. As shown in Xu Ying's and other residents' accounts, the traditional assumption that caring for others is woman's work had continued in the PRC. By reducing her responsibilities to the realm of care, summing them up as an extended version of housework, and labeling them trivial and random, Xu Ying feminized her work in the RC, implicitly placing it on a lower level. Most residents and even cadres themselves arbitrarily connected the peripheral status of the RC with its "feminine" status, emphasizing that the RC was full of unpaid female retirees, volunteers whose "housework" was merely extended to the neighborhood.

From the RC to the Community: Failed Attempts to Replace the Parental Role of the Work Unit

The RC entered a new phase after the early 1990s, when the fear of Fenghuang's "death" fell upon Hadong. Among local residents, the death of the work unit meant the death of a "parent," as shown in their frequent description of themselves as "abandoned children" (*meiyou yangde haizi*). The RC increasingly received special attention from the government amidst the breakdown of the work unit, emerging as a new form of urban governance at the very moment when the loss of the "parent" was being met with sorrow, anger, and desperation among the residents of Hadong. Replacing the RC with the Community became one of the state's most important efforts to compensate for the loss of that "parent." The government has tried to regenerate the RC (which is considered far from a counterpart to the work unit) so that it may acquire the paternal authority that the work unit once had. The state's campaign of building community has thus amounted to a series of governmental actions.

To begin with, as mentioned earlier, the realm of administration that the new Community is required to encompass has been extended to include a variety of themes. Every Community office now has ten to fifteen cadres, including one director, three or four deputy directors who take charge of the one-child policy and "environment and hygiene" (*huanjing weisheng*), and other social workers who deal with social security programs for laid-off and unemployed workers, the minimum livelihood guarantee (*dibao*), public security, and care for the disabled.

The government has also addressed wide-ranging concerns about the treatment of new cadres. In Hadong in the late 1980s Community cadres first received formal wages from the government. The wage of a Community director increased from 30 yuan in 1987 to 150 yuan in 2000 and 900 yuan in 2008. As of July 2008, a deputy director earned 800 yuan and a general worker 529 yuan per month. Cadres have also benefited from pension and medical insurance, which offset their relatively low wages.[8]

In addition, cadres have increasingly had their own offices, though in three out of eleven Communities in Hadong, cadres were still doing their work from home. Songhua Community became an object of envy among other Community cadres because of the renovation of its space in early 2008. It was the first office in Hadong where the director's office and other cadres' offices are separate from one another. "How fancy the office is! Songhua cadres look more authoritative now. Residents won't look down on them," said Lin Liping, a director of Jianguo Community.[9]

Nevertheless, these actions have ended up separating Community cadres from their neighbors by failing to invoke the parental role that the work unit once played even as they imbue the Community with a different kind of authority. The new parental role of the Community has been considered incomplete, however, owing to the absence of "patriarchal" power. First, the Community is seen as a "caregiver" while the former work unit was a "job provider." Community cadres have suggested job opportunities or implemented job training for impoverished workers, issued them the "preferential certificates for reemployment" (*zaijiuye youhuizheng*), and provided them with unemployment allowances (*shiyejin*) or the minimum livelihood guarantee (*dibao*). Yet cadres have never given these impoverished workers an actual job, which is what they want more than anything else. In 2006, for example, Jianguo Community reported that it had successfully found new jobs for 101 out of 459 registered laid-off and unemployed workers living in its neighborhood. Out of those 101 people, however, 56 were listed as "temporary workers" (*linshigong*), without specific categories of employment, and the 45 others included peddlers, community guards, cleaners, salesclerks, and repairers, none of which is considered a real job. Although part-time, temporary, and casual work (*dagong*) has become widespread with the breakdown of the work unit and the growth of the service sector, what workers call a "real" job (*gongzuo*) is still limited to "full-time, permanent, formal sector, *danwei* [work unit] employment" (Henderson et al. 2000: 48).

Second, local residents consider the middle-aged laid-off female workers who have become the new Community cadres as no better than the old "grannies" of the RC. In this sense, most residents have found it hard to swallow the fact that Community cadres now receive formal wages from the government. Leaving after making a fruitless trip to a Community office, one retired man grumbled: "Former cadres were not paid for their service at all. They worked voluntarily. Why do these women earn money while absent from their office so often? How can they get 800 yuan? Huh! Even adult men in Hadong have a hard time making 500 yuan if they work hard outside." In other words, the "feminine" position of the RC still haunts the new Community. Through media coverage, the government attempts to add a family flavor to community by highlighting cadres who earnestly take care of local residents. Yet this effort is doomed to fail because residents are unwilling to accept the idea of a family without a breadwinner. Even worse, it divides Community cadres from their neighbors, who are reluctant to acknowledge their increasing authority.

In and Outside the State

What makes the new Community cadres even more vulnerable is that the state has never fully embraced them even as they have become increasingly alienated from local residents. Although the state has imbued their work with increased authority, this does not necessarily mean that they have been seen purely as government officials. The Community has not been entirely incorporated into the state apparatus but is located both *in* and *outside* the state, as is suggested by the complex meanings of the very term "community." This section sheds light on the liminal position of the Community in state bureaucracy.

The Ignorant People

At each Monday meeting during which the officials of the street office transmit instructions from higher levels of government to the Community cadres, attendance is taken for the more than one hundred cadres. Even a little bit of noise from them is considered evidence of their "low" quality (*suzhi*), even though the street office staff members often carry on private cell phone conversations throughout the meeting.[10] The chairman frequently concludes the meeting with an admonitory speech: "I know that most of you are laid-off workers. The state gave you your current position. The state also raised your salary recently. Do you know what this means? You should raise your own quality [*suzhi*]. If you don't use your brain, how can we let you do this work? If you don't observe the rules, how can we let you transmit state policies to ordinary people?"

Community cadres have been incorporated into the state apparatus to a greater extent than ever before, as I noted in the previous section. Yet the insufficient education of these cadres has made their position in the state bureaucracy highly problematic. The professionalization of Community cadres, to which the chairman was alluding, has been a very strong theme running through the campaign of building community (Pan 2002; Shi 2006a; Wang 2006). The campaign has emphasized endlessly that Community cadres should be "reborn," acting no longer as mere messengers of the government but as social workers equipped with professional knowledge and skills. In *Studies on Community Building in Urban China* (*Chengshi jiceng quanli chongzu*), Shi Weimin writes: "It is true that Community cadres are lacking in both the knowledge for Community work and the capacity for self-governance. For a long time, most of the RC cadres consisted of old retirees. Our mothers and grandmothers did the Community work for some decades. Although these comrades are filled with the spirit of sacrifice, not only are they older, but also their cultural and educational level is low. It is thus difficult for them to assume the new task of community self-governance" (Shi 2006a: 153).

Yet it is middle-aged, mostly female laid-off workers, as well as young college graduates, who have taken over the posts formerly held by "grannies" in the Communities. This phenomenon has been more noticeable in poor neighborhoods, like Hadong, where young college graduates are unwilling to come to work. In particular, since the early 2000s, the government has introduced the new system of "public posts" as a way of reemploying large numbers of laid-off workers (see introduction). At the time of my visit, with the exception of (deputy) directors, who were chosen in local elections, cadres in eleven Hadong Communities had been selected primarily through the system of "public posts." One of the cadres in her early fifties said to me: "Don't you think that the socialist state is still good? The system of public posts is what the state has created to protect [urban] laid-off workers like me. Who else invents a job for me these days? Other companies usually don't want me because I'm too old. The public post means that I work for the state. It is therefore safe. If you work outside [in the private sector], some bad employers run away without paying you your salary." A public post is thus considered a product of the governmental policy of privileging urban laid-off workers. Community cadres often explained the policy to me as an example of how the Chinese state has not abandoned the people— particularly workers who have been laid off.

Such governmental protection, however, does not mean that the state has embraced their "simplicity," which was once celebrated as a quality of "the people" in political campaigns throughout the Mao era. "The more a person knows, the more reactionary she or he will become [*zhishi yueduo yue fandong*]." Thus the fifty-seven-year-old Community director Yin Xiuzhen began her conversation with me by using a well-known saying from the Maoist period when I met her in the Xiangnan Community office. Born in Shanghai, Yin Xiuzhen was the only director in Hadong who had graduated from junior college (*dazhuan*). "Education?" she exclaimed. "It was useless in Mao's era!" Before she came to Fenghuang factory, Yin Xiuzhen had been at a factory in Shenyang, a city in northeast China. "I used to be a technician," she told me. "But I was assigned to Shenyang as a worker. It was amidst the turmoil of the Cultural Revolution. Chairman Mao said that technicians should learn from workers just as the students who went to the countryside learned from peasants. It was not until 1978 that I finally went back to being a technician." Yin Xiuzhen continued: "Workers and peasants are people of no culture [*meiyou wenhua*]. This means that they are pure and simple. That's why they were encouraged to lead the nation during the Cultural Revolution. By contrast, intellectuals thought of everything in overly complicated ways. They needed to simplify their thoughts by learning from workers and peasants."

"What the hell did they learn from *us?*" A Community cadre, Zhang Yan, interrupted Yin Xiuzhen. A laid-off worker from Fenghuang factory, she challenged Yin Xiuzhen in self-denigrating terms: "What the hell did the intellectuals learn from those who had no knowledge? When I was a student, the only thing I learned was the sayings of Chairman Mao. I didn't gain any real knowledge. How can those who have no culture lead the country? We workers had no scientific knowledge. We all know why the planned economy crashed." She then quoted a common saying: "No scientific knowledge, no development!"

Her self-deprecatory account seemed at odds with the ubiquitous nostalgia of workers for Mao's era, when, they insisted, they experienced full membership in society. In chapter 1 I demonstrated how workers' memories returned ceaselessly to the Maoist past and how they routinely invoked the honor and pride they once had as "the people." Through their memories, these laid-off workers have attempted to recall their membership in a wider society, a membership they have felt deprived of during the transition to a market economy. Nevertheless, this socialist nostalgia of these workers always seemed to coexist with a sense of shame and despair. Their nostalgia for "the people," which was a source of pride and honor, went hand in hand with their self-description of "the people" as naïve and backward. Their claim that "we the people" built the new China ran parallel to their sense of guilt that it was "we the people" who ruined China's growth. Although nostalgia represents a quest for "certitude" (Rofel 1999: 136), the workers' invocation of "the people" revealed tensions and fissures rather than bestowing that certitude. The saying "No scientific knowledge, no development" has taken on a hegemonic power among urban laid-off workers, including Community cadres, whose lack of education so negatively affects their capacity for survival in post-Mao China.

Not surprisingly, Community cadres have accepted the demand for professionalization as the stream in which they must swim, even though they can drown in it. In particular, computer literacy has been held to represent the professionalization that they should strive for. This varies from writing reports on community work to filing the lists of holders of the reemployment certificate or the recipients of the minimum livelihood guarantee. In August 2007, only two out of eleven Community offices in Hadong had computers; workers in nine Communities had to go to the street office for all their computer work. Yet despite the lack of computer resources, higher-level government officials have emphasized proficient word processing as the primary evidence of professionalism. The discrepancy between this demand and the reality has often been the object of self-mockery among Community comrades. The day before one meeting in the street office, some of the Community cadres were talking about an episode that had occurred when a new social worker was being selected in Hadong. One of cadres remarked: "It's said that ten people wanted the position at first. Seven out of ten submitted the paper application in the end. Yet only three were left after the news that an exam would follow. Wei Yonglan [a deputy director of the street office] called in on them to check whether they could actually do computer work or not. The first applicant said, 'I've never used Microsoft Word, though I can do an Internet search.' The second applicant typed only one word in ten minutes. The third applicant typed thirty words in the same time. That's why the third one was finally chosen!"

Nevertheless, laughter frequently turns to fear in the daily business of these cadres. Jiang Yun, whom I mentioned briefly earlier in this chapter, is a social security worker who deals with *dibao* in Jianguo Community. She was laid off from a box factory in the mid-1990s. At the suggestion of an official in the street office, she decided to take the exam for Community cadres. Though overwhelmed with debt resulting from her husband's heart surgery, she continued to learn basic computer skills at her own expense and finally came to work in the Community starting in 2004. Nevertheless, Jiang Yun is overwhelmed by fear whenever she sits in front of a computer. She said to me: "Another exam is coming soon. As you know, I'm so old that I can't keep up with every request from the higher-level governments. The government wants young folks. My sight is growing dim with age. It's hard even to see the computer screen. Like my husband's, my heart isn't good either. Last week when you were in Beijing, I caused the computer to shut down. It was infected with a virus. I was about to report the list of *dibao* recipients to the street office. How urgent it was! I felt as if my heart stood still for a moment. It was beating so fast, even after I went back home. I had to visit the hospital after all that."

Jiang Yun and many other Community cadres spent their youth amidst the upheavals of the Cultural Revolution. The impossibility of receiving an education during that period has made their survival in the new market economy both difficult and painful. In becoming cadres, however, they are presumed to be subjects who are not inviolable and self-knowing but inherently lacking and in need of constant readjustment (see Yan 2003a: 511). "Go back home!" is something that these cadres frequently hear from higher authorities. In the meeting in which Jiang Yun was urged to purchase the magazine *Community* (*Shequ*), Jiang Shunjie, a deputy director of the street office, shouted at her and other Community cadres: "Read a paper, a magazine or whatever. What if you can't progress while your society progresses? Is there any other choice except your going back home? If our district is redeveloped sometime in the future, it will be filled by new residents who have high quality [*suzhi*] and high education. How will you be able to support them unless you raise your quality?"

Nevertheless, most Community cadres are willing to accept their problematic position in the state apparatus. Although they are constantly scolded by higher-level officials, these cadres have also been stimulated by improved working conditions and, more important, their membership in the state. Incorporated into the bureaucracy more fully than at any time in the past, they have attempted to embrace the authority of the state as their own. The tendency to seek security through membership in the state is more palpable in the case of middle-aged cadres who used to work in state-owned enterprises than among newly arrived young cadres. Yet the desire of the former for membership has never been easy to achieve. Community cadres are as much excluded from as included in "the state" of their imagination, as I discuss in the next section.

"Only You Can Do This Work!"

One early October morning in 2006, Chen Yuhua, one of the cadres in Jianguo Community, was sweeping garbage into a bicycle cart. Residents were drying cabbages and green onions in the sun in preparation for winter, and every street in Hadong was littered with discarded rotten vegetables mixed with coal ashes. "There must be some volunteers who can help you with cleaning. Otherwise, why don't you hire more cleaners?" I asked Chen Yuhua. She responded with a sigh: "Who can help us these days? Residents are resentful because we Community cadres receive a salary from the government. Higher-level government officials don't care about us. We have to do this work ourselves. I can't help it." She added self-mockingly, "This is 'self-governance' [*zizhi*], isn't it?"

It is through the governmental emphasis on "self-governance" that Community cadres are squeezed out of the position of state agents. As noted earlier, the Community, like its predecessor the RC, has been officially referred to as "a mass organization of self-governance at the grassroots level" (Shi 2006b: 4-5) though it in fact serves as the lowest-level urban administrative unit. In Mao's era, the motto "self-governance," much like another popular motto, "self-reliance," was selected as one of the survival strategies of the socialist regime when it faced economic isolation from capitalist countries. Once a measure for promoting socialist mobilization, the motto is now getting fresh attention. As I mentioned earlier, scholars are reconsidering what it means to be a citizen in relation to the nation-state through the idea of "community self-governance."[11]

Nevertheless, the remarkable contrast between the increase of scholarly concern with "community" and the near absence of the practices related to it in local, particularly poor neighborhoods is intriguing. In Hadong, it was not until an inspection by the district government was drawing near that I had any sense of the campaign of "community self-governance." Having learned of the inspection, Community cadres began to produce a good number of files filled with documents, including reports on the condition of Community self-governance and public opinion polls, as well as proceedings of the Community Representative Assembly, the Community Council, the Community Hearings, the Community Coordination Committee, the Community Consultation Committee, and so on. I stopped asking cadres what these strange committees were all about when I noticed their reluctance to answer. Not surprisingly, the most active participants in these committees were not citizens in general, as studies of community assume, but local cadres appointed by the state. In all these reports and proceedings, the cadres filled in their own names, adding the names of a few residents who had good relationships with them.

Apart from this paper display of community activities, I never saw any events or heard any remarks about "community self-governance" in street-level government. Many Community cadres viewed the concept as "not expecting any help from the state," in the words of one of them. A government meeting provides a good example of how higher-level officials employed the claim of "self-governance" to pass their burden on to Community cadres. On October 23, 2006, deputy director Wei Yonglan asked Community cadres to report their current situations during the weekly meeting of the Guangming street office. Using this "rare" opportunity, cadres began to vent their frustrations about the disposal of garbage.

The eldest, Xu Ying, a director of Jiangbei Community, first complained about the harsh living conditions in her neighborhood: "More than a month has passed since our broken water pipes were repaired. But water still doesn't come out. Neither the police office nor the street office would take responsibility for this, although five hundred households have no water to drink. Epidemic prevention remains a mess. Cockroaches are everywhere! Residents are raising a clamor, saying that they will be poisoned to death. As you know, our office used to be a child care center for the Fenghuang factory's number one shop. The office may go at any moment. Its floor is rotten, and water is leaking in. Didn't you [the street office] say that the office was temporary?" The director of Lianhe Community then spoke up: "Public toilets as well as dustbins are full. Not surprisingly, no resident will pay the cleaning fee. A disposal truck stops by the entrance of our neighborhood only once a week. We have no money to pay to get the truck to come more often."

Some Community directors stressed how they used their own money for this purpose. The director of Linjiang Community, which was notorious for having the most garbage in Hadong, said: "To pump out the filthy water, we [Community cadres] have used up the monthly 50 yuan that the street office offers us for managing the Community as well as 30 percent of the security fees. We also took money out of our own pockets. For pumping, we spent 50 yuan to borrow a truck from Fenghuang factory. As you know, Fenghuang went bankrupt last year, and we needed to find private companies for help. Those companies, however, demand at least 80 yuan. We can't afford it. In addition, it is not easy to find a cleaner who is willing to crush a block of ice with waste mixed in." This meeting disintegrated in utter confusion as Community cadres began to burst out simultaneously with similar frustrations. Eventually Wei Yonglan spoke:

> Listening to your stories, I can appreciate that you are working in extremely harsh conditions.
>
> I feel sad to learn that you pay out of your own pocket to take care of the garbage. The problem is that the [higher-level] government won't pay for this matter. I know the reason why some of the Community directors said nothing today. You thought that you would rather solve the problem yourselves than create a burden on the street office.
>
> I feel sad whenever I finish this kind of meeting. You are working in adverse conditions without water, electricity, and heating. I know that most of you have caught colds. Yet we [the street office] can't help you because 90 percent of you are in similar situations. When I showed anger at another meeting of the street office, director Li Yuming [of the Guangming street office] said to me, "Do you think that I feel comfortable in this situation?" Director Li Yuming says that he feels sad whenever he comes back after visiting other Communities in good condition.
>
> The superior authorities wouldn't take real action even if director Li Yuming and I reported these problems to them. One day last week, I finally let loose my indignation to the authorities. I said: "Our area is so different from others. Located in the urban periphery, our area is crowded with orphans, psychopaths, and patients who shit everywhere. You should come and see what happens here. Our area is even worse than the countryside."
>
> Today I wrote down all the troubles that you mentioned. Thanks again for all your labor. But in reality, there is no way that we can get help from the superior authorities. It's time for you to show your capacity for self-help [*zizhu nengli*]. As I have said ten thousand times, only *you* can do this work!

After the meeting, some of the Community cadres approached Wei Yonglan. They said to her, as if with one voice: "We won't tell you about this kind of problem anymore. We know very well how you care about us and support our work. Yet we also know that you can't help us with this matter. We won't tell you from now on."

Ultimately it is the Community cadres—the most "exemplary" people among the poor residents—who are supposed to demonstrate their capacity for self-help voluntarily. Not every type of self-help, however, is praised as an expression of voluntarism. If an act of self-help ends up causing a problem for the government, it is not even called "self-help." In other words, "worthy" self-help is not unconditional, often reckless loyalty to the state, but more rational, prudent support of it. At the meeting just described, for instance, Community cadres stressed that they had used up all the subsidies provided by the government to deal with their garbage problem. Although Wei Yonglan expressed deep gratitude for their sacrifice, when she met those cadres a week later, she emphasized that their sacrifice should be based on law. "The Street Office has given you 50 yuan every month," she reminded them, "so that you can purchase any miscellaneous products for your office. Yet I know that you have spent this small amount of money on pumping out filthy water or purchasing heaters for your office. As director Li Yuming stressed, however, funds earmarked for specific purposes are not to be transferred at will [zhuankuan zhuanyong]! Your accounts should be transparent when the higher-level government inspects them at the end of the year. Last year, numerous problems were found in the nearby Communities when the district government visited them without notice." Eventually Wei Yonglan suggested that the Community cadres donate money themselves to improve their decaying neighborhood. She made an example of Xiangnan Community, in which officials contributed their own money to fix the water pipes on nearby streets. "This is the very expression of high quality [suzhi] and good manners!"

Practicing "community self-governance" has been painful and complex in Hadong. As for the problem of garbage, Community cadres have attempted to cope with it by increasing their workload. Consider an example from Jianguo Community. In 2007 the Guangming street office set a total of 12,000 yuan as the target figure for the cleaning fee to be collected from local residents. The figure was calculated on the basis of the total number of households (835 households × 3.6 yuan × 4 quarters). Nevertheless, Community cadres estimated that the actual amount they could collect from residents would be less than 10,000 yuan. Residents' resistance to paying the fee, as well as the high mobility of rural migrants, made it difficult to achieve the target figure, as we shall see in chapter 6. The street office granted a "favor" to each Community, allowing it to use around 70 percent of the collected fees for dealing with its own garbage problem. Because of the limited budget, Community cadres were able to hire only one elderly cleaner from the countryside, paying him 400 yuan a month. Only a rural migrant was willing to do the work of gathering all the garbage from more than eight hundred households and transporting it to eleven garbage bins for a low wage. Some of the remaining budget was spent on insecticides and tools for cleaning. Cadres also saved some money to provide treats for a few volunteers who were willing to help them or to offset the loss of community supplies, which were vulnerable to theft.

Given this tight budget, cleaning became one of the primary duties of all Community cadres—whether their supposed responsibility was social security, policing, disability, the environment, or the one-child policy. Discouraged by his hard job, the migrant cleaner often disappeared without notice. Yet Community cadres had no choice but to do the labor themselves while waiting for him to return, since no one else was willing to take on that kind of work for so little money. In addition, Community cadres received little help from local residents, who remembered that the old grannies of the RC had not been paid for their community service. Almost daily these cadres would go to every street with besoms, shovels, and carts in order to clear away heavy snow and crush "trash ice."

Thanks to this spirit of "self-help," that year Jianguo Community was awarded the title of a "model community" (*biaobing shequ*) with a prize of 300 yuan. Honored as an "advanced individual" (*xianjin geren*), director Lin Liping received 200 yuan from the street office. She told me: "The street office praised us [Community cadres in Jianguo] for our capacity for self-help [*zizhu nengli*]. We were praised because we built our own office and solved the garbage problem ourselves, while other Communities sought help from the street office. That's why director Li Yuming likes our Community." In other words, Jianguo Community was saluted by the state as a "model community" for bearing the burden imposed on it in the name of "community self-governance." Community cadres achieved the approval of the state and positioned themselves within the state apparatus only through the *denial* of support from the state.

Creating viable communities has been encouraged as a buffer against the dispersal of the state's redistributive functions. Yet I have shown in this chapter how the neoliberal technique of governing poverty through community has prompted "the will to survive" rather than "the will to empower," and the remapping of state practices rather than their retrenchment. The meaning of community self-governance has not been based on the partnership between the state and community so much as it has been reduced to the mere shifting of the state's workload to the local level. In particular, I have highlighted how the remapping of state practices is made possible by and through the peripheral, feminine, and liminal position of a specific group, the Community cadres. Varying kinds of responsibilities that the government should take in institutional ways have been piled onto the shoulders of these street-level cadres, whose membership in the state apparatus has been questioned rather than confirmed.

In Hadong, Community cadres have remained the most active participants in the building of community. These middle-aged female laid-off workers, historically positioned in a peripheral realm, and now located both in and outside the state, have attached themselves to the old Maoist doctrine of self-reliance in order to cope with their liminal, fragile position. Sweeping garbage alone in the street, one cadre in Hadong told me in a self-mocking tone: "Chairman Mao died long ago. Yet his teaching is forever true. We should rely on our own effort [*zili gengsheng*]." In this vein, the concept of "community" has ended up being less a force for mobilizing citizens as a willing partner of the state than a form of valorizing the citizens' obedience to sovereign rule. This valorization is the result of the refashioning of the lowest level of the state apparatus, the Community, which is staffed mostly by laid-off female workers, to be simultaneously in and outside the state.

The fragile position of Community cadres is deeply connected to the historical specificity of the "subjects" whom one party—whether the state or other social agencies—seeks to empower. If community self-governance or empowerment is a technology for constituting citizens out of subjects, as Barbara Cruikshank notes, it should be emphasized that the "subjects" have been living—and will continue to live—in highly gendered and historically embedded circumstances. In modern China, intellectuals fashioned the "subjects" as "the people" before they ever called them "the citizens," as they are known today. Whereas in European societies the state's subjects are presumed to be autonomous and self-knowing in the Enlightenment tradition (Yan 2003a: 511), throughout the socialist history of China, "the people" have been considered "a blank sheet of paper" (Mao 1958) that can be freshly painted, whether as full-blooded revolutionaries, patriotic masses, modern educated subjects, national women (*funü*), and so on. The authoritative painters of this "blank" paper have, in most cases, been state agents or intellectuals rather than "the people" themselves, though the latter, as the "masters" of the country, were sometimes given a paintbrush in the Mao period. The gendered and developmentalist tensions embedded in "the people" have loomed large at the very moment when those who had been designated as "the people"—laid-off female workers in this case—are newly "painted" as "the citizens" amidst the reconfiguration of urban governance through community. As shown in this chapter, the dilemma of Community cadres arises from the fact that they still rely on the baffling claim to be of "the people," and on the techniques based on the concept, to prove that they are voluntary, self-motivating "citizens."

Before concluding this chapter, I should stress the *temporality* of the Community cadres' dilemma. The government through community that I have discussed here is historically contingent. The dilemma that Community cadres in Hadong experience will have different nuances and specifics in the future. In many rich neighborhoods in China's big cities, young college graduates are increasingly replacing "granny cadres" (Pan 2002) or uneducated, middle-aged cadres, although this change has been slow in shanty neighborhoods on the urban periphery. These young "professionals" do not share the history of "the people," which inspired most "uneducated" cadres in Hadong to endure their sacrifice and grapple with their membership in the state. In July 2008, when I was about to leave Hadong, three young women in their mid-twenties arrived after passing an official exam for social workers. Simply called "college students" by local residents, these young cadres did not agree to be "daily cleaners" in the streets. Instead they suggested that they should take responsibility for doing computer work in the office while the older cadres cleaned up refuse outside. These young "professionals" will rewrite the ethnography of practicing "community" as globally circulating techniques intersect with specific historical and regional factors in new ways.

• • •

One early April morning in 2007, four Community cadres in Hadong were shoveling waste in the streets as usual. Their faces were flushed with heat, and their shoes were already soaked with muddy wastewater. Sun Yufen, a rural migrant, passed by, returning home after making her rounds of the neighborhood collecting scraps of old metal from a nearby rail yard. Sun Yufen began to chat with her brother Sun Yuming, who was sitting in the street playing poker with his friends, and his wife, Zhang Yujian, who, off from work that day, was cutting up a plastic pipe to use as a flowerpot. Zhang Yujian and Sun Yufen were urging Sun Yuming to go out to work. Making an excuse, Sun Yuming replied: "The police control is now stricter than ever. Avoiding daytime work is a way of saving money." None of them paid any attention to the Community cadres, who were clearing away garbage right next to them. The angry faces of the Community cadres presented a striking contrast to the unperturbed expressions of these rural migrants. Tired of shoveling, Jiang Yun, one of the cadres, began to grumble, "I would rather go out to pick up garbage [scrap metal] than labor like this." Another cadre, Zhang Lijun, agreed with her; Looking at Sun Yufen, she opined: "Rag picking allows freedom. At least I wouldn't have to be criticized by high-level officials every day."

Rural migrants, whom these cadres envied, at least for the moment, constitute the other poor—a group once proclaimed to be a part of "the people" but which has proceeded along a very different path from that of urban laid-off workers. They are the subject of the next chapter.

CHAPTER 5

Inclusive Exclusion

One evening in October 2006 I was preparing dinner with Sun Yufen, a forty-five-year old migrant woman, who had returned home after collecting plastic bottles. Sun Yuming, her thirty-five-year-old brother, and his two younger buddies stopped by her house to get some cigarettes on their way to work. They were going to sell used tires, which they collected in the nearby countryside. Seeing a foreigner for the first time in their lives, Sun Yuming's friends did not conceal their curiosity about me. They wanted to know how I, a foreign student, had come to this peripheral shantytown and made friends with a "peasant" like Sun Yufen. Instead of patiently listening to my story, these young friends asked whatever questions popped into their head: "Are there many used tires in South Korea?" "How much money do people earn by reselling those tires there?" "How much money do Koreans spend buying food each day?" "How can we go to Korea for work?"

Sun Yuming said nothing at all during this conversation. His silence made me uncomfortable, because I had been counting on him to introduce me to his friends. Sun Yuming knew about my project, though only roughly; for almost three months he had seen how I wandered around the streets of Hadong and met residents there. Instead of introducing me, however, he suddenly asked me whether I had read a novel, *Ren yu lang* (Man and Wolf). He said: "As you know, I only graduated from elementary school. Yet I know one book, which has made a deep impression on my mind. It is *Ren yu lang,* although the title might be a bit different. The book was once read in my school. Although I've almost forgotten the thread of the story, throughout my life I have felt how the life of a wolf is similar to that of a peasant. We peasants are not human beings. We are no better than wolves, who desperately struggle for survival every day. What is your research for? You chose the wrong research site. Why are you hanging around in the city although you said you would study poverty? It is of no use for us to have this conversation before you read *Ren yu lang.*"

Although I was upset by his remarks, which felt like scolding, I decided to seek out the book, expecting that I might have a deeper conversation with him after reading it. Yet I failed to find it, even though I looked for it in every likely place in Harbin—in bookstores, libraries, and even flea markets. In fact it was impossible to find a book that a man in his mid-thirties only vaguely remembered, and even the title of which was unclear to him. I did, however, see a book titled *Lang tu teng* (Wolf Totem, 2005) displayed in every bookstore. Noted as the biggest best-seller in China since Mao's *Little Red Book,*[1] *Lang tu teng* vividly captures the lives of the nomadic herders of Inner Mongolia, who fight off wolves, but also learn from them, in their own struggle for survival. The book was written by an "educated urban youth" (*zhishi qingnian*) who had volunteered during the Cultural Revolution to go to the borderland where wolves and herders meet. The author eulogizes the sacredness and wisdom of the wolves as well as the courage and adaptability of the Mongolian herders, in contrast to the "sedentary" lives of Han Chinese.

When I met Sun Yuming again a few weeks later, I told him I had read *Lang tu teng,* though not *Ren yu lang.* Sun Yuming apologized to me, seeing how I had struggled to find the latter. "I told you about the book at that time only because I didn't want my friends to bother you with such stupid questions," he told me. "It seems that the book *Lang tu teng* praises a wolf. Well, urbanites have ridiculous tastes. Do they really want to live just as wolves do? Do they think that wolves have chosen a harsh life because they want it? Wolves, like us peasants, are beings who can't survive without desperately struggling to do so." With this remark he did not summon the ruthless wolves depicted in *Ren yu lang* or *Lang tu teng* so much as he pictured wolves as the social outcasts they were in his mind.

Rural migrants are not entirely outside the state's concerns in contemporary China. Although Sun Yuming compared what he called "peasants" in the city to desperate wolves, China's rural migrants have not been banished into the distant forest. They are more fully incorporated into urban life than ever before. Never in all the time since China's widespread social and economic reforms began has there been such an outpouring of heartfelt care and attention given to rural migrants in the cities.[2] The dramatic shift in the government's and the people's concern for this formerly neglected group in less than a decade is nearly great enough to eclipse the long-time discrimination against and stigmatization of rural migrants, who have been widely regarded as "dirty, silly, poor, aimless, uncivil, congregating, and money-driven" (Zhang 2001: 32). This shift is not limited to ritual gestures on the part of the government, such as offering train tickets for migrant workers to visit their hometowns at the Lunar New Year or letting their representatives participate in the National People's Congress. It also includes legal and institutional reforms: compensating for industry disasters affecting migrant workers, punishing employers who refuse to pay wages owed to their workers, and improving official efforts to help rural migrant workers newly arrived in cities to find secure jobs. The policy reform regarding rural migrants was embodied in Premier Wen Jiabao's personal intervention in helping a migrant worker collect his unpaid wages, an action that led to a massive media blitz in late 2003.[3] Yet despite the state's increasing concern for rural migrants, most of them, like Sun Yuming, identify themselves as "wolves" or "nonhuman beings" who have been totally abandoned by Chinese society.

In this chapter I examine how rural migrants continue to describe themselves in a way that magnifies their abandonment and abjection, regardless of the social assistance directed toward them. This differs from the tendency of urban laid-off workers to lay claim to the title of "the people" while grappling with their relationship to the original author of that claim, the Chinese state. The rural migrants I spoke to in Hadong were not interested in either the old ideological rhetoric identifying peasants as "the people," and thus the masters of the country, or the state's new ideological description of migrant workers as "an active industrial army spurring the nation's economic development."[4] From "(powerless) common people" (*laobaixing*) to "wolves," poverty-stricken rural migrants in Hadong produced their "downtrodden" identity in ways that differed from the state's attempts to see, name, and count them.

These rural migrants identify themselves as powerless outcasts because they have been not merely excluded but, to borrow from Giorgio Agamben, "excluded through inclusion" in a socialist fantasy that both guarantees their rights and yet simultaneously limits them through numerous reversals, modifications, and exceptions (1998: 18). In the case of rural migrants, unlike urban laid-off workers, this politics of "inclusive exclusion" began with the founding of the PRC, through the state's political eulogy for and its de facto abandonment of peasants (Cohen 1993; Kipnis 1995).

In order to delve into the experience of "inclusive exclusion" that rural migrants commonly narrate despite the sheer diversity of their experiences, I construct my arguments through the ethnography of one person, Sun Yufen, mentioned at the beginning of this chapter, a forty-five-year old migrant ragpicker who had lived in Harbin for thirteen years. I first met Sun Yufen in August 2006, when she was chatting with neighbors on a street corner as she darned her worn socks. When she suddenly asked me, a stranger, to help her go back to her hometown, I had no way of knowing that this chance encounter would transform me into a pseudo-lawyer and even a lay real estate consultant for a year.[5] I construct Sun Yufen's narrative around my conversations with her and the many people with whom she and I inter-acted: her extended family and neighbors, real estate agents, and government officials in urban and rural areas. This ethnographic approach allows me to highlight my point that rural migrants experience exclusion not through some specific categorization but through a series of processes. This is the very reason why many of these migrants ignore and even scorn recent gov-ernmental attempts to woo them by depicting them positively.

This chapter consists of four parts. The first part focuses on the demo-graphics of rural migrants in Hadong. Despite their diversity, there is one name by which rural migrants identify themselves and one another: "peas-ants." I discuss why these migrants persist in using the term although many of them have never farmed in the countryside and have spent most of their lives in the city. Next I introduce the story of Sun Yufen's arrival in Hadong and examine how her relationships with urbanites have made her life there an unequal, insecure, and painful experience. In the third part I detail Sun Yufen's struggle to take back her "stolen" rural land, where she wished to return and put an end her travails in the city. I then turn to Sun Yufen's eventual decision to settle in the city and her struggle to find urban housing, an attempt frustrated by urban regimes that included her through exclusion.

I make it clear that I was deeply involved in Sun Yufen's struggle to obtain urban housing as well as her fight to regain her rural land. I do not think that my presence in the struggle created any distinct exception in her life trajectory, since Sun had visited her former home to retrieve her "stolen" land many times before I met her in Hadong. Rather, I mean to emphasize how I came to a better understanding of Sun's social sufferings through my own feelings, particularly of confusion, rage, and frustration.[6] I appear in my account at moments when my presence helped develop my insights into Sun's "inclusive exclusion."

Rural Migrants on the Urban Periphery

In Hadong, the beginning of the breakdown of the work unit in the mid-1980s coincided with the arrival of rural migrants. Although the household registration (*hukou*) system has been relaxed in recent years,[7] the absence of urban *hukou* has long deprived most rural migrants of their right to urban space and urban housing. As Li Zhang explains, "migrants are not entitled to any state-subsidized housing and are also prohibited from constructing their own housing in the city" (2002: 319). In Harbin, urban *hukou* is provided only to wealthy migrants who can afford to purchase commercial or commodity housing (*shangpin fang*), typically priced at more than 150,000 yuan.[8] Thus any illegal housing built by migrants is vulnerable to official threats and even forceful demolition (e.g., Zhang 2001; Xiang 2005; Siu 2007). The situation in China, as I have noted, is in contrast to that in many other Asian countries and in Latin America, where large numbers of rural migrants have constructed illegal communities in cities and have often positioned themselves as "the urban poor," that is, as political subjects in conflict with state power (e.g., Paley 2001; Goldstein 2004; Cho 2005).

In China, however, a new political space is being formed in unexpected ways. As we have seen in the case of Hadong, the dilapidated residential space of the former work unit in the urban periphery has become a place where two differently impoverished groups meet: urban laid-off workers and pensioners mired down in their "urban shantytown" on the one hand, and on the other, newly arrived rural migrants seeking low rents and permissive housing regulations. These two groups have had no choice but to live in the same areas, as they cannot afford to pay the escalating housing costs in other neighborhoods.

In Hadong the rural migrants, who in most cases hold one or more jobs, fall into three main categories. The first category consists of people who live on informal, non-factory work—hawkers, ragpickers, rickshaw men, janitors, repairmen, service workers, and so on. Their origin is diverse: they come from the nearby countryside and also from villages in south China, as far away as a thousand miles or more. The typical residential structure in Hadong—single-story housing (*pingfang*)—offers a favorable environment for their informal work. For example, Sun Yuming and his half brother have made a small business of collecting used tires and reselling them to processing plants. A little courtyard in their rented house is always full of used tires that they have collected while making the rounds of nearby villages. During winter, when it is hard to collect tires, the Sun brothers become "rickshaw men." Their street in Hadong becomes an assembly line on which they make rickshaws. Sticks, boards, tents, nails, and saws are scattered all over, despite the protests of Community cadres (figure 5.1). The migrants who belong to this category constitute about 65 percent of the migrant population.

The second category comprises temporary workers in factories. They work not only in downtown Harbin but also in Hadong, where at the time of my stay about eighty small-scale factories that produced environmentally noxious materials were concentrated to avoid governmental control. For example, Jianguo Community contained sixteen small-scale repair shops and factories,[9] which produced doors and marble and household accessories or processed machinery and plastic fiber. Fourteen of these sixteen shops and factories employed only rural migrants, whose numbers varied from four to twenty per worksite. In the wake of the state's emphasis on environmental protection in recent times, the governmental regulation of these factories has become increasingly scrupulous; actual inspection is nominal, however, because these factories constitute the most significant source of the fees that local cadres are required to collect to meet the quotas demanded by the higher levels of government (see chapter 6). The migrants in this category constitute about 25 percent of the total.

FIGURE 5.1. Making rickshaws in Hadong (November 2006)

The final category of rural migrants consists of peasants who rent the land of peri-urban farmers (*cainong*). Despite the high rents for this land,[10] these peasants have chosen to rent out their own land back in the countryside and grow vegetables on others' land nearer the city, which eventually provides them with greater profits owing to the larger demand and higher purchase prices for vegetables in the city. For example, Xu Yuling and her husband came from Binxian, about ninety miles from Harbin, after renting out their own fourteen *mu* of land to their neighbors for 1,400 yuan a year. In Hadong they rented housing for 110 yuan a month and nine *mu* of land for 2,700 yuan a year. They sold vegetables directly to the morning market in Hadong or to a middleman who frequently came to their field. The migrants who belong to this category constitute about 10 percent of the total.

In other words, what characterizes rural migrants in Hadong is their diversity. Tied to the work unit system in which life and labor were merged together (Dutton 2005: 164), urbanites in Hadong have accumulated shared experiences despite the fact that their memories are always marked by tensions and fissures, as I discussed in chapter 1. Rural migrants in Hadong, however, have had no shared events through which they could construct their own collective memories: their places of origin range from nearby villages to far-off regions requiring a two-day train trip; their length of stay in Hadong varies from a month to more than a decade; they do various kinds of work, from rag picking to farming and factory labor.

Nevertheless, as we have seen, there is one name by which most rural migrants identify themselves collectively: "peasants" (*nongmin*). Almost all the migrants in Hadong call themselves "peasants," although many of them, like Sun Yuming, have spent most of their lifetime working in the city. In the first place, the use of the term "peasants" has to do with the *hukou* system. It is still difficult to change one's household registration from rural to urban unless one obtains a college degree, gains secure employment from a big corporation or the government, or purchases commercial housing. One can easily discern eugenic nuances in such social barriers. Also, given the increasing rural-urban gap, one might guess that those who have been unable to change their residential permit are mostly poor, less educated people. They have continued to call themselves "peasants" because even though they live in the city, their condition is not very different from that of peasants in the countryside. Finally, the rural migrants' persistent use of the term "peasants" arises from their attitude toward the term "urban," as I show through Sun Yufen's narratives in the next section.

"Urbanites Raised by the State" versus "Peasants Raising Themselves"

In the summer of 2006, when I started my fieldwork in Hadong, every street corner was a site of erupting anger among urban residents. Stepping outside their homes after breakfast, elderly people instantly began to moan about their misfortunes. "How can my monthly pension be only 600 yuan after thirty years' labor? How can the state treat us like this?" they would say. "The state is going down the wrong path these days. I'm a child abandoned by my parents. Yet I still believe that they will come back to take care of me if they get better." Streets in the evening were crowded with recently laid-off workers arriving home from days spent doing casual labor (*dagong*). "Factory workers continue to be let go, but white-collar workers suck up all our money while sitting idly at their jobs," they would complain. "I've heard I'll be excluded from the minimum livelihood guarantee [*dibao*]. The government says I should find work. Do you know how many rich frauds live off *dibao* secretly?" Angry urban residents raised their voices in the streets, in the markets, and even in government offices. In the eyes of Sun Yufen, however, their anger was nothing but the grumbling of those who have everything: "It is all so unfair. Peasants farm their whole life to feed urbanites. Still, the state doesn't give us a pension. If we don't grow beans, how can they eat tofu? If we don't grow corn, how can they eat corn noodles? We peasants are barely able to eat steamed buns, picking up waste in the city, but the urbanites eat the best rice [*huangliang*]. It's because the state raises them."

Sun Yufen was a seasonal rural migrant whom I met without a screening by Community cadres. It was during the first stage of my fieldwork. To avoid unnecessary misunderstandings, I tried to meet residents on an official basis, having local cadres introduce me to them, rather than setting up my own criteria for meeting people. The only people to whom Community cadres introduced me, however, were urban *hukou* holders, particularly disabled *dibao* recipients. But in the afternoons, when the cadres were often away from their neighborhood attending various meetings, I enjoyed chatting with local residents on street corners. Sun Yufen was always sitting on the corner. After collecting scraps of old metal, having lunch, and taking a nap, she always came out on the street with worn socks, gloves, or clothes that she would mend. I had first introduced myself as a college student who had come to conduct a social survey (*shehui diaocha*),[11] and Sun Yufen recited her misfortunes to me so frequently that I could remember almost every detail.

Her hard luck stories always began with smoking. "I can't stop smoking," she would say. "My children have grown up. They should get married.

But I have nothing—neither home nor money." Sun Yufen started smoking when her husband, tormented by gambling debts, killed himself when she was thirty-one years old. Things got worse the following year, when she was hit by a car owned by a telephone company. The compensation of 850 yuan that she received was not even enough to pay for her hospitalization. Lying in bed for two years, Sun had to sell most of her household goods to pay for medications. After her recovery, she found that the village government had taken away her land. Going to a city seemed to be the only solution for raising her ten-year-old son and eleven-year-old daughter. Sun Yufen found a home in Hadong, where Sun Yuming, her younger brother, had come earlier and started a small business collecting and reselling used tires. "Thirteen years have passed since then," she told me. "I thought Hadong would be a temporary place for me. I never realized that I'd still be stuck here."

I was first intrigued by the distinction she drew between "urbanites who are raised by the state" and "peasants who must raise themselves." The governmental initiatives that offended urban residents during that time led Sun to legitimate the distinction. To name just a few of these policies, there was the "buyout" (*maiduan*) system, under which laid-off workers in Fenghuang had to sever their relationship to their work unit completely after receiving a lump sum payment (see chapter 1). In order to qualify for a pension later in life, these laid-off workers had to pay an insurance premium for themselves until they reached the age of retirement. Given the soaring cost of living in the city, *maiduan* was considered by most urbanites absurdly inadequate to meet their needs. Yet the idea of receiving money upon leaving a job was astonishing to Sun Yufen. She also remarked on another benefit available to city residents, the minimum livelihood guarantee (*dibao*), which was given to poor urban residents whose income fell below the local poverty line (see chapter 3). She asked me: "Do you know that the government gives money to the urban folks? They live off *dibao* in their own homes. But I have neither housing nor food to eat." Soaring grievances over *dibao*—ambiguous criteria, inadequate payments, and an unfair screening process—did not prevent her from assuming that the urban poor were living like nobility.

Setting aside all other benefits, however, what Sun Yufen was most envious of was the pension given to urban retirees. On the eve of the Spring Festival in 2007, I was preparing dinner with Sun. "Rich people have as many as sixteen to eighteen dishes today," she assured me. "We need to make at least six to eight dishes." Sun was pretty determined. When we were almost done with the cooking, her daughter, Xueqiao, and son, Xueguo, came home after shopping in a nearby bazaar. Indicating her two children, Sun said proudly to me, "They are my pension [*laobao*]!" Soon afterwards, however, Sun reflected sadly: "Why do we peasants have no pension?[12] Small or not, urban people get it anyway when they grow old. In the countryside, you had better kill yourself when you get old. Otherwise you become a burden for your children. My children have never done anything bad in their lives. But why do they have to feel such pressure? I don't want to trouble them. I feel guilty every time I look at my children."

FIGURE 5.2.   Sun Yufen returns to her home in Hadong after working (November 2006)

For Sun Yufen, her expectation of familial support had been crippled not only by her position in relation to that of other urban retirees living on their own pensions but also by the contrast between her two children and other urban youths who, she thought, must have received better care and education. Xueqiao and Xueguo spent their days as children selling vegetables with their mother in the market rather than attending school as did most of their urban counterparts. Twenty-five-year-old Xueqiao was now a saleswoman selling ceramic goods in Harbin. With only an elementary school education, and without urban *hukou,* she had to be satisfied with temporary work in factories, shops, or restaurants. Twenty-four-year-old Xueguo could visit his mother only once a month because he worked at a construction site far away from Hadong. Sun was always worried about their future. "Neither my son nor my daughter has a partner," she said. "My family is so poor that they can't even imagine dating. As you know, my children are good and honest. But they have no money. A granny tried to find a husband for my daughter. But I froze when she asked too many questions about my money, house, furniture, land, etcetera. My son says that he will get a wife after saving 10,000 yuan and that it will take ten more years. How can I help him? I feel that I'm nothing." Every time Sun talked about her children's marriage prospects, her urban neighbors attributed her anxiety to a sort of peasant habit. One old woman said to me: "Sun Yufen's children are only twenty-four, twenty-five years old. Why is she so worried? Yes, early marriage is common in the countryside. *Peasants* [emphasis added] think differently from urbanites." In Sun Yufen's narrative, however, her anxiety readily evolved into a sense of guilt that she had done nothing for her children, and finally into frustration regarding her own insecure future in which she could expect nothing from them in return.

In all, every moment in her daily life reminded Sun Yufen of her "destiny" as a "peasant." It seemed meaningless to remind her that peasants, as well as urban workers, used to be invoked as "the people" in the Maoist past. Yet Sun Yufen and other poor rural migrants tenaciously use the term "peasants" not because they have become used to "the mentality of peasants," as many urbanites I met would claim, but rather because they incessantly confirm their "otherness" in their relationships with "the urban." Sun Yufen and other poverty-stricken migrants experience rage, frustration, and depression in their confrontation with all that is "urban": urban policies that do not take into consideration the settling of migrants in the city, urban residents who are "raised by the state," and urban discourses that ceaselessly distinguish between "us" (urbanites) and "them" (peasants). In contemporary China, the term "peasants" has become a self-disparaging expression of this "otherness." In this sense, rural migrants are "peasants" *in* and *through* society, even in the city.[13] Nevertheless, Sun Yufen never ceased her struggle to get out of Hadong. It was through this struggle that Sun came to confirm her "otherness" and nurture her sense of abandonment and abjection. During my fieldwork, the struggle recommenced with her efforts to recover her "stolen" rural land.

Unable to Return to the Countryside

"I will go back home if I can take back my land." The thought of returning to the countryside revisited Sun Yufen every time she got hurt by her life in Harbin. The daily struggles she faced there exacerbated her frustration with the "disappearance" of her land. "The bastard [village secretary] took my land without saying a word to me. He insists that I gave up the land myself [*zidong fangqi*]. It's too absurd. How could I give up the only pension I have?"

The loss of her land dated back a decade or more, when the car accident following her husband's sudden death left Sun Yufen recuperating at her mother's home. In the meantime, there was a flood in Binxian, her late husband's hometown. The village government took away her "abandoned" land of seven *mu* in order to rebuild houses washed away by the flood. When she returned to Binxian two years after the car accident, she saw new houses standing on her land. Crying and protesting were of no use. Her husband was gone, and few household goods were left because she had sold most of them to cover the cost of her medicine. Her sisters- and brothers-in-law could only say that they had not informed her immediately because they had not known when she would be coming back. Absorbed by the precariousness of her new situation and feeling quite helpless, Sun even failed to mention the obvious fact that she still had her household registration in Binxian.[14] Relocating was the only option left to her. Nevertheless, she continued to visit Binxian periodically afterwards to insist on her rights to her land.

Many urbanites see the hardships of rural migrants in the city as bearable because the migrants have land that they can return to. This is true in the case of migrants who work part of the year in the city and go back to their land in the farming season. Out of the thirty-five rural migrants whom I interviewed in Hadong between October and December 2006, twenty-four still had land in rural areas. Yet only seven out of the twenty-four alternated between the city and the countryside to farm their land. For the other seventeen migrants, land was no longer an issue. Ten out of these seventeen migrants, in their thirties, had been allocated such a small amount of land (less than four *mu* per household) that they gave it to their parents or in-laws in exchange for taking care of their children. The other seven migrants had already rented or "sold" their land, albeit illegally, to their families or neighbors a long time before they migrated to Harbin. These migrants considered land nothing but the source of a little extra income that supplemented their meager earnings in the city. Their land in the countryside rented for only 100 to 150 yuan per *mu*. Given the fact that the average amount of land allocated to them was only eight *mu,* the total income they received from rent was only 800 to 1,200 yuan *per year,* which was comparable to the average per capita *monthly* income (936 yuan) of urbanites in Harbin in 2006.[15]

Significantly, eleven of the thirty-five rural migrants whom I interviewed, including Sun Yufen, no longer had land in the countryside. It should be noted that the recent process of urbanization in China has led to a massive loss of land for 4.5 million people, who are commonly called "displaced peasants" (*shidi nongmin*) in governmental and scholarly accounts (Wang 2006: 88). The urbanization process has accelerated the expropriation of rural land belonging to peasants who have migrated to the cities; their land has been taken not only for public facilities but also for private factories and new houses built for urbanites displaced by redevelopment in the cities. Scholars have also examined the predatory role of local government in expropriating the land of peasants in order to attract domestic and foreign investors, and thus to increase its own profit. China's land law asserts that the ownership of rural farmland resides with the "rural collective," but without defining whom exactly that comprises (Ho 2001; Brandt et al. 2002; Chen 2002). Not surprisingly, ownership by the collective has often been changed to ownership by local cadres, who then abuse their power in concert with the government (Guo 2001; Cai 2003; Cao and Yu 2006).

The story of Sun Yufen is less about this large-scale, visible expropriation, which has aroused the collective protests of peasants in many regions, than it is about a more mundane, often invisible takeover of rural migrants' land that happens quietly while the original contractor is away working in the city. By law, peasants, regardless of their current place of residence, can exercise both the land-contracting right (*tudi chengbao jingyingquan*) and the right to use an urban residential quarter (*zhusuodi shiyongquan*), as long as their household registration remains in the rural district (Liu and Chen 2006). The land belonging to rural migrants becomes vulnerable to takeover, however, during a long absence. This is not only because local cadres may attempt to use collective land for more entrepreneurial purposes but also because of the structural predicament of China's land administration, which reviews land allocations infrequently, despite the fact that the rural population is in a constant state of flux. In any case, for rural migrants, losing land represents a loss of their birthright, which serves as an "equivalent of the state provision of grain and pensions given to urban residents" (C. K. Lee 2007: 209).

In addition to her migrant status, Sun Yufen's gender has also determined her loss of land entitlement. For rural women in China, land rights are often lost through divorce or the death of the husband. Analyzing land allocation since the decollectivization of the early 1980s, many scholars have examined long-standing ambiguities surrounding women's claims to the land as well as gender disparities in access to land resources (Judd 1992, 1996; Jacka 1997; Li 2002). Ellen Judd notes that when a daughter marries, any allocations of land originally in her name in fact remain under the control of the household head, who is commonly her father, even though she has little land allocated to her in her husband's village (Judd 1992: 346). The recent land reforms, which reaffirmed thirty-year leases and put an end to redistributions with the aim of better securing land tenure rights for rural migrants, have paradoxically made land rights for women more vulnerable by preventing newly married women from applying for new allocations (Hare, Yang, and Englander 2007; Chen and Summerfeld 2007). Zongmin Li (2002) stresses how the land rights of widows are put at risk when the late husband's family insists on use rights according to traditional practice. In other cases the village collective simply withdraws the land.

In the case of Sun Yufen, neither the village collective nor her in-laws deprived her of her land. Nevertheless, the death of her husband—in addition to her absence owing to hospitalization—made it easier for the village government to take away her land and build new homes on it. More than a decade had gone by since the land passed out of her control, but Sun still held a grudge against her in-laws as well as against her neighbors, who were reluctant to help her at the time of the loss. "After my husband was gone, nobody in the village was willing to assist my family," she told me. "Of course, my husband's sister and brother expressed sympathy for my situation. However, they worried that I might rely on them to raise my children. When the village government attempted to build houses on my land, they could've come to tell me in advance. But they didn't."

When Sun Yufen asked me to help her reclaim her land, I could not say no. Although I concluded later that agreeing might have been as irresponsible as refusing, I did not want to veil myself as a "disinterested" scholar and explain that I was neither a lawyer nor a reporter but merely a foreigner who was not familiar with Sun Yufen's situation. Given the land law, it seemed unequivocal that she should have the right either to reclaim her allocation of land or to receive compensation for its loss.[16] Encouraging me to help, Sun's neighbor said: "In the first place, we peasants don't know the law. Second,

FIGURE 5.3. Sun Yufen returned to Binxian in pursuit of her lost land (December 2006)

we don't have connections [*guanxi*]. Finally, we don't know what to say even if we realize that there is a problem." I could not deny that I might be better prepared than Sun Yufen in these three respects.

In mid-December, Sun and I arrived at a small mountain village (of about two hundred households) in Binxian after lurching along in a packed bus for hours on frozen unpaved roads. Wang Jun, a younger brother of Sun's late husband, greeted us. Because the village secretary was out of town, the three of us first went to see Xun, a leader of the small group (*xiaozu*) under the authority of the village committee. Sun asked for land to compensate for what she had lost.

> XUN: No lands are left. Wait until we find surplus land.
> SUN YUFEN: How can I wait? Where can I find work at my age? Nobody wants me in the city.
> XUN: Nobody can touch the matter of the land against policy. How could we dare to give out land as we like?
> SUN: If so, how could you dare to build a house on my land?
> XUN: You're no better. You gave up your land. You left, didn't you?
> SUN: Who gave up the land? Because of the car accident, I was lying in bed for two years. I couldn't do anything during those years.

My young son and daughter had to deal with my urine and feces. I didn't dare to spend even 2 yuan. How can you say that I just left? My family lives from hand to mouth. My children have grown up, but they can't even think of marriage because they have no money. I wanted to kill myself. But my daughter asked me not to do that. She said: "Mom, please. I already have no father. I don't want to be an orphan."

Sun Yufen burst into tears after delivering this speech. Feeling awkward, Xun suggested that we visit the township government (*zhen zhengfu*). Agreeing to go the next day, Sun Yufen and I spent the evening in conversation with her husband's family members. Although they sympathized with Sun, they thought that her attempt to reclaim the land was futile. "The matter of the land happened ten or more years ago. How is it possible to reclaim the land now?" said one of her in-laws. "Mr. Yang, a neighbor, came back to request his land. He was in the city for twenty years, wasn't he? Rumors are flying that he ran away after being beaten by the village secretary," said another. One of Sun's sisters-in-law added: "The land was worthless [*buzhiqian*] before. Nothing was left after one year's farming. So, many people deserted it and rushed to the cities. But the price of corn has gone up, grain taxes have been waived.[17] That's why they come back and request the land. Yet the land allocation is over." Although Sun Yufen was with her relatives, it seemed that she was not one of them. On the issue of land conflicts, she was on the opposite side. The total size of a plot of land in the village had been decreasing year after year. Wang Jun and his wife had received four *mu* each at the latest land renewal in Harbin in 1998. But the wife of Jin, a son of Sun Yufen's sister-in-law, had received only one *mu* when she moved to this village on her marriage three years earlier. In order to farm, Jin's family had to rent the land of a neighbor who had migrated to Harbin. Although Sun Yufen's relatives understood her desperation, any benefit to her could be to their disadvantage, or at least to the disadvantage of their offspring, whose land allotment would be further reduced.

The next morning Sun Yufen, Wang Jun, and I visited the township government office to meet with the deputy director. His cold manner made us feel embarrassed from the outset. The deputy director remained unmoved while listening to Sun Yufen, who narrated her life story through tears. "The government acts only in terms of law, policy, and documents," he remarked. What he meant by "law, policy, and documents," however, was different from my understanding, which was based on the land law enacted in 2003, under which one is entitled to maintain one's land contracting right for thirty years, provided one remains a member of the collective.[18] In contrast, his under-standing was based on a document published by the Harbin government,[19] according to which a person who did not participate in the land renewal in 1998 is regarded as having abandoned his or her land contracting rights. Central government law should have overridden his municipal-level docu-ment. Nevertheless, he responded: "Central and local policies do not neces-sarily correspond to each other. I just follow instructions from the superior authority. Anyway, rural land is owned not by the state but by the collective. You had better talk to the village secretary."

Back in the village, Sun Yufen, Wang Jun, and I caught Wei, the village secretary, just as he was about to leave his office for the remainder of the day, having heard that we were on our way to visit him. Wei first repeated what we had heard from the township government: Sun's "self-abandonment" of her land as well as her absence at the time of the land renewal in 1998 left her with no claim. He even made an unsubstantiated argument that Sun's household registration did not belong to this village anymore because her husband was dead. Again, Sun Yufen began to tell her story through tears. Yet I eventually put myself forward because her tears did not seem to be of any use in countering Wei. My explanation failed to persuade him to withdraw his baseless argument until I showed him my identification card. Upon learning that I was not Chinese, he softened his manner and began to talk about land allocations and compensation, telling Sun: "Let's see. No decision has been made about land yet this year. You're a special case because your land was taken for building houses. A land allocation will be avail-able to you in the event that there is a land renewal next year. If there is no renewal, you will receive compensation based on the value of the land during the period when your land was taken. But I can't promise you anything for sure, since you didn't participate in the land renewal in 1998."

On our way back to Harbin, Sun Yufen and I felt so elated that we went out for a nice meal together. "Poor people usually die young. I have to eat as much as I can when I'm alive," said Sun, finishing off a couple of the dishes that we had ordered. She was cheerfully asking about commonalities between China and South Korea, my home country, and between her and me. "Is the countryside big in Korea?" she wanted to know. "Are there lots of chickens, pigs, and cows in the countryside? Are there more good people than bad people?" For Sun Yufen, these common points seemed to connect the two of us not as a poor migrant from a poor country and a college stu-dent from a wealthy country but as equal human beings.

Sun's joy and mine were short-lived, however. The Spring Festival came and went, and still there was no news of a land renewal. Sun Yufen became anxious after a call from her brother-in-law Wang Jun, who claimed that Wei, the village secretary, had lied to us because he thought I was a reporter. I felt frustrated and sad when Sun took off her underwear and showed me her wounded leg. "See. My leg is like this. It still hurts me. I have no hope of living unless the matter of the land is resolved."

In late March 2007, Sun and I returned to Binxian to meet Wei for a second time. He did not even show up to meet us. Sun Yufen, Wang Jun, and I had walked along muddy roads for an hour to see him, in vain. Wei's son said that he had gone to Harbin, while his wife suggested that he might be staying in a nearby village. The next morning I finally had a conversation with him by phone. He told me: "Regardless of any law, the document produced by the Harbin government in 1998 is the yardstick for land compensation here. The document states that people who left before the land renewal in 1998 are excluded from compensation. As land allocation is getting more difficult, it is impossible to follow the central law just as we are told. But considering her pitiable circumstances, I may take care of Sun particularly [*teshu zhaogu*] at the time of the next land renewal." Wei was dangling the possibility of a special, paternalistic intervention on Sun's behalf in the very matter in which he had ignored the right she deserved by law. Desperate, I contacted a friend of mine, a legal affairs reporter, who stressed that the only barometer in land compensation was whether one was a member of the collective or not. Nevertheless, he advised me: "It's time for you to stop. Even a provincial-level reporter is doomed to lose in this kind of matter. You are neither a Chinese citizen nor her family member. The government won't be happy about your presence." Although he tried to be polite, he assured me in an irritating tone that this was none of my business. Staring at my helpless, clouded face, Sun Yufen said simply, "It's time to go back." She recognized that we had reached the limit of our endeavors to reclaim her land, and she was ready to return to the city.

What intrigued me about Sun Yufen's struggle for her land was that she was willing to accept either monetary compensation or a reallocation of land. Claiming her land rights did not necessarily mean returning to the countryside where she had lived with her husband. Binxian was her husband's home, and he was no longer present. Upon her marriage she had moved to her husband's hometown and had lived there for ten years. The more carefree life of a newlywed faded as she endured his suicide, the car accident, and the loss of her land. Fond memories were displaced by the recollection of her starving children, and of having to sell most of the family's household goods in order to survive. Furthermore, unlike some successful migrants who return to build a new house and show off their wealth in their hometown (Jeong

2000; Sargeson 2002), Sun Yufen had visited her former home to beg for her lost land. As implied in the conversations with her in-laws, Sun's permanent return would not be entirely welcomed by other peasants who suffered from the scarcity of land. Finally, without her husband, Sun Yufen's claim was regarded by her in-laws as no stronger than that of any other peasant. The countryside refused to accept it.

Unable to Settle in the City

I visited Sun Yufen again one month after our return from Binxian. To my surprise, she was holding a commercial flyer for real estate in Harbin. It was from Elegance Life Garden, the new complex where Chen Yuhua and many other residents of Hadong were attempting to purchase an apartment (see chapter 2). Sun Yufen said to me: "My land is gone. But I can't live here all my life. My children should have housing in order to get a good spouse." Sun made the difficult decision to buy a house in Harbin, despite the many difficulties she had had with members of her family who had also migrated there (as well as with urban neighbors with whom she did not get along), because she expected to receive help from them. Sun Yufen's brother Sun Yuming, who was living across the street from her, came to work in Harbin at the age of twelve, as I noted earlier. Sun Yuming and his wife, a temporary worker in a pharmaceutical factory, had helped Sun Yufen settle in Hadong. Every night Sun Yufen went to Sun Yuming's to watch her favorite television shows. Sun Yuguo, her thirty-three-year-old half brother, had worked as a truck driver for years after his discharge from military service. Bringing his fiancée to live with him, he had recently settled in Hadong and started to collect junk tires along with Sun Yuming. Sun Yufen's mother had also come from her hometown to stay with Sun Yuguo and his fiancée. It was Sun Song, her forty-year-old younger sister, of whom Sun Yufen was most proud among all the members of her family. "Sun Song is rich," Sun Yufen told me. "She has an apartment as well as an urban household registration. Her husband is a teacher raised by the state. I envy her. Her husband took her to a nice restaurant on Women's Day on March 8. Where is luxury like that in the countryside? I used to eat two eggs on my birthday. That was all." Arranged by a distant family member from Harbin, Sun Song's marriage was to a teacher who had polio and who had worked as a repairman while at college. Sun Yufen seldom went to Sun Song's, because she felt her poverty whenever she walked out of Sun Song's high-rise apartment. Instead, Sun Song sometimes visited Sun Yufen and gave her some money before leaving. Sun Yufen had decided to purchase an apartment because she was confident of generous support from her siblings.

As I mentioned in chapter 2, the new multistory apartment buildings (*loufang*) quickly became a desirable location for nearby urban residents, most of whom have lived in single-story housing (*pingfang*) throughout their lives. For them, single-story houses no longer represent the socialist workers' village.[20] Paralleling their lowered status, such housing is now derided as a "slum," where residents must go outside to use public toilets even on freezing winter nights. In contrast, apartment buildings, with their blueprints displayed in model apartments, introduce these former workers to the "real" city, where every household has its own private toilet, access to sewer lines, and a boiler for heat and hot water.

Nevertheless, not everyone is encouraged to enter the gates of this "real" city. Public narratives of desire, as we have seen, are suffused with the theme of power—the power "to differentiate among those deemed appropriate subjects of these imaginations and those cast as inappropriate" (Rofel 2007: 24). From the outset, Sun Yufen's desire for an apartment was considered "inappropriate" by her urban neighbors, by her family, and even by herself. Community cadre Chen Yuhua laughed at her for being interested in the housing. "How can a peasant afford an apartment?" she exclaimed. "She is successful even if she can buy a single-story house here." Sun Yuming, Sun Yufen's brother, did not even want to discuss her plan. "Just leave her alone. She will come to herself," he told me. Although most people already knew of Sun Yufen's intention, she asked whomever she spoke to—including me—to keep it secret: "People will make a fuss about this. They will say that a rag-picking migrant woman cannot buy an apartment. What if I can't get housing because of that rumor? I have a plan. For the down payment on my house, I will borrow 30,000 yuan from Sun Song, 20,000 yuan from Sun Yuming and Sun Yuguo, and 10,000 from other relatives. But I won't tell my plan to anybody. If they suspected my plan, the housing company wouldn't accept my application."

The unstable material conditions affecting her migrant family prevented Sun Yufen even from knocking on the door of the "real" city. In early May 2007, Sun and I visited the model apartment to inquire about any necessary qualifications for a mortgage. What she wanted was an apartment measuring thirty square meters—the smallest one. A sales expert began to explain the requirements in detail, although Sun's bad breath and shabby clothes seemed to make her uncomfortable. The sales agent told Sun: "People who come from out of town can purchase housing. But someone with a Harbin household registration should act as a guarantor for you. It'll be best if your guarantor is a public servant." Sun Yufen responded delightedly: "Yes. I have my sister. She has Harbin household registration [*hukou*]. She'll take care of everything!" Sun was acutely aware that she would not make the cut without a connection to an urban resident. The sales expert, however, asked about more than just the connection.

> SALES EXPERT (DUBIOUSLY): Do you have a steady income?
>
> SUN YUFEN: No, but my sister's husband is a teacher. He can be a guarantor.
>
> AUTHOR: Sun's daughter has a steady income.
>
> SALES EXPERT: The purchaser should have fixed work [*guding gongzuo*] in Harbin, and the work unit should issue a certificate of work [*gongzuo zhengming*]. So not you but your daughter should be the purchaser.
>
> SUN: No problem. Xueqiao, my daughter, has worked in Harbin for more than six years. She's working very hard. She will be able to get the certificate.
>
> SALES EXPERT: How much is her salary? Does it amount to more than 1,000 yuan?
>
> SUN: No. She gets 800 yuan a month.
>
> SALES EXPERT: In that case you need 50,000 yuan for a down payment. Then you can pay 300 to 400 yuan in monthly payments for twenty years. However, the final decision regarding qualification is made by a bank. You should check.
>
> SUN: No problem. My sister has money. Let me bring her!

Every procedure turned out to be more complicated than Sun Yufen had thought. Fear suddenly overtook her—the fear of not knowing how to proceed. For more information regarding the proposed mortgage, Sun and I went to a nearby bank, but soon after we entered the building, she became impatient and said: "Let's go out. I want to smoke." Puffing on a cigarette outside, she continued: "I'm really an idiot, aren't I? I know nothing. A three-year-old baby would be better than me. I have no idea how things are going." In fact, Sun's original plan was simple enough: borrowing money from relatives, making the down payment after construction was complete, and paying the monthly mortgage bills out of her children's salaries. None of the elements of her plan was guaranteed, however. First, she had not even talked with her family about lending money for the down payment. Second, she had not known that she would be required to pay a portion of the down payment within a few weeks. Third, her children had little idea of their expected ongoing financial responsibility for mortgage payments. Above all, Sun failed to submit the certificate of work which she had promised that Xueqiao would obtain from her company. A week later Sun told me: "Xueqiao says that her boss refused to issue the certificate. I don't know why. Xueguo [her son] says the same thing." During a private conversation with Xueqiao later that evening, I found that she had not even raised the matter with her boss. "Sister," she told me, "it is impossible to ask my boss for the certificate. I've worked less than a year in the shop. It's been less than four months since my brother found his new job [*dagong*]. Both he and I are temporary workers. Also, we are people who have come from out of town [*waidiren*]. My boss wouldn't do me a favor."

What compelled Xueqiao not even to broach the subject? What has led Sun and her family to agree that they do not deserve their dreams? And despite all expectations to the contrary, why did Sun still try to enter the "real" city? Why did she keep pursuing her dream when in the end it only reminded her that her actions were "inappropriate"? I believe that the fear, hesitancy, anxiety, and frustration that poor migrants like Sun experience when they attempt to be not only *in* urban space but also *of* it arise because they are not excluded from the city but are included "through exclusion" in it. That is, although government power is exercised in the name of the well-being of the entire population, the poor still experience a state of exclusion from the very site where they are formally included.[21]

Poor rural migrants like Sun are not simply expelled to the margins of the political order. Instead they are incessantly included through a media blitz that spotlights their misery, through paternalistic slogans that tout their protection from legal wrongdoing, and even through laws that prescribe their rights. These processes of inclusion, however, coincide with processes of exclusion that differentiate them from urbanites and discourage their settling permanently in the city. Sun's desire to reclaim her land in the countryside, as well as her subsequent desire to purchase housing in the city, were encouraged by laws that guarantee her rights to do so. In practice, however, the law's executors implement a myriad of local modifications, exceptions, and puzzling turns of phrase that limit Sun's choices. According to Agamben, this is the very nature of every law. He quotes a sentence from "Before the Law," a parable that Kafka introduced in his novel *The Trial:* "How can we hope to 'open' if the door [law] is already open?" Kafka's parable, Agamben notes, presents "the pure form in which law affirms itself with the greatest force precisely at the point in which it no longer prescribes anything" (Agamben 1998: 49). With this denial of prescription, the open door destined for Sun Yufen eventually excludes her by including her.

Now that her pursuit of a settlement has amounted to nothing, Sun Yufen remains in her rented room in Hadong, paying 130 yuan a month. Her life goes on. She gets up at four a.m. and picks up scraps of old metal while making the rounds of sites where single-story public housing was recently pulled down to make room for new commercial apartments. In the afternoon, she, along with her neighbors, makes tiny tassels for decorating liquor bottles—another side business that provides a bit more income. After dinner with Xueqiao, who comes directly from work, she watches *The Nanny* (*Baomu*), her favorite television show, in Sun Yuming's home. Her dream world in which virtue wins and vice loses finally gains its realization on TV.

I conclude this chapter by pointing to a significant gap between the state's increasing concern for rural migrants and the abandonment that rural migrants like Sun Yufen still experience in their everyday lives. The central government has mobilized both spectacular performances and institutional reforms for rural migrants in recent years in the wake of growing anxiety about economic polarization. Almost on a daily basis, television news reports numerous policies and activities planned by the central and local governments to protect the rights of rural migrants. Yet never did I see Sun Yufen and her family tune in to the news channel, though I watched TV with them many times. They had no interest in identifying themselves with the category of "rural migrants" who featured so prominently in nightly newscasts.

The gap between the politics of rights as established at the national level and as ignored among rural migrants themselves becomes more understandable when one sees rural migrants' lives not in a momentary snapshot but through a series of processes in which hope, anger, and depression alternate throughout long, desperate struggles. Sun Yufen's struggles are not an expression of her "misery," as it is often depicted by the media in attention-grabbing images that legitimate the inherent powerlessness of migrants and the state's paternal care for them. Rather, they produce a wide variety of emotions. During her quest to recover her lost land, Sun burst into tears in front of a roomful of government officials. She nearly wept for joy when a village secretary hinted at the possibility of compensation. She walked down muddy roads in vain to meet a government secretary who had run away to avoid seeing her. Often she realized her precarious position both as a woman and as a widow in the presence of in-laws who no longer supported her fight for land. In the process of seeking new housing in the city, Sun was buoyant while examining the blueprint of a model apartment. She made plans in her own way, she felt fear in front of those who requested expert knowledge and qualifications, and she faced the ridicule of her family members as well as of her urban neighbors. It was therefore in her own struggles and not in a newspaper or in nightly news bulletins that Sun Yufen encountered "the law," "the state," and "the government." When she returned to her shabby room after all these struggles ended, Sun Yufen felt that "rights" had never belonged to her. She said: "I have no rights. Only officials [*dangguan*] have them. They have rights to do whatever they want. Law? Useless! Officials have the right to make any excuse whenever they violate the law."

I would argue that Sun Yufen's despair runs deeper because of her experience of "inclusive exclusion." Her in-between status is painful precisely because she is not merely being excluded but is excluded "through inclusion" in a post-Mao fantasy that liberates peasants from their bond to the rural land and even attempts to protect their rights in the city. Sun Yufen feels frustrated because the path of belonging is not closed but supposedly open. This "openness" leads her to try to gain access to the path until she realizes in despair that it is closed to her. In short, her "bare life," as Agamben puts it, "remains included in politics in the form of the exception, that is, as something that is included solely through an exclusion" (Agamben 1998: 11).[22]

In fact, the "inclusive exclusion" that I highlight in this chapter is not experienced by rural migrants alone. Many urban laid-off workers find themselves caught between the state's promise to protect them and their increasing de facto exclusion as they are expelled from their lifetime employment, left mired in their shantytowns, and, like rural migrants, dubbed a "weaker social group" (*ruoshi qunti*). Nevertheless, a signifier like "wolf" does not emerge among these urban laid-off workers because they, unlike rural migrants, once shared a sense of membership, a sense that they received protection from the state in accordance with the ideological acclaim for "the people." This past experience of membership and protection has led these workers to associate their poverty with a feeling of loss rather than with a feeling of total abjection.

More significantly, this difference between rural migrants and urban laid-off workers does not simply demonstrate the heterogeneity of poverty. Difference does not describe something that merely remains different. To paraphrase Jacques Rancière,[23] it is always possible to recruit from the poor an army against the poor. In the next chapter I demonstrate how the relationship between urban laid-off workers and rural migrants moves toward a tension, and even an antagonism, between them in tandem with the state's practices of dividing the poor as well as the historically accumulated tension between the urban and the rural.

CHAPTER 6

Dividing the Poor

One early December morning in 2006 I was reading *Life Daily* (*Shenghuo bao*), one of the major newspapers in Harbin. An article on the front page immediately caught my eye because it reported a dispute that occurred in Hadong. According to the article, the conflict arose when a rural migrant, Mrs. Hu, refused to pay the security fee to Community cadres. The reporter writes: "Mrs. Hu thought it was illegal for Community cadres to collect the security fee in place of the police.... A severe dispute then transpired between Mrs. Hu and two female Community cadres [Li Shun and her daughter-in-law]. Mrs. Hu insisted that the two cadres had even mobilized their own family and assaulted her and her husband." The violent incident eventually landed both the Hus and Li Shun's son in a nearby hospital for a few days.

I found this dispute interesting because the collection of community fees had become a breeding ground for anger among local residents in Hadong during that time. For more than a decade, street-level officials had been collecting from their residents community fees, which include a security fee, a cleaning fee, and a service fee. Colloquially known as *shoufei,* the collection of community fees has been a major sticking point between the street-level government and residents, both urbanites and rural migrants. Because the amount of some of the fees is left to the discretion of the street office, government officials have paid significant attention to the collection. Nevertheless, residents have seen how the local government, which they thought would take care of them in place of the collapsed work unit, has been incapable of improving their living conditions. Even as residents have witnessed mountains of uncollected garbage accumulating and crime increasing, the amount of the fees has risen. The ongoing dilapidation of the neighborhood has led local people to view the collection as extortion from the poor.

I was curious about how street-level government officials and local residents narrated and circulated the *shoufei* incident. My first assumption was that such a controversy would gain political significance, with the potential for uniting poor urban residents and rural migrants against adverse circumstances. The local version of the incident, however, was not about "the state" versus "the poor" but about "the urban" versus "the rural."

At first, Community cadres voiced their grievances over the collection of community fees (hereafter *shoufei*). "I spent all day collecting fees. I'm tired of quarreling with residents over *shoufei*," said one cadre, while another told me: "The Street Office shouldn't impose target figures on us. We are told to take money out of our own pocket unless we achieve the target figures. How absurd it is! I hope we won't have to collect the fees again." Yet their complaints directed at high-level government were quickly overshadowed by their condemnation of the Hus. "How savage they are! It's said that they called up young gangsters to attack Li Shun and her son," one cadre informed me. Another insisted, "The reporter has no idea how savage out-of-towners [*waidi ren*] are." Although these cadres did not know exactly where the Hus came from, they assumed that the Hus must be "out-of-towners," in light of their "savage" acts. One cadre said with a sigh: "I'm sure that the Hus bought off the reporter. These days, rural migrants have more power than we urbanites do."

For their part, urban residents, including laid-off workers and older retirees, first blamed the Community cadres and then, more vaguely, "the government." One informant told me: "She [Li Shun] brought misfortune on herself. What the hell has she done for us except take our money?" Another declared: "The government should stop collecting any fees. Look, robberies happen every day in this neighborhood. Who would willingly pay the security fee?" Nevertheless, they mostly ended up blaming rural migrants' "bad" habits. "Why do these rural folks [the Hus] come and make a fuss here instead of farming in the countryside?" questioned one resident. "It was not until rural migrants came here that this kind of disturbance was widespread," another told me, advising: "You should be careful when you meet them [rural migrants]. We urbanites are poor now. But we can live by borrowing some money from our family or friends. However, rural migrants have no connections like these. Without money, no one knows what the hell they will do to others!"

Rural migrants whom I met seemed relatively uninterested in this incident. Most of them were not familiar with the Hus, who had been living in Hadong for only two months. It was not until after I raised the subject with Sun Yufen (see chapter 5) that I heard some of her opinions. Sun said to me: "I'm sure that the incident occurred because people look down on migrants like me. We migrants pay the [security] fees regularly because we're afraid of being punished. But urbanites don't care. Some of them have never paid at all because they are good at arguing. It's so unfair!"

Today the political, economic, and sociocultural boundaries between "the urban" and "the rural" have become more destabilized than at any other time in China's socialist history. The household registration system that restricted the movement of rural people to the city has been relaxed; the work unit system that once formed enclosed territories for urban workers in the city has collapsed. Furthermore, the social distinction between urbanites and rural migrants has broken down in the cities, including Hadong, because of factors such as business partnerships, intermarriages, or the common schooling of their children. These conditions led me to anticipate that the blurred boundary between "the urban" and "the rural" would be evident in Hadong, where impoverished urbanites and rural migrants lived in the same neighborhoods and together experienced spatial segregation, marginalization, insecurity, and social inequality.

The *shoufei* incident nonetheless demonstrates the tenacity of the boundary. It ended up reinforcing the belief of urbanites, including both government officials and poor residents, that rural migrants are uncontrollable and dangerous. Despite, or because of, living under the common condition of poverty, urbanites and rural migrants in Hadong have not become friends, let alone formed a political coalition against state power, as in many other Asian and Latin American countries (see, e.g., Paley 2001; Goldstein 2004; Cho 2005). An emphasis on the differences between them mostly overshadows their common perception that they are poor and stuck in the same wretched space.

In this chapter I examine what I call the processes of differential impoverishment: why and in what ways the urban poor and rural migrants in Hadong have reinforced the distinctions between them rather than recognizing their commonalities. In particular, I scrutinize the workings and outcomes of "dividing the poor," which I find is one governmental intervention for recruiting from the poor an army against the poor (see Marx 1972). China's urban poor are not merely excluded from the wider society; they are prompted to voice their grievances not against the state but against other poor people. Thus impoverished urbanites and rural migrants in Hadong are divided by themselves as well as by state officials. Despite living in the same wretched space and engaging in the same kinds of temporary, precarious work, both groups aggravate their misery by insisting, on one side, that rural migrants "work like hell and take all the jobs in the city" and, on the other, that urban workers are "still raised and fed by the state."

What I call dividing the poor is not a singular, intentional project of state bureaucrats. Rather, as I show, it has been made possible through the "porous array of intersections" of various governmental interventions.[1] In this chapter I pay particular attention to the temporality of state policies, disjunctive layers of state actions, and the positionality of state agents in order to show the contingent ways in which dividing the poor comes into being. In the decaying neighborhood of Hadong, urban laid-off workers, rural migrants, and street-level state officials have restabilized the distinction between the urban and the rural while encountering a variety of state policies that were established at different times in the past and enacted for different purposes. Even in the present, the division of the poor is realized differently at each level of state bureaucracy. Particularly in street-level government, the dual position of Community cadres, who are urbanites as well as state bureaucrats, unwittingly plays a key role in directing local responses to state appropriation not toward "the state" versus "the poor" but toward "the urban" versus "the rural."

Such attention to the actual performance of governmental interventions finally leads me to highlight a number of ruptures inherent in governing, as I show how state officials are incapable of dealing with the "uncontrollability" of rural migrants, the very outcome of the differential administration of the poor. Dividing the poor produces such conflicting outcomes precisely because it is unintentional. It may contribute to state governance by disabling the potential of the poor to unite against state power. Yet it often creates a "hole in the system" by placing rural migrants outside the purview of state governance and triggering their flight from it. Studies of government programs directed toward laid-off workers and rural migrants in China often draw attention to the production of entrepreneurial and self-motivating subjects through the intersections of gendered claims, socialist legacies, or pro-market rationales (Guiheux 2007; Won 2004; Yan 2003a; Yang 2008, 2010). My approach is slightly different. Rather than focusing solely on how subjects are governed, I attend to how governing sometimes fails, thus emphasizing the precarious and patchy nature of state governance (see also Cho 2011).

The Historicity of Differential Impoverishment

To understand the tensions pertaining to the lack of communication between urban laid-off workers and rural migrants, I provide in this section a historical analysis of how the urban and the rural were both imagined and experienced in Hadong. These groups did not begin their new interactions "as blank slates" (Pieke 1996: 44) to each other. Although rural collectivization and the urban work unit system firmly restricted the mobility of both groups, political policies and programs occasionally gave each one some sense of what the other was like.

Older Retirees: Relief at Not "Being Sent to the Countryside"

It is an irony that older retirees in Hadong, who assert that there is a distinct gap between the urban and the rural in their narratives, have mostly come from the nearby countryside. When Fenghuang began to recruit workers on a large scale in the early 1950s, they could become urban residents by entering the factory. It was a time when the household registration (*hukou*) system had not reached its complete form; movement between the city and the countryside was relatively free, at least until the mid-1950s.[2] Older retirees in Hadong describe their departure from the countryside as a stroke of good fortune. "My family had nothing to eat in the countryside. It so happened that I came here to find work. At that time, however, I never realized that my relatives would be stuck in the countryside while I became a permanent urbanite," Song Guoqing, a retired worker, said to me.

Even before the *hukou* system was finalized, however, the countryside was already considered empty space, useful for "cleansing" the ill effects of urban space on city residents. In November 1948, even before the PRC announced its establishment, the Committee of Northeast China (Dongbei Weiyuanhui) started the compulsory migration of the "idle" urban population to the countryside. Between 1948 and 1949, the authorities sent 9,370 Harbin households (31,886 people) to the countryside, citing the need to "ease the urban burden, solve urban unemployment, make the idle population participate in labor, and promote rural development" (Li and Shi 1987: 223).[3] The "idle" population included unemployed workers, casual laborers, coolies, rickshaw pullers, and other poor people.

After the formation of the PRC, this migration effort continued in concert with the Party's decision to reduce the workforce in the cities. The nationwide "downsizing" (*jingjian*) of the early 1960s is a dramatic example. About 20 million rural people moved to cities during the feverish industrialization drive of the Great Leap Forward. Nearly half of them, however, eventually returned to their home villages when natural disasters followed the failure of the campaign (Brown 2012: 119–22). According to the government document "Decision by the Party to Further Streamline the Workforce and Reduce the Urban Population," Harbin was assigned the task of reducing its population by 460,000 people between 1961 and 1962. A total of 492,000 people were sent to the countryside during that period (HSZ 1999). Although this nationwide drive peaked in the early 1960s, the governmental decision to downsize had been made even prior to the Great Leap Forward. In the Taiping district, of which Hadong was a part at that time, about ten thousand people in all were sent to the countryside in 1955, 1957, and 1969 (TQ 1992). On January 28, 1958, the *Harbin Daily* reported: "Taiping residents who chose to migrate went to two counties to participate in rural production and settle there. A total of 153 households (448 people) went to the countryside. Most of them had been jobless for a very long time. Some of them were seasonal laborers, cart pullers, and street vendors. Others were temporary workers or young peasants who had blindly come to the city." Despite some privileging policies such as resettlement stipends and fair wage compensation, it was not easy to persuade these people to go. A retired cadre who directed the migration campaign in the Harbin government once commented to me: "People were discontented with this decision. Going to the countryside was considered to be as unbearable [then] as it is now. But complaints were of no use. We officials persistently made them obey through [our] political work."

Urban Laid-Off Workers: The Tortuous Experience of Going "Down to the Villages"

Whereas many older retirees in Hadong had lived in the country before coming to the city, most laid-off workers in their fifties, who came of age during the Cultural Revolution, encountered the countryside through a unique experience, the drastic mass movement known as "up to the mountains, down to the villages" (*shangshan xiaxiang*). During the Cultural Revolution, the government sent more than 17 million students to the countryside to learn from the peasants and to alleviate urban unemployment (for details, see Bernstein 1977; Ding 1998). The number of sent-down youth peaked at 5.4 million in the period from 1968 to 1970, the middle stage of the Cultural Revolution (Bernstein 1977: 39–40).

Although the sense of mission and the spirit of self-sacrifice are evident in many documentary films of that period, going to the countryside was not necessarily voluntary among those who went. Chen Yuhua, a Community cadre whom I introduced in chapter 2, is one of those who avoided the mission for fear of a harsh life in the countryside. "I graduated from a middle school in 1971," she told me. "Policy had become more relaxed in those days. I could go to the countryside or not. I decided not to go. But people from my father's work unit always kept coming to me to persuade me to go. How persistent they were! I got a severe cold in the nick of time. My father said that I might not have to go to the countryside if I had a disease. So I went through an examination at the hospital. I explained my desperate situation to the doctor. Fearful of criticism, he avoided giving a definite answer and merely suggested that I wait for his diagnosis at home. But he finally issued a certificate that I had pneumonia. Thanks to the certificate, I could avoid going to the countryside!"

Many other workers in Hadong, unlike Chen Yuhua, decided to go to the country either out of passionate commitment or because they faced severe unemployment in the city. For them, "down to the villages" (xiaxiang) remains one of the most significant moments in their life because it was a never-to-be-repeated experience. Chen Yuhua's sister proudly recalled living in a distant village for three years: "Xiaxiang was an unforgettable experience. I volunteered to go to the USSR border. I used to bring films from the propaganda bureau and show them in the village. They were mostly about war and imperialism. But some of them came from North Korea, the USSR, and other eastern European countries. Peasants loved those films!"

What is notable in their stories is not only their being sent "down to the villages" but also their mass exodus from the countryside (McLaren 1979; Gold 1980).[4] Li Yalin, a security guard in Hadong, spent six years reclaiming the northernmost regions of Heilongjiang, widely known as beidahuang. It was his family name, Li, that rescued him in the maelstrom of the rush back to the city. "It was not easy to return to the city in the late 1970s," he told me. "But I was lucky anyway. In the countryside, I met a girl who also came from Harbin. Her family name is Li, the same as mine. At that time her brother succeeded in returning to the city by passing a college exam. My girlfriend helped me to use his name as if I were her brother. So I was able to get out of the countryside [by claiming] that I could inherit her father's position in his factory!"

A wave of remembered adventure and relief swept over many laid-off workers in Hadong with whom I spoke who had experienced the sent-down movement. The countryside is incessantly conjured up and often romanticized in their narratives, all the more so because it no longer remains a lived experience for that generation; "only once, never again," as Li Yalin said to me.

Rural Migrants: Envy of Sent-Down Youths Who Could Leave

Although for many urbanites the countryside was often evoked as the site of an unforgettable memory, for most rural migrants in Hadong, the country is far from being a place they can point to with pride in their narratives. From the start, it has been inseparable from a status they are ashamed of, that is, being "peasants." "The countryside has nothing, the city has everything. What am I supposed to tell you about my home?" This was the first response I received from Yang Meimei, who worked in a small furniture factory in Hadong, when I asked her to tell me more about her rural hometown. For Yang Meimei, urban sent-down youths who came to her village were nothing but strangers who remained only briefly rather than settling there. She told me: "In the early 1970s, about thirty urban youths came to my village. They stayed for three years, though all of them returned to the city. At first they didn't touch the thin porridge we peasants usually ate. They wouldn't eat it until they'd almost starved to death. They mostly dated each other. Sometimes a sent-down boy and a pretty rural girl would go with each other and even get married. But they would agree to a fake divorce for fear that the husband would not be allowed to return to the city. It was common that she lost contact with her 'ex'-husband after he left."

Yet having seen the urban youths as strangers does not necessarily mean that these youths meant nothing to those who remained in the countryside. Rural migrants now in their forties and fifties witnessed at an early age how desperate the urban youths were to flee from their village. Later, coming to the city for work themselves, these migrants saw that many of the urbanites who had once farmed with them now enjoyed conditions superior to those available to the migrants as new arrivals in the city. They often highlighted the contrast between those who were able to leave and those who had to remain in the country. Li Jing, a rural migrant in his mid-thirties, once said to me: "When I was young, around twenty urban youths from Harbin came to my hometown. After experiencing the bitterness of rural life for a little while, they all returned to Harbin. 'Down to the villages' was a kind of 'workout' [duanlian] for them. They learned from rural life, hung around for two or three years in my village, and then ran away to the city. After that, they got jobs and housing in the city. They even became government officials! Basically, their life is different from our peasant life. Who distributes work for peasants? They fled after a three-year workout, but we had to remain stuck in the countryside. The city and the countryside are completely different."

Narratives of Fear

So far I have shown how contrasting perceptions of "the urban" and "the rural" were shaped by the personal experiences of people in Hadong. Direct contacts with migrants through occasional political events, and indirect knowledge of them through news reports about the city and the countryside, have imbued urbanites with a sense of superiority in comparison to "peasants" while reinforcing a sense of perpetual marginality among rural migrants.

Such historically inflected perceptions have been a source of fear and anxiety among many urban residents when "peasants invaded" their already decaying neighborhoods, confirming their own already waning social and economic position. For example, Liu Xing, a man I met while interviewing *dibao* recipients, felt that rural migrants had exacerbated the misery of urban laid-off workers like him by being more competitive. "I was in Fenghuang factory for seventeen years," he told me. "At the factory, I was only responsible for the work which the workshop director ordered me to do. I was trained to follow orders. Skill? Education? Experience? What do they expect me to do? This society urges me to be a carpenter, though I used to be a mason. It also urges me to fix a window frame without any time to practice doing it. This society gives me no chance of serving in an apprenticeship [*xuetu,* as in the Mao era] until I master new skills.

"Now," he continued, "we laid-off workers are completely inundated by rural migrants in the labor market. Of course they are worse off than us when they first enter the city. How shabby and inexperienced they are! However, they know no fear. They really do whatever comes along. How capable they are! Without them, who would clean the windows of skyscrapers? We urbanites wouldn't do that. We don't work that hard until we are starving to death. We look right through them, but we end up falling behind them. They work like hell and finally buy a new house. Look at this neighborhood. Unable to find any work that they are capable of, most urbanites stay indoors. Retirees, laid-off workers, jobless youths."

The fear and anxiety that arise from urbanites' relationships with rural migrants recall what Arjun Appadurai (2006) calls the "threatened majority."[5] According to him, this phenomenon emerges when majorities are mobilized to "think that they are in danger of becoming minor (culturally and numerically)" (2006: 83).[6] In fact, urban laid-off workers are not so much "majorities" as "in-betweens"; they were once treated as "majorities," honored as "masters of the country," but are now witnessing their decline from a place of superiority. This in-between position exacerbates the fear and anxiety of the urban poor. They have experienced downward mobility while remaining in the same urban space that has historically been considered superior to the countryside. Still attached to "the urban," these impoverished workers witness their waning status in the city through their direct encounters with rural migrants, the "peasants" whom they have held in contempt throughout China's socialist history.[7] Looking at a migrant man who passed by carrying a heavy bundle on his back, an old retiree said to his friend and me: "Now this place makes me sick. I want my granddaughter to leave here and live in better circumstances. I shudder at the mere thought that her fate may become like that of the rural migrant."

During my fieldwork, urbanites' fear of rural migrants increased with the occurrence of some tragic event. I learned of six violent or suspicious deaths in or near Hadong. Among the six, a laid-off worker had killed himself, and a drunken retiree was found frozen to death on the street on the eve of the Spring Festival. Their deaths were mostly spoken of among local residents as the natural outcome of a "mental disorder" and "chronic alcoholism," respectively. As for two of the other four victims, the greatest concern among local residents was to discover who had murdered them. In the first case, a retiree from Fenghuang factory was found burned to death; three houses, including his, had burned down in a fire. Although some residents speculated that the fire must have been a result of his carelessness, others suspected rural migrants of arson. One said: "Rural migrants have low 'quality.' They throw away cigarette butts anywhere. I saw a young out-of-towner puffing on his cigarette in front of his [the dead man's] house before the fire occurred." The second case involved a migrant family near Hadong, where a migrant man in his mid-thirties, who ran a small-scale factory, was found murdered along with his wife and daughter. People did not hesitate to point the finger at a migrant as the suspected criminal. "It is obvious that the murderer is a rural migrant," said one resident. Another added, "We urbanites do not have the nerve to commit such a horrible murder." In the first case, however, the fire turned out to have been caused by a faulty stove. It was reported that the retiree had been using a small electrical stove with old wiring; it ignited, and the fire spread in moments. In the second case, as many local residents expected, the killing indeed turned out to have been committed by a migrant youth. It was reported that he had worked in the factory run by the dead man and his wages had gone unpaid for almost a year. What interested me about these cases was how some urbanites' fear of rural migrants prevented them from appreciating the effect of their harsh living conditions. The question of what had caused the tragic events was overshadowed by the question of who had killed whom. The fear of the poor for the poor prevented them from paying serious attention to precipitating factors such as dilapidated housing and unpaid wages, which they all had experienced or were likely to experience.

Accordingly, this historically informed tension makes local practices of dividing the poor different from those pursued by the central government in recent years. In the next section I examine the shifting modes of governing urban poverty in state policies and then return to Hadong to discuss how the policies are reformulated in the actions of street-level government officials who are themselves not only state bureaucrats but also urban residents.

Living Urbanites versus Laboring Migrants

As addressed in the introduction, poverty as an economically impoverished condition does not necessarily correspond to poverty as a social problem for government. This argument is significant in understanding how, against the backdrop of the nation's enduring urban-rural divide, impoverished urban workers and rural migrants are often not lumped together as the urban poor but instead are governed differentially. In the post-Mao era, it is important to note that nationwide governmental interventions for urban poverty started not in the early 1980s, when rural migrants began to flood into the cities in large numbers, but in the mid-1990s, when urban workers started to experience massive layoffs during the country's widespread restructuring of state-owned enterprises.

Not until the early years of the twenty-first century did migrant workers become a crucial target for state welfare policies as China's new leaders acknowledged the role of these workers in upholding the nation's economic position as the world's factory. Not since China's economic reforms began had there been such an outpouring of heartfelt care and attention given to rural migrants (see chapter 5). Helping and protecting migrant workers in the city was the linchpin of the leaders' overall push to pursue growth based on a strategy of keeping wages low. In addition to their economic motivations, I found policymakers increasingly concerned about globally circulating discourses of human rights, citizenship, and good governance. One government official whom I met in Beijing told me, "In order to keep its leading status around the world, China must not neglect the basic rights of migrant workers." In January 2003 the State Council issued the first in a series of documents that would emerge that year effecting policy changes focused on migrant workers. This document—"Notification on Improving the Work of Managing and Providing Services to Peasants Who Move to Cities for Work"—fundamentally altered the official policy on migration (Xiang and Tan 2005: 8; Davies and Ramia 2008: 142).

Even in this case, urban laid-off workers and rural migrants are governed differently. Since the mid-1990s urban laid-off workers have received significant attention from successive central governments through a variety of programs such as the re-employment project, pension and medical insurance reforms, the minimum livelihood guarantee, unemployment allowances, housing subsidies, tax breaks, and micro-financing. Whereas some of these government programs have supported the overall quality of life for these workers, subsequent institutional reforms in support of rural migrants were mostly work-related. Issued by the State Council and the Ministry of Labor and Social Security between 2003 and 2006, governmental policies for rural migrants include settling unpaid wages, improving working conditions, institutionalizing labor contracts, enacting employment injury insurance, and job training (ZLSN 2004–2007). All these policies focus on the *labor* of rural migrants, not on their lives in general. The State Council officially defines rural migrants as "new labor forces who have emerged in the course of industrialization and urbanization amidst our nation's reform," addressing their "contribution to the modernization of our nation."[8] Without urban household registration, rural migrants are considered to be no more than a "floating" population who come to cities in search of work and then return to their homes in the countryside in search of a more meaningful life.

In short, the poor are divided by state policies into *living* urbanites and *laboring* migrants. Rural migrants are considered "deserving" citizens in the city as long as they work. In Hadong, however, the central government's labor-centered approach to migration has left street-level government officials with more questions than answers about how to manage rural migrants within their residential area. The labor-centered policies have had little influence on the living conditions of rural migrants. As I noted in chapter 5, what characterizes rural migrants in Hadong is their sheer diversity: their work ranges from informal, non-factory work to temporary work in factories and even farming. Governmental concerns such as lawsuits over unpaid wages and the participation of workers in labor unions hold little relevance for rural migrants whose work is informal and who labor temporarily in small-scale private factories. Although numerous official documents regarding the protection of migrants have been transmitted to the local government, officials in the street office (*jiedao*) and the Community (*shequ*) under its authority actually have little power to protect them.

Gui Yang, who was in charge of migration-related work in the street office, looked uncomfortable when I asked how she discharged her responsibilities. She wrote down three tasks she performed: establishing a labor union for rural migrants in local non–publicly owned companies; informing rural migrants how to obtain their legal rights and helping them sign an official labor contract with their company; and visiting and expressing appreciation to poor rural migrant families during the Spring Festival and other holidays. After listing these tasks, Gui Yang gave vent to her complaints: "It's been less than two years since these policies were made. In fact they are more one-time events than policies. Look at the rural migrants in Hadong. They are unskilled, uneducated, lower-class [*diceng*] people. Without a formal job, these people are working at this and that. Nobody knows when they will quit and leave. What can we do for them?" When she contemptuously described rural migrants as "unskilled, uneducated, and lower-class," I wondered if Gui Yang was troubled not by the fact that street-level officials could do nothing to protect rural migrants but by the question, why do we urbanites have to protect them?

Dual Position of Street-Level Officials

Early one morning in October 2006, Chen Yuhua, a Community cadre, was cleaning the streets in Hadong. As usual, a few urban residents stopped her to complain about mountains of garbage and frequent robberies in their neighborhood. Chen responded: "Don't blame us [officials] for these problems. Like you, I'm also troubled by them. I'm a resident here too. Out-of-towners have a low-quality character [*suzhi*]. They don't know how to dispose of garbage properly." After her conversation with the residents, Chen Yuhua turned to me and said, "They [out-of-towners] are not like us [urbanites]." Spending a great deal of time in the Community office, I found that local cadres talked about rural migrants the same way that impoverished urbanites did on the street. For example, Community cadre Huang Lihong complained to me when she heard that some rural migrants had shown interest in purchasing a new apartment in a complex that would be built in the south of Hadong: "There should be some regulation to distinguish us from out-of-towners in purchasing housing. If we pay 200,000 yuan for housing, they should pay 300,000 yuan for it. We urbanites are mostly laid off. We are becoming no better than beggars. However, peasants work like hell in the city and eventually purchase housing. These days, urbanites are trying to go to the countryside to make money!"

Both Chen's and Huang's complaints become understandable if one is reminded that they are not only street-level government officials whom local residents often criticize but also neighbors who agree with their fellow urbanites about "dangerous, uncontrollable, and reckless" rural migrants. With this emphasis on the dual position of Community cadres, I turn to scholarly studies on the everyday practices of state agencies, a significant focus of anthropological analyses of the state (Gupta 1995; Gupta and Sharma 2006). Rather than presuming the state to be an overarching entity, anthropologists have inquired into how "the state" is substantiated through the "banal" practices of local bureaucracies: "What the state means to people...is profoundly shaped through the *routine* and *repetitive* procedures of bureaucracies" (Gupta and Sharma 2006: 11). Centering on *routine* performance, however, these studies give little attention to the fact that "the state," which local residents encounter in their everyday routines, is not represented through forms such as speeches, slogans, and documents but embodied through *living people*. These people are not simply "bureaucrats" but are imbued with multiple identities.

In Hadong, street-level government officials—particularly Community cadres—have a dual position. They are state agents who keep an eye on any unlawful acts of local residents; but they are also urban residents who feel fearful about and overwhelmed by the increasing number of rural migrants in their neighborhood. As I noted in chapter 4, most of the Community cadres in Hadong are middle-aged female laid-off workers who face as many economic difficulties as do their neighbors. Most having lived in Hadong for decades, these officials disrupt the presumed distinction between "the state" and "the poor." Some of them still have a family network in the countryside, and in many instances only a decade or so has passed since they achieved urban citizenship after the expropriation of their land. Nevertheless, these officials actively participate in restabilizing the distinction between "the urban" and "the rural" while seeking a palpable target to blame for their social and environmental suffering. Far from burying their antagonistic feelings toward rural migrants in private conversations, they spread those feelings through their everyday practices. Witness Chen Yuhua's mentioning to residents the "bad habits" of rural migrants. When a crime is committed, these officials begin to gather dusty files on rural migrants in their area even before police officers come to request them. They thus play a key role in circulating and amplifying the signs of fear that urban residents have produced as they have unavoidably come to live together with rural migrants. These signs of fear, as Sara Ahmed argues, increase in affective value through their circulation as well as through a history that makes them stick: "The more they [signs] circulate, the more affective they become, and the more they appear to 'contain' affect" (2004: 120).

In the next section I return to the dispute over *shoufei*—the collection of community fees—which I introduced earlier in this chapter. Focusing on this example, I show how the dual position of street-level state officials is played out in dividing the poor in Hadong. These officials' disparate relationships to impoverished urbanites and to rural migrants eventually reveal how very volatile the seemingly banal practices of local state bureaucracies are.

"Whoever Provokes the Government Cannot Win!"

Shoufei has created tension between the local government and residents, both urbanites and rural migrants. In the case of commodity housing (*shangpin fang*) included in newly built residential compounds (*xiaoqu*), the fees do not need to be paid separately because they are automatically charged by property management agencies (*wuye guanli*) (Zhang 2010). In Hadong, however, which mostly contains work unit–based single-story housing (*pingfang*), Community cadres are required to go door-to-door collecting the fees. For convenience, these cadres usually collect the security fee[9] (12 yuan) once a year instead of doing it every month. At the same time, residents are expected to pay a cleaning fee (*weisheng fei*)—3.6 yuan per quarter—in addition to the security fee, for a total of 26.4 yuan. Community cadres attempt to collect as many fees as they can, particularly from rural migrants, whose presence is fairly unstable. These attempts do not reflect any avarice on the part of Community cadres but represent solely the quotas demanded by high-level government. As I noted earlier, every year the street office imposes target figures for three community fees—a service fee (*wangdian fei*) in addition to the security fee and the cleaning fee—on each community.[10] Given the absence of many homeowners, migrant tenants have become targeted by Community cadres, who are under pressure to meet their quotas. Not sure when these migrants may leave Hadong, the cadres often urge them to pay community fees for the whole year. It is not surprising that every rural migrant I met complained, "Government officials haven't done anything except take my money."[11]

The violent dispute between a rural migrant family, the Hus, and Community cadre Li Shun's family, which I recounted at the beginning of this chapter, occurred in the wake of exactly this type of disagreement over the collection of community fees. Senior officials in the street office interpreted the incident as an instance of "the floating population" (*liudong renkou*) challenging the state. Against the backdrop of the incident, these higher-level officials attached great intensity to the signs of fear—depicting rural migrants as threatening or dangerous—which Community cadres had circulated in their everyday practices. A meeting between Community cadres and senior officials in the street office was held a week later, after the incident had been reported in the paper. Deputy director Wei Yonglan brought up the matter after she had listened to all the reports from Community cadres about the fees they had collected toward fulfilling their targets. In a distinctly grave tone, she expressed the government's stance toward the dispute:

As you know, a shameful incident happened in relation to the collection of community fees. A reporter wrote an article without understanding the real circumstances. His article was no better than reversing black and white. Although the condition of our side [Li Shun's son] was much more serious, the reporter described it as if both sides had received wounds of the same degree. His false report embarrassed high-level officials in the district and city governments as well as in the People's Congress. I dispatched some officials to the newspaper right away. The chief editor called in the reporter to make him apologize to our people. He also admitted his prejudice, in writing.

The family who caused this incident belongs to the floating population, without an urban household permit. We found that they ran away a few days ago, knowing that this incident would end up unfavorably for them. They were ignorant of the law [fawang]. They found a connection, provided him with a gift, and even paid him money. Yet they finally ran away because every circumstance turned out to be adverse for them. We [the government] are working out the matter now. Because they are from the floating population, this matter needs a lot of time and effort. But I am pleased to say that the city congress, the city government, the district congress, and the district government have rewarded us for our work with full support.

Faced with this kind of incident, you [Community cadres] should deal with every matter lawfully. Even if your counterpart acts barbarously, you shouldn't respond in the same way. You should not deal with the matter in private, as they do. You should elevate your "quality" [suzhi]!

Finally, I want to remind you that the government will catch the family by any means and inflict severe punishment on them. Our neighborhood is not a place where everyone can come and behave however they want. If we [government officials] do not deal with this matter properly, people will think that the government is incompetent. I repeat, you may put your minds at rest on this matter. The government will show you how we deal with the matter properly so that it can't threaten us. We will show you that whoever provokes the government cannot win!

It is interesting to see how Wei Yonglan's speech differs from a more recent call by the Chinese regime for "building a harmonious socialist society" (*hexie shehui*) (Zhang 2010). As I noted earlier, criminalizing rural migrants is no longer common in public media or government documents, which demonstrate increasingly warm support for them. Yet as a senior street-level officer who had worked in and lived near Hadong for more than a decade, Wei Yonglan was desperate to find a scapegoat to blame for the decay of the neighborhood. Her primary focus was not on how important migrant workers were for the nation's development, as promoted in official government documents, but on how they had "ruined" her territory.

Above all, I find that Wei Yonglan's speech is, in itself, a manifesto for what Carl Schmitt (2007) has laid out as the "friend-enemy" distinction.[12] Her speech invokes the popular Maoist notion of "struggle" (*douzheng*), which the party-state's more recent call for "harmony" (*hexie*) opposes (Zhang 2010: 215). In the *shoufei* incident, Hu's family came to be considered "the enemy" who must be fought and driven away in order to preserve the state's authority. Wei Yonglan attempted to show the "competence" of the government by highlighting her will to catch and "inflict punishment" on the Hus. The rural migrant family in this case was defined purely as an "enemy" who would threaten state sovereignty if not "managed properly." Furthermore, contrary to Michael Dutton's argument (2005) that the division between friend and enemy has been entirely displaced by the divide between the legal and the illegal in post-Mao China, what Wei Yonglan's speech reveals is that the two parts of the binary are not completely distinct but continuous with each other.[13] Wei Yonglan never forgets her emphasis on lawfulness in dealing with the incident. But as she claims fiercely that she (and other government officials) will surely find and punish the "barbarous" family, showing that "whoever provokes the government won't be able to win," it is hard to determine whether she is a government agent focused on law or a warrior determined to expel evil from the land. If rural migrants are turned into "enemies," who, then, will remain as "friends" in the government of local cadres? Let me introduce another ethnographic example involving *shoufei* to answer this question.

Strategic Comradeship

On August 6, 2008, cadres in Jianguo Community had already gone into emergency mode over security concerns as the Beijing Olympics drew near. Harbin is about 750 miles from Beijing. No Olympic events were taking place in Harbin. Nevertheless, a tense atmosphere could be felt throughout the city, including in Hadong. In line with the state's directive that no embarrassing incidents should take place around the time of the Olympic Games, street-level officials became increasingly sensitive about security in their neighborhoods. They began to patrol the streets of Hadong wearing red armbands. I accompanied them, though I was worried that this would make me look like another cadre to residents. The atmosphere of the patrol was not as tense as I expected, however. "What are you doing? Has anything happened here?" people who were sitting around the alleys asked Community cadres. "No, we are just taking a stroll," a cadre responded blandly. On our way back to the Community office we ran into Li Jun, a patrol guard in the Community. He was picking up garbage on the street. Community director Lin Liping asked him, "Are you okay now?" Laughing, Li Jun replied, "Well, what can I do even if I'm not okay?" as the other cadres joined in the laughter.

Back at the Community office, Lin Liping explained to me how Li Jun had become a target of ridicule among the other cadres: "As usual, Li Jun was collecting the security fees yesterday. He asked Jie Mei to pay the fee. Jie Mei is one of the most annoying people in our neighborhood." I asked, "Is she a native of this place?" and Lin Liping answered, "Yes, she is a laid-off worker." She continued: "You don't know how awful she is. She has never paid any community fees. People just go away without a word whenever she runs off at the mouth. Every word she speaks is a curse. Li Jun went to see her yesterday to ask for the fees. Of course his effort was in vain. But Li Jun was so angry at her that he cursed her on the street. He said in front of other residents that he would cut off her arms and legs. Who knew that Jie Mei was shitting in a public toilet just at that moment? She was listening! You can imagine what the next part of the story was. Li Jun was totally beaten by her. He was physically assaulted by that woman!"

Community cadres treated this incident neither with embarrassment nor with resentment but with light mockery. They spoke with delight about how a bulky man like Li Jun was ruthlessly beaten by a woman ten years younger than he. Although for almost two decades Jie Mei had never paid the community fee, Community cadres considered her merely an "annoying" person, and although Jie Mei cursed and even beat Li Jun violently, these cadres treated her as a cranky neighbor rather than as their enemy. Their narratives about Jie Mei were very different from those about the Hus, the rural migrants who fled town after their dispute with the Community cadres. The Hus' violent act, unlike Jie Mei's, was considered an intolerable crime committed by "savage out-of-towners," even a serious challenge to the government. Rarely do intimate conversations between rural migrants and Community cadres take place in Hadong. Therefore, once any conflict occurs between them, it is easily transformed into an episode of "uncontrollable violence," as we have seen.

By contrast, Community cadres and urban residents, including laid-off workers, remain united under the common category of "urbanites." Their relationship, of course, is not necessarily amicable: endless quarrels between them are highly common in Hadong. Urban residents burst out with their grievances whenever they happen to meet Community cadres in the street. "See this garbage outside? What is the purpose of the cleaning fee, which you take out of our pocket? What the hell are you doing for that money?" Back in the office, complaints spill out of cadres' mouths: "I can't stand these nagging residents anymore. What they pay for the community fee is only around 20 yuan a year. But they always threaten not to pay the fee. Damn it!" Nevertheless, the tension between Community cadres and urban residents rarely devolves into violent antagonism. What is commonly seen between them is negotiation and compromise in an endless game of seesaw.

Instead of viewing urban residents as inevitable foes, these cadres develop diverse strategies to get them to pay the community fee. For example, they bring in intermediaries to negotiate between themselves and residents, seeking out people who have a good reputation among local residents and who can thus persuade them to cooperate with community work and conform to expectations. The mediators also remind residents of the potential disadvantages they may encounter if they are not supportive of the cadres. On one early June morning in 2007 I was working in the Jianguo Community office. Five residents came in to argue with director Lin Liping. They criticized her for arranging public posts for only a few residents with whom she was well acquainted. "As you know, all of us are laid-off workers," they said to her as if with a single voice. "Why are you discriminating against people?" Lin Liping retorted: "People do to others as they would want to be treated. How do you expect us to give you more if we don't receive any support from you? You never showed up for any community work. You always threatened not to pay the community fee. How can I enthusiastically inform you about any available jobs? Isn't it only natural that I should want to help those who support our work?"

Most urban laid-off workers find it hard to ignore this potential advantage—or disadvantage—in their relationships with Community cadres. Street offices and Communities function as employment agencies for laid-off workers, and trade unions, the Women's Federation, and the Young Communist League, which were ideological apparatuses at the local level in the Mao era, organize job training courses or post recruiting notices for urban laid-off workers. As Antoine Kernen and Jean-Louis Rocca argue, however, the social work performed by such intermediary organizations has created highly fragmented "administered cells." Furthermore, "each cell has its 'own' unemployed to find new jobs for, its 'own' nearby jobs to define, its 'own' *xiagang* [laid-off workers] to recommend and its 'own' poor to support" (2000: 48). Given this "cellularization," the local Community office is the only agency that can compensate for the limited connection among cells. In Hadong, job listings from official intermediary organizations are first transmitted to the street office, which then forwards these listings, along with job listings from other companies, to every Community through a weekly meeting. Community cadres frequently publicize job listings by posting them in the office or on public walls in their neighborhood. The more attractive positions, however, are frequently heard of first by family members of Community cadres or their "good" neighbors. One resident said to me: "I'm not satisfied with what Community cadres are doing these days. But it isn't good for me not to get along well with them. After all, they support people who support them."

Given this reckoning of gains and losses, collective boycotts against local cadres are often reduced to calculated acquiescence. In May 2007 about ten households, all of them urban residents in Jianguo Community, decided not to pay the community fee. This protest was short-lived, however. Han Quanwei, who had participated in the boycott, told me later: "Director Lin Liping came to see me last Saturday night. She said that she was sorry she had not seen me for so long. She asked if my husband was getting better and if my son's studies were going well. Regarding the collection of community fees, she didn't bring it up at all. She and I had a very good conversation that night. Well, Lin Liping came to see me again three days later. At that time she brought up the problem of collecting the fees. She said how hard it was to collect the fees door-to-door. Face-to-face with her, I could not say anything that would hurt her. I learned later that Lin Liping had also visited other families. You know, we residents have known her so long. How could we act so harshly to her?"

In all, it is strategic comradeship that ties urban laid-off workers to street-level government officials. Although the urbanites, like rural migrants, frequently view the collection of community fees as extortion from the poor, they respond to it in a greater spirit of compromise. Whereas rural migrants have in effect been excluded from the paternal bond to the state, urban workers served as both ideological representatives and the main beneficiaries of the socialist regime. For many rural migrants, the title of "the people" was considered nothing more than an "empty slogan," as one of them insisted, while that very same title filled many urban workers with a sense of honor and pride, as well as a sense of social and economic protection. Even when these workers deplore that the state has now abandoned them and they are no longer respected as "the people" by the wider society, they are still forging a basis for negotiation with the government by invoking the claim of being "the people." Yet what is the outcome of this effort? Do local officials' actions of dividing the poor ultimately contribute to state governance by complicating the potential tension between the poor and the state? This is a point to which I now turn in concluding this chapter.

Throughout this discussion I have shown that being "poor" is in itself no premise for solidarity or resistance. Although poverty is a common condition that has existed in every historical period, any experience of poverty is deeply specific and contingent. Michael Hardt and Antonio Negri (2001, 2004) view the poor as the foundation of what they call "the multitude," which aims at a totality presupposed by its very multiplicity. Ethnographic research, however, calls for a deeper engagement with this multiplicity per se by probing the production of misrecognition and even animosity among the poor.

In Hadong, although the social distinction between urbanites and rural migrants has been destabilized as the two groups experience intermarriage or the common schooling of their children, this distinction has been restabilized on the epistemological map of many impoverished urbanites. They have witnessed their waning status and downward mobility as they have unavoidably come to live together with rural migrants, the "peasants" they long considered inferior to them. Their fear of the other poor is informed by the historical rural-urban tension, in fleeting but vivid encounters as well as in various institutional barriers. In light of such historical baggage, signs of fear circulate through local projects of "dividing the poor," differentiating these projects from those pursued by the central government. Increasingly conscious of migrants' importance for the nation's development as well as for China's status as a "proper" global leader, policymakers and elites have recently formulated a number of policies for protecting the rights of rural migrants, although these focus mostly on their labor rather than on their lives in general. In a decaying neighborhood on the urban periphery, however, state governance is exercised differently through the dual position of street-level officials—who themselves are not only state bureaucrats but also urban residents who, like their neighbors, feel fear at the encroachment by increasing numbers of migrants. With their complex identities, these officials produce dissonances in the normal workings of state bureaucracy by establishing strategic friendships with urban laid-off workers while making rural migrants a highly visible target to be blamed for neighborhood decline. Informed by the historical rural-urban divide, and exacerbated by the differential workings of state intervention, cultural and political Othering (Siu 2007) eventually persists among the urban poor, weighing them down with social suffering.

It should be emphasized that dividing the poor is not an intentional project of certain individuals. Rather, it is the result of a heterogeneous assemblage of institutional policies that have historically built up physical and emotional tensions between the city and the countryside, the disparate and often contradictory governmental techniques at central and local levels, and the dual position of street-level state officials. In this sense, dividing the poor, which may contribute to state governance, is achieved not through the scrupulous workings of state bureaucracy but by a more contingent interplay between state agents and their counterparts. I agree with Tania Li that "governmental interventions configure ways of thinking and acting not by operating alone, but by working as part of a constellation," which often leads to messy but real consequences (2007: 28).

The story of the Hus, the rural migrants who ran away after having a violent dispute with Community cadres, illustrates the "messy" consequences of these governmental interventions. In early March 2007, more than two months after the *shoufei* incident, Lin Liping (the director of Jianguo Community) and I visited Li Shun, the cadre who had fought with the Hus. Li Shun's community in southern Hadong is a sparsely populated area where small-scale factories and farmlands are scattered in a disorderly fashion. The community looked almost empty, since most of the migrants had returned to their homes in the countryside for the Spring Festival. "They are not coming back until the Qing Ming Festival," said Li Shun.

Li Shun spent the Spring Festival that year in a depressed mood. "I had to borrow some money to spend during the Spring Festival," she told me. "I had to give up on buying even candy and peanuts." For her family, community work remained their basic meal ticket: Li Shun's husband had hurt his leg in his late twenties and remained a seasonal laborer throughout his life. Thus he had no job in a work unit (*dingti*) for his son to inherit; like his father, Li Shun's son also remained a temporary worker. Now, Li Shun's family were barely getting by on the low wages that Li Shun and her daughter-in-law received for their community work.

After the *shoufei* incident, however, Li Shun lost her interest in that work. Caught up in the altercation, Li Shun's son almost lost the sight of his left eye. The Lis spent more than 10,000 yuan for his medical expenses, adding to the total debt of her family. With a deep sigh, Li Shun complained to Lin Liping and me: "Both the police and the street office have refused to be responsible for this incident anymore. They are passing the buck to each other." In the months that followed, I witnessed Li Shun anxiously waiting for deputy director Wei Yonglan or other officials in the street office to provide some help; I never saw her receive a satisfactory response from them.

In the end, Wei Yonglan's resolute promise made during the meeting did not come to pass after all. Although she insisted that the government would make an example of any challenge to state authority, the Hus simply ran away and never came back. They left under cover of night, when people rarely go outside in freezing weather. The police, in fact, gave up chasing them because, as one official said, nobody was killed in the incident, and they considered it nearly impossible to find rural migrants, who worked here and there without formal registration. Acknowledging that there had been no progress in the handling of the incident, Wei Yonglan complained to me: "The Hus belong to the floating population. They're out-of-towners without urban *hukou*. Migrants like the Hus go away after renting a few months here. No one knows where they leave for. There is no way to control them."

In fact, the uncontrollability of rural migrants is precisely the result of the state's selective management of urban poverty. It arises from the predicaments inherent in the political economy of modern China, where rural people have no choice but to be perpetual migrants (Cho 2009). Significant disparities between the urban and rural sectors, which I noted earlier, have led to a massive rural-to-urban migration. This structural problem, driven by China's political-economic relations, has been transmuted into the "cultural" problem of "uncivil and uncontrollable" rural migrants, as the signs of fear circulate through state interventions as well as urbanite-driven narratives. Yet the very uncontrollability of rural migrants, as the outcome of state governance, unexpectedly opens up a space in which migrants can disrupt state authority. Excluded from the paternal bond to the state, these rural migrants ignore, run away from, or even respond violently to local government officials. When the Hus fought with Community cadres and fled by night, local government officials helplessly witnessed the predictable outcome of their management of rural migrants. Furthermore, Community cadres like Li Shun observed the consequences of making high-level state officials "friends" while making their rural migrant neighbors "enemies."

Conclusion

In April 2007, at the height of my fieldwork, I was asked to give a talk in a student forum at the Harbin Institute of Technology, where I served as a research fellow. I decided to introduce students to anthropology, which was a field unfamiliar to many of them. Titling my talk "Seeing Like an Anthropologist," and using my fieldwork in Hadong as an example, I demonstrated how anthropological perspectives help us to rethink many unwarranted assumptions about the poor and their "dependency."

The scale of the forum was much larger than I had anticipated. More than two hundred students filled the lecture hall on that night. Half excited and half nervous, I began to tell my stories in front of an audience. I projected photos of Hadong onto a screen as I described the suffering experienced by many urban laid-off workers and rural migrants in the decaying neighborhood portrayed in the images.

The one-hour talk went smoothly. The question-and-answer session that followed did not. The agitation began with a question from a student in the back row. With a very serious expression on her face, she posed a query that at first seemed unrelated to my talk: "As you know, China is a country with a very rich history. Countries such as Japan and South Korea paid tribute to our emperor for so long. Today, despite recent economic growth, our country is still surpassed by these other countries. What do you think of our nation's poverty? Why do you think China has come to be left behind? Should the Chinese people be blamed for that?"

Her question aroused the entire audience, prompting a heated debate about "why China is still poor." Without waiting for my answer, several students began talking at once, sharing their opinions on the subject. Though embarrassed by my inability to control the forum, I myself was struck by her question, which identified the different "poverties" at play. Whereas I had focused on poverty among urban laid-off workers and rural migrants, her question centered on the nation's poverty. Whereas I was concerned about the impoverishment of people in Harbin, her concern was for the Chinese people as a nation.

As this anecdote reveals, there are distinct layers of poverty in China. It illustrates how questions about the personal experience of poverty often overlap with very different questions about how to overcome the nation's poverty through continuous processes of development. This conflation highlights the need to study China's management of urban poverty as a prime site for subject formation. Managing urban poverty is not simply a technical project for alleviating the economic problems of certain individuals. It is part of a subject-making project aimed at cultivating self-managing, responsible citizens qualified to direct the nation's drive toward modernization. Such a project seems likely to revitalize a modernizing mission pursued by Chinese intellectuals a century ago. Nevertheless, today's mission is more complex than ever before. Impoverished urban workers whom government officials and intellectuals attempt to "enlighten" are not merely needy and excluded bodies. They are former representatives of the socialist regime. Once celebrated as the masters of the country, these workers are now the shadowy subjects of a "reemerging" China.

This book has focused on the impoverishment of these onetime representatives of socialism. I have examined how they experience and respond to their downward mobility as their country is emerging as an economic superpower. I have also explored how their penury is managed in a country where the official claim of socialism persists despite massive pro-market reforms. The unique, historically informed processes of impoverishment in China have prompted me to situate the management of urban poverty as a primary domain where the relationship between the nation-state and its subjects is being reconfigured in an atmosphere of great tension.

A unifying thread throughout this book has been ethnographic attention to "the people." Since the PRC's founding in 1949, the maxim "Serve the People" has defined the country, representing a conviction that gives both voice and leverage to urban workers. Nevertheless, as I have argued, any claim of belonging to "the people" is historically contingent, and has become contentious since the nation's market-oriented reform has transformed many urban workers into the "new urban poor" (Kernen and Rocca 2000). While impoverished workers invoke their sacrifices for the nation, expecting more help from the government, local officials simply calculate their poverty, positioning them as recipients among the poor as a whole. While these workers are engrossed in nostalgia for "the days of Chairman Mao," many government officials and local scholars attribute their "problem" to the "tragic" history of that era, discovering the origin of their "dependency" in the history of Maoist socialism. While these workers in the country's northeast highlight their region's contribution to national development, public media accounts mock northeasterners as lacking a spirit of enterprise. And while some laid-off workers have responded to the state's call to work in the government sector, they find themselves framed as being in need of constant reeducation and readjustment.

In this book I have positioned the historically informed category of "the people," not the standardized category of "the poor," as an object of inquiry in order to reclaim the historicity of poverty. Such an attempt, however, does not deny the fact that China shares many of the complexities of urban poverty with other societies around the globe (Wu 2009; Wu and Webster 2010). The problems facing China's impoverished urban workers and rural migrants do not seem very different from those facing the 1 billion people who, according to Mike Davis's estimate (2006), live in the city slums of the global South: run-down housing, overcrowding, pollution, and decay. Since China undertook its market reform in the late 1970s, massive and uneven urbanization processes have accelerated the dilapidation of working-class neighborhoods as well as the burgeoning of upscale gated communities. Ecological suffering has become unavoidable when large numbers of rural migrants flood already decaying working-class communities or village enclaves in the urban periphery. China's urban poor also share job insecurity, marginality, territorial stigmatization, and the punitive gaze of others, all of which are viewed as afflicting precarious proletariats in neoliberal North Atlantic societies (Bourdieu 2000; Bourgois 1995, 2002; Wacquant 2008, 2009). The socialist labor-allocation system under the planned economy is now stigmatized as a "problem" of excessive government (Hoffman 2010: 8–9) and is blamed for depriving workers of an opportunity to develop the capacity for self-management. Such similarities shared by the poor across borders have prompted an unprecedented degree of global concern about poverty in recent times. Massive campaigns for humanitarian aid as well as worldwide movements against market violence have been undertaken in the name of alleviating global poverty.

Nevertheless, I have chosen to emphasize the historicity of China's urban poor rather than homogenize the experiential condition of the poor within a neoliberal political economy. I argue that paying insufficient attention to the historicity of poverty creates a danger of presupposing the persistence of poverty as a self-evident truth, reproducing received categorizations of the poor and missing the complexity of inequality as individual lives intersect with a changing political economy. It thus threatens to take the edge off our insights about how to react effectively to economic polarization, systemic violence, and increasing inequality with which many scholars and activists mournfully characterize our contemporary world.

My emphasis on the historically informed category of "the people" is neither a strategy of "defending the local," which Michael Hardt and Antonio Negri find damaging to our search for real alternatives, nor mere nostalgia for a Maoist past that many Chinese are reluctant to recall. By detailing ethnographic scenes in which urban workers have not entirely shifted from being "the people" to becoming nameless, ahistorical poor bodies, I have tried to provide complex but necessary analyses of the forces that enable poor people to find their commonality or disable them from doing so.

The claim of belonging to "the people" is replete with ambivalences and contradictions. To begin with, it has prompted impoverished urban workers, particularly in northeast China, to forge a conviction that the state will not—and should not—abandon them, despite the pro-market restructuring of China's urban political economy. The ongoing distinction between the Party and the people (*dang-qun guanxi*) in China allows impoverished workers to engage in direct negotiation or confrontation with the state, a relationship that has been made invisible in many neoliberal settings around the globe (Goode and Maskovsky 2001; Cho 2005). Such a distinction prevents them from being entirely converted into "numbers," that is, into a regularized population without history, and at times may even lead them to formulate strategic alliances with local government officials.

The floating signifier "the people," however, is subject to volatile uses, with contradictory outcomes. In their attempts to grapple with the claim, workers have often aggravated the precariousness of their state through the paternalistic, patriarchal, and developmental tensions embedded in the category of "the people." In particular, as I detailed in chapter 2, the nostalgic myth of "equal" poverty under socialism in the past has unexpectedly resonated with the recent neoliberal quest for wealth. This phenomenon has prompted workers' "nonconformist" pursuit of better housing, often weighing them down with social suffering. In addition, these workers have encouraged the state's practice of dividing the poor by making "the people" an exclusionary claim of their own and often developing antagonism against rural migrants, another group that is heir to the title of "the people" in the Maoist sense, despite their shared experiences of poverty in the city (chapter 6).

Above all, I argue that the enduring tensions surrounding the claim of belonging to "the people" reveal the contingent, porous, and often contradictory ways in which impoverished workers experience and respond to their changing positions in their new relationships to the other poor as well as involve themselves in state projects for governing poverty. The specter of "the people" haunts the management of urban poverty in northeast China. Grappling with the floating signifier, impoverished urban workers do not necessarily fall subject to but continuously struggle against new modes of government directed toward them. Such struggles produce volatile and often paradoxical outcomes that confound the government's plans.

In the summer of 2011 I revisited Hadong to meet close informants of mine. Every road was clogged with garbage that people simply tossed away. Community cadres had just about given up on picking up the trash because, as Lin Liping (chapter 4) remarked, "this area will disappear soon." Lin told me that the street office had recently selected a real estate company to build a high-rise apartment complex in part of Hadong. Some Community cadres had accompanied employees from the company to help them measure the size of every house. Already swamped with a heavy workload and exhausted by the sweltering heat, these cadres frequently ignored the growing tensions relating to compensation between real estate employees and local residents.

No mournful voices were heard in the disappearing village. It has been a long time since Hadong's reputation as the "honored workers' village" faded away. Most urban workers welcomed the demolition of the "shantytown," expecting compensation, the amount of which they did not know for sure. Chen Yuhua (chapters 2 and 4), who moved out though her house in Hadong remains, was extremely concerned about how much compensation she would receive for the unlicensed shack that her family had added to their original housing. Cao Guiying (chapters 2 and 3), whose house did not belong to the residential compounds of Fenghuang factory, was exempt from all the fuss about demolition. She was half relieved because her poverty-stricken family really had nowhere else to go, and half annoyed because her family would miss the opportunity to receive allegedly sizable compensation. Unlike these urban dwellers, rural migrants were busy searching for any rented housing nearby. Sun Yuming eventually decided to return to the countryside, while his sister Sun Yufen (chapter 5) was anxiously waiting for her children to come up with a plan. Her daughter brought me to church and asked me to pray for new housing for her family.

"The people" turns out to be a term of both inclusion and exclusion in the process of demolition as well as in the management of poverty. The precarious bond between the Chinese state and impoverished urban workers has persisted while excluding the other poor, that is, rural migrants. Such a bond, however, is no longer passed on to the next generation. Having grown up under the nation's market reform, today's generation is not imbued with the sense of paternal intimacy that the state once cultivated under the Maoist slogan of "Serve the People." Without any particular identity, many children of impoverished workers have been reduced merely to what the mass media often call "the second generation of the poor" (*pin er dai*).

Many children of urban laid-off workers and rural migrants whom I have met in northeast China as part of my new research project are thinking deeply about their "poorness" and constituting their subjectivities by forging multilayered relationships with their parents' generation, China's changing education and population policies, and a shifting global political economy. Like precarious youth in other capitalist societies, these young Chinese are experiencing the inheritance of poverty with little prospect of escaping from it, and are being overwhelmed by the neoliberal emphasis on independence and an entrepreneurial spirit. Living under a rapidly growing economy, however, and yet still shouldering the historical weight of state socialism, they are ambivalently considering their future, as their parents did, but differently from them. The fact that neither regular work nor housing, which their working-class parents had expected to receive, is no longer a given makes these young people and their parents extremely anxious. Yet the country's emerging status as a global economic superpower prompts them to persist in the expectation that they will enjoy wealth someday, though not right now. Such expectation often fades away, however, as China, the world's factory, continues to provide the types of jobs that never appeal to young people. Most of these young people are college graduates produced by the dramatic increase in higher education enrollments in recent times.

Will this precariously situated youth create a new term in place of "the people" to "identify the basic antagonism or antagonistic struggle" in which they are commonly caught despite the numerous differences among them (Žižek 2008: 157)? Or will they, more inexorably than their parents did, reproduce and newly produce lines of distinction, such as the city versus the countryside, the "first-rate" city (*yiliu chengshi*) versus the "second-rate" city (*erliu chengshi*), and the post-1980s generation (*baling hou*) versus the post-1990s generation (*jiuling hou*)? Further ethnographic research will provide deeper insights into these questions. The experiences through which their parents renegotiated their former status may inform and shape the negotiations of these young people.

● Notes

Preface

1. The statistical quagmire of the state's measurement of unemployment rates renders it difficult to quantify them (Solinger 2001). According to the official statistical data, Harbin's unemployment rate has been less than 4 percent since 2000 (http://www.stats-hlheb.gov.cn). This number, however, excludes most unregistered unemployed as well as the laid-off (*xiagang*). Given this fact, many of the Chinese scholars whom I met during my fieldwork unofficially estimated that the unemployment rate in many cities in the northeast—including Harbin—was probably as high as 20 percent.

2. In this book, except for large areas such as Harbin, Binxian, and Hadong, all names of places, persons, and government offices are pseudonyms.

3. To maintain confidentiality, I will avoid referring to the products of this factory.

4. For the first three months of research, rather than set up my own criteria for meeting my subjects, I simply met with the poor residents to whom Community cadres introduced me. (I capitalize "Community" to distinguish the government office from the neighborhood covered by its administration.) These strategies, however, were not merely a necessary condition of my research; they allowed me to explore in what way state agents situate urban poverty and categorize "the poor." As I show in detail, rural migrants have been excluded from their consideration. Via the informants I met through state agents, I was introduced to other groups, thus extending the number of my research subjects.

5. Used metaphorically, according to Johan A. Lindquist, a "train station" is an ideal place for observers to study mobility by remaining in place. It allows us to consider "not only who is travelling where, but also, for instance, what particular routes are available, who is selling tickets, how the local pickpockets work, and what the police are doing about it" (Lindquist 2009: 10).

Introduction

1. As he asserts, the official class label belied inequalities among workers: "As economic inequalities of property were supplanted by the new inequalities of occupational rank, many cadres found class designations useful as a way of reducing popular consciousness of this change" (Kraus 1981: 38).

2. In a similar sense, William Hurst explains the specificity of labor relations (*laodong guanxi*) in China. Rather than referring to collective bargaining or employment contracts, "labor relations" were in fact indistinguishable from work-unit

membership. In the Mao period, therefore, labor relations were "a basis for urban household registrations and a key to guaranteed employment for one's descendants" (Hurst 2009: 13).

3. The existence of antagonistic classes is central to the Marxist concept of "class." Marx writes, "Insofar as millions of families live under conditions of existence that separate their mode of life, their interests, and their culture from those of the other classes, and put them in hostile opposition to the latter, they form a class" (Marx 1972: 124).

4. In the Hegelian Master-Slave dialectic, the Master's certainty is not purely subjective and "immediate"; it is "objectivized and 'mediated' by another's, the Slave's, recognition" (Kojève 1980: 16).

5. Of course, not all studies emphasize the uniqueness of "class" in China for that purpose. In her study of stratification in Harbin, Carolyn L. Hsu (2007) insightfully addresses how ordinary people reinterpret the state-centered narratives of class. Her use of the terms "ordinary people" or "Harbiners," however, obscures the positionality of subjects, thus leaving us unable to examine in what different ways, and in what particular moments, differently positioned people respond to class and classification.

6. The New Youth intellectuals coalesced around the revolutionary magazine *New Youth* (*Xin Qingnian*) during the New Culture Movement of the mid-1910s and 1920s. Whereas intellectuals in the late Qing discussed China's slave status in relation to the invasion of foreign powers, the members of the New Youth targeted the "slave mentality" of the Chinese people themselves (Chen 2003).

7. Mao's populist faith in the masses was also contrasted with Leninism— and, more broadly, Soviet-style socialism, which defended the sacrosanct status of the Party and the primary role of educated elites in leading the country (Meisner 1999: 43–44).

8. In 2009 China's per capita GDP was only $3,744. It placed eighty-sixth out of 164 countries ranked according to World Bank data (http://finance.fortune.cnn.com/2011/02/17).

9. The initial effects of the reform actually strengthened the work unit system. As the central government abandoned austerity socialism and provided enterprises with incentives, businesses were allowed to retain larger shares of the surplus they generated, thereby improving workers' living standards (Perry and Wong 1985: 12; Walder 1986: 224–27; Naughton 1997: 182–83).

10. See Kim (2000) and Lee (2010) on the ambiguity of resistance in the case of China's peasants.

11. Then-premier Zhu Rongji first acknowledged the existence of urban poverty in a 2001 working report of the State Council on "marginal groups" (Wu et al. 2010: 2).

12. In 2009 the total number of rural migrant laborers (*waichu nongmingong*) was 145.33 million. National Bureau of Statistics (March 2010), http://www.stats.gov.cn/tjfx/fxbg/t20100319_402628281.htm.

13. "If we restrict ourselves to the sovereign-subject relationship, the limit of the law is the subject's disobedience; it is the 'no' with which the subject opposes the sovereign. But when it is a question of the relationship between government and population, then the limit of the sovereign's or government's decision is by no means necessarily the refusal of the people to whom the decision is addressed" (Foucault 2007: 71).

14. Some scholars have discussed the significance of "the population" as a strategic alternative for marginalized groups. For example, Partha Chatterjee theorizes "the population" as a form of political belonging through which marginalized groups access public services. In India, he argues, "classic" citizenship represents a modernist ideal that applies only to elites, while subalterns must play on their status as "populations" in order to secure social welfare. Belonging to "the population" thus opens strategic "possibilities" for the poor, who are in need of protection but inaccessible to a liberal political discourse of citizenship and individual rights (Chatterjee 2004: 50). Nonetheless, becoming "the population" has never been viewed as a "possibility" by China's urban poor. Unlike India's subalterns, China's impoverished workers experienced a historical moment in which they were celebrated and rewarded as "the people," that is, as the "masters" of the country. They grew up in a country that "blatantly displayed subalterns and brought them to voice" rather than merely repressing their voices throughout the socialist regime (Rofel 1999: 286).

15. Therefore I am wary of the inclination among some scholars and members of the public to criticize China for not being enough of a "civil society" or sympathizing with the Chinese people for not achieving "citizenship" fully enough. To draw on Jean-Louis Rocca's critical approach to modernity in China, the problem arises from the erroneous comparison between the concrete situation of China and the ideological vision of "the West" (Rocca 2002a: 54).

16. In contemporary China, "community" (*shequ*) refers to both the lowest-level division of local urban government and the geographical locale, or neighborhood, covered by this administration. I capitalize "Community" to distinguish the government office from the neighborhood covered by its administration.

1. In Search of "the People"

1. The spatial politics of the past, which reinforced social relations of privilege and stigmatization, still haunts the present. Harbiners commonly say "Nangang is a paradise [*tiantang*], Daoli a world [*renjian*], Daowai a hell [*diyu*]" when they want to highlight the unequal, spatially hierarchical distribution of social and economic resources in the city.

2. I use the term "place-name" to suggest that place as a symbolic referent has greater significance than place as a bounded territory.

3. The description of the land as "empty" is dominant in both popular and scholarly accounts of northeast China. Given the fact that the region was populated by several nomadic tribes throughout China's history, the description reveals a great deal of Han Chinese bias.

4. The migration was encouraged by the Chinese authorities, who thought that the presence of migrants would undergird China's sovereignty in Manchuria against threats from Russia, Japan, and other foreign powers. After the 1920s, migration was encouraged by the Japanese, who needed to recruit cheap Chinese labor for their mines and factories.

5. From 1995 to 2001, 43 million workers were officially registered as laid off (*xiagang*), including 34 million from the state sector (Giles, Park, and Cai 2006: 61–62; see also http://www.atimes.com/atimes/China/GI14Ad03.html).

6. China Compendium of Statistics, 1949–2004 (data for 1965–2004), and www.stats.gov.cn (National Bureau of Statistics of China).

7. GDP increased from 24.9 to 1.83 trillion yuan in Jiangsu, from 12.4 to 134 trillion yuan in Zhejiang, and from 18.6 to 2.24 trillion yuan in Guangdong. It increased from 22.9 to 800.9 billion yuan in Liaoning, from 8.2 to 362 billion yuan in Jilin, and from 17.5 to 551.2 billion yuan in Heilongjiang.

8. Threatened by social instability prompted by increasing regional inequalities and broad labor unrest, the central government launched the "Revive the Northeast" (*zhenxing dongbei*) program in 2004, centering on the restructuring of state-owned sectors (Chung, Lai, and Joo 2009). The effect of the program, however, has not yet been felt among local people whom I met in the northeast.

9. Ortner explores the location of "class" in the United States, where race and ethnicity have been dominant discourses of social difference. Questioning the basically classless notion of identities, she argues that class is "hidden" in the dominance of race and ethnicity, and "requires more intellectual archaeology" (1998: 13).

10. *Maiduan* is a system in which the work unit "makes a lump-sum payment when an employee forfeits any future claim to enterprise resources" (Hurst and O'Brien 2002: 350). The system was popular in larger firms with more favorable business environments from the mid-1990s through 2008 (Hurst 2009: 79).

11. The official amount was 1,570 yuan.

12. The Harbin census for December 1934 notes: "Fifty-five percent of the entire population is jobless in the suburbs of Taiping [of which Hadong is a part]. They fled from famine in Shandong and Hebei provinces. Some are ragpickers, while others are seasonal laborers" (TQ 1992).

13. Taiping district, to which Hadong had belonged, was absorbed into Daowai district in 2005.

14. In government documents, the decision is described as "Moving Factories from the South to the North" (*nanchang beiqian*) (HS 1991; HSZ 1999).

15. "New Year's Message" ["Yuandan xianci"] (FR January 1, 1990).

16. The spirit of "selfless sacrifice" loomed large in workers' accounts during that time. For example, one worker wrote in the factory's newsletter in 1990: "It has already been twenty-seven years since Chairman Mao announced 'Learn from Lei Feng Day.'...Selfless sacrifice is the very embodiment of human dignity. Comrade Lei Feng once said, 'Man's life is limited while service to the people is unlimited.' We workers should act like Lei Feng. Face our comrades warmly like the spring breeze! Face our work intensely like the heat of the summer! Face individualism indifferently like falling leaves in autumn winds! Face our enemy cruelly like the coldest weather!" ("Let Lei Feng Spirit Carry Forward" [Rang Lei Feng jingshen fayang guangda], FR March 1990).

17. Situating the claim of "the people" in the despair of *dongbei ren* oftentimes allows workers to enter into an emotional alliance with other groups of people in the northeast, who also bear grudges over increasing regional inequalities. During my stay in Harbin I encountered this emotional alliance among a wide array of intellectuals, government officials, and even entrepreneurs. Sympathy arises when they complain about poor wages or scant government support for businesses in comparison with their counterparts in the south.

18. The famous saying of Deng Xiaoping was articulated on his tour of southern China in 1991. Deng was attempting to remobilize support for his policy of reform at the very moment when many CCP leaders were trying to return to a more planned economy and isolationism in the face of severe sanctions from the international community following the Tiananmen incident in 1989.

19. "Cap" (*maozi*) is a historically informed political metaphor from the Maoist era. In political campaigns, particularly during the Cultural Revolution, numerous people were forced to wear dunce caps as well as humiliating signs in public. Yet the political metaphor has been widely used in other situations, for example, "Let's Take Off the 'Cap' of Long-Term Losses," the title of an article in the factory's newsletter (FR March 1987).

20. Today China's enterprises are commonly classified into state enterprises and non-state enterprises rather than SOEs and COEs. This reclassification reflects the growth of the non-state sector. With the exception of the COEs, the non-state sector consists of community-owned enterprises, cooperatives, individual-owned enterprises, private corporations, and foreign joint ventures (Sachs and Woo 1996).

21. At this early point, Fenghuang comprised only state-owned sectors (*gongchang*).

22. Workers who entered *gongsi* at that time still remember the slogan "Go the May 7 Road, all go to work!" (*zou wuqi daolu, dou canjia gongzuo*). The "May 7 Directive" is a letter Mao wrote to his designated successor, Lin Biao, on May 7, 1966, in which Mao proposed a comprehensive plan for turning the whole country into "a great school of Mao Zedong Thought" (*Mao Zedong sixiang da xuexiao*), where "all personnel, no matter whether they worked in the areas of agriculture, industry, the military, commerce, service professions, or Party and government organizations, must study politics, military affairs, and culture, and must take part in the criticism of the bourgeoisie, while all engaging in sideline work to supplement their regular professions" (He 2001: 514).

23. *Gongsi,* a colloquial term for a variety of COEs in Fenghuang, is derived from this name. In 1990 the Fenghuang Service Corporation was renamed the Fenghuang Industrial Corporation (*Fenghuang gongye gongsi*).

24. To Yu Jixiang's sorrow, both her eldest son and her husband had died of cerebral hemorrhages ten years before I met her.

25. In the 1980s, retirees from the *gongsi* received only 27 yuan a month.

26. Salary differences between the *gongchang* and *gongsi* were also evident, though they are difficult to compare owing to insufficient data. For reference, in Harbin, the yearly wages of the SOE workers increased from 492 yuan in 1952 to 898 yuan in 1980 and 19,946 yuan in 2006. By contrast, the yearly wages of the COE workers increased from 421 yuan in 1952 to 725 yuan in 1980 and 8,304 yuan in 2006 (HTNJ 2008).

27. The 2005 buyout policy was the second and last. The first buyout policy was carried out in 2001, when only about one hundred workers left Fenghuang after receiving 500 yuan for each year of service. Those who applied for the buyout during that time had in fact left Fenghuang much earlier in search of market opportunities. They remained in the work unit (*guaming*) in name only.

28. The amount of the unemployment allowance increased from 277 yuan in December 2005 to 320 yuan in August 2007.

29. *Cainong* literally means vegetable farmers. Yet people in Hadong used the term to refer to their peri-urban status.

30. A crucial difference between the Shengli members and other peasants in the countryside was that they were required to return their land to the collective when they reached retirement age (fifty-five for women and sixty for men), while peasants generally are entitled to retain their land-contracting rights for thirty years, provided they remain members of their collective.

31. Lin Liping was transferred to a port office when the office expropriated her land. She moved and worked in a bicycle factory until she was laid off in 1996. She received a position as a Community cadre just as the government was beginning to change the form of urban governance amidst the breakdown of the urban work unit system (see chapter 4).

2. Gambling on a New Home

1. As early as 1978 Deng Xiaoping proposed this argument to spur China's economic reform saying, "It should be accepted that certain areas, enterprises, workers, and peasants attain high income and an affluent life through an industrious attitude and efficient management" (Deng 1983: 142). When ordinary people refer to his remarks, however, they rarely bring up his emphasis on "industrious management."

2. From the founding of the PRC, China emulated the Soviet model of development, which concentrated on heavy industry. Not surprisingly, investment in the production of consumer goods and housing was assigned a low priority. The shortage of consumer goods was particularly noticeable in northeast China, where most products needed for people's daily lives had to be supplied from other regions of the country because the development of the region was so completely centered on heavy industry.

3. Unequal access to housing existed among work units as well as within each work unit. For example, most workers from small-scale, collectively owned enterprises near Hadong had to give up the thought of being assigned housing early on. These workers either waited for their spouses to receive housing from the state-owned enterprises where they worked or simply stayed with their parents who had already received housing from the state-owned enterprises.

4. Data from the National Development and Reform Commission, www.sdpc. gov.cn.

5. In the Maoist era, the social status of intellectuals was highly precarious. Mao did not conceal his distrust of the expert knowledge offered by intellectuals and disregarded their suffering, particularly during the Cultural Revolution (Meisner 1999: 43). Given the wealth and influence they accrued after the reform, it is no wonder that these intellectuals are now contemptuously called "snakes with glasses" (*yanjing she*) by angry impoverished workers.

6. "Booming Real Estate Sector Puts China at Crossroads," *Xinhua,* March 1, 2010, http://www.chinadaily.com.cn/china/2010–03/01/content_9521206.htm#.

7. Liu Liu's novel *Woju* ("Dwelling Narrowness," 2007) was quickly adapted as a TV series in 2008. This popular drama vividly demonstrated the anxiety, desperation, and conflicts faced by those who were struggling to find housing in the city.

8. I thank Lisa Hoffman for this insight.

3. On the Border between "the People" and "the Population"

1. Data from the National Bureau of Statistics of China, http://www.stats.gov.cn.

2. For an English translation of the "Bulletin," see Tang, Sha, and Ren 2003/4: 115–16.

3. "Summary Table of *Dibao* Recipients in Hadong" (internal material of the street office). Apart from income, other items in the table do not represent national formulas but rather are based on modifications made in Harbin by local officials.

4. Since it was first mandated in the 1986 Law on Compulsory Education, the principle of free education has applied to six years of primary school and three years of junior high school. "China Pledges Elimination of Rural Compulsory Education Charges in Two Years," *People's Daily,* March 5, 2006. In cities, however, it is increasingly common for parents to send their children to better schools at their own expense instead of having them assigned to nearby schools.

5. Generally, China's undergraduate colleges are classified as first class (*yiben*), second class (*erben*), and third class (*sanben*), according to their quality. First-class colleges require applicants to have higher scores on the national college entrance examination than do those of the second class, which in turn are superior to those of the third class. After taking the entrance exam, students apply for the next level down if their application is rejected by higher-level colleges. In most cases, to bring in more money, second- and third-class colleges require higher tuition or a longer period of study than higher-ranking institutions. For this reason, the families of students who selected a second- or third-class college are not qualified for *dibao.* My thanks to Chen Junwei for his explanation.

6. "Methods Regarding the Minimum Living Standard Scheme for Urban Residents," Harbin government document 161, July 11, 2007.

7. Data from Harbin Bureau of Civil Affairs, http://www.hrbmzj.gov.cn, and its documents 9 and 43 (2006), and from internal materials from the Daowai district government and Guangming street office (July 2007).

8. For example, the government is supposed to provide 25,000 yuan to a *dibao* family whose eviction compensation amounts to 45,000 yuan.

9. The presumed income (*xuni shouru*) refers to an income standard that is computed on the assumption that anyone who is of working age has a full-time paying job. The use of presumed income in calculating *dibao* eligibility has persisted in many local governments although it has been criticized by scholars as being one of several common "local policies" (*tu zhengce*) that run counter to the instructions of the central government to calculate actual income (Hong 2004: 123). As of July 2007, the presumed monthly income in Harbin was calculated at 439 yuan.

10. I borrow the term "machine" from Gilles Deleuze and Félix Guattari (1987). What they call "machines," unmoored from mechanistic connotations, refers to a series of devices for social subjection or enslavement. The users of the calculating machine—*dibao* recipients—experience subjection in the sense that they are required to follow its directives even though they have no means to access the enigmatic power of the machine.

11. "The Income Standard for Individually Owned Business or Flexible Work," Harbin Bureau of Civil Affairs, document 29, March 15, 2004.

12. See Solinger (2009: 320–22) for detailed procedures used to judge whether or not a household deserves to receive *dibao*. Public notice is one part of the overall procedure.

13. Summary report of *dibao* work in the first half of 2008 (internal material of Daowai district government in Harbin).

14. See "Zhongguo renmin zhengzhi xieshang huiyi gongtong gangling" [The Common Program of the Chinese People's Political Consultative Conference], in *Jianguo yilai zhongyao wenxian xuanbian* [Selected Important Documents since the Founding of the People's Republic of China], vol. 1, Zhonggong zhongyang wenxian yanjiushi [Institute for Documentary Studies of the Central Committee of the CCP] (1948; Beijing: Zhongyang wenxian chubanshe, 1992), 1–13.

15. See, for example, Xie Jihong, "Dibao zaoyu ganga: baiwanfuweng chi dibao, dibao qingnian bu shangban" [The *Dibao* System Disgraced: A Millionaire on *Dibao* and Young People on *Dibao* Refusing to Go to Work], *Renmin wang,* August 9, 2003; Xiaolu, "'Ningyuan chidibao, buyuan zaijiuye' kaoyan laodong guangrong'" ["I'd Rather Eat on *Dibao* Than Get Reemployed" Puts the Glory of Labor to the Test], *Tongling Daily,* April 28, 2008.

16. See, for example, "Daqingshi bufen xiagang renyuan fangqi jiuye yilai dibao" [Some Laid-Off Workers in Daqing Give Up on Getting a Job and Depend on *Dibao*], *Daqing wanbao,* November 26, 2002; Huang Huo, Hou Dawei, and Shi Zhiyong, *"Jiuye buru 'chi dibao'"* [Getting a Job Is Not as Good as 'Eating on *Dibao*'], *Liaowang xinwen zhoukan* 14 (2006): 46–47.

17. Liu Yibin, "Xuyao fansi de 'dibao lanhan' xianxiang" [The Phenomenon of the 'Dibao Sluggard' That Needs Reflection], *Zhongguo qingnian bao,* August 11, 2003.

18. Xiaolu, "'Ningyuan chidibao.'"

4. The Will to Survive

1. In scholarly accounts in the PRC, one may readily note how the idea of "community" has generated widespread debates on what it means to be a citizen, for example, how community organizations can be diversified and voluntarism inspired, how the Community can be transformed from the mere messenger of the government to an active partner with it, or how grassroots democracy and "good" governance (*shanzhi*) can be realized by inducing participation and self-governance (Xu 2001; Wu 2001; Fei 2002; Chen 2004; Bai 2006).

2. "'Minzhengfu' zai quanguo tuijin chengshi shequ jianshede yijian," document 23 (Beijing: Minzhengbu, 2000).

3. Article 111 of the Constitution of the PRC, cited in Shi (2006b: 4–5).

4. See the Organic Law of the People's Republic of China on Urban Residents' Committees (1990).

5. Lacking guidelines for encouraging "self-governance," government documents are inundated with criticisms about not accomplishing this goal successfully. For instance, the document "Views of 'the Ministry of Civil Affairs' on the Condition of Community Building and the Arrangement of Work in 2002" ends by stating that "[the] Community has not yet realized the self-governance of local residents" after enumerating all the contradictions related to "a lack of participation."

"'Minzhengfu' bangongting guanyu shequ jianshe gongzuo qingkuang he 2002 nian gongzuo anpai de yijian," document 1 (cited in Shi 2006a: 152).

6. The data are limited to the state-owned sector within Fenghuang factory. During that time, the state-owned sector had about five thousand employees and two thousand retirees.

7. "Thanks to the Factory for Its Concern for Us" [Ganxia gongchang dui women de guanhuai], FR, May 1990.

8. The wages of Community cadres are still low if one considers that the average monthly wage in Harbin was 2,127 yuan in 2008.

9. When I visited Jianguo Community in August 2009, Lin Liping took me to a new building under construction and happily showed me the empty space that would become her own room in the new office.

10. *Suzhi,* roughly translated as "quality" in English, is not a novel term in China, but it acquired "new discursive power" amidst the nation's massive socioeconomic reforms (Anagnost 2004: 189). Ann Anagnost stresses that *suzhi* is "not something that naturally inheres in the body but is rather something that must be built in the body" (193). *Suzhi* is thus operationalized in extremely hierarchical ways. In the Monday meetings in Hadong, the *suzhi* of high-level officials was never discussed even though they were noisier than the Community cadres.

11. For example, Fei Xiaotong, a renowned Chinese anthropologist, rethought "the self" as a significant node of moral configuration when he connected it to the possibility of "grassroots democracy" (*jiceng minzhu*) while arguing, "It is the residents themselves who know their own desire and request more [self governance] than anyone else" (Fei 2002: 15–17).

5. Inclusive Exclusion

1. See http://www.abc.net.au/rn/bookshow/stories/2008/2239944.htm.

2. For the policy reforms relating to the rural-to-urban migration, see Chan and Zhang (1999). Their study demonstrates how the *hukou* system and governmental actions related to it have made strikingly more difficult the permanent settlement of rural people in the city, though many of these people have been de facto urban residents for years.

3. During his inspection trip to Chongqing in October 2003, Wen Jiabao met Xiong Deming, wife of a migrant worker, who told him that her husband's boss had withheld 2,300 yuan of his salary. Xiong's husband was reimbursed within six hours of her conversation with the premier. *People's Daily Online,* November 12, 2003.

4. This phrase is frequently used in government documents dating from 2003.

5. As João Biehl noted in his work on a homeless woman in Brazil, the ethnography of one person is more than the description of that person's life. Seeing the woman not as an exception but as a "patterned entity" (2005: 13), he addresses the various circuits in which her intractability gained its form.

6. Similar cases are found in many other ethnographies. To cite just one example, Jean Briggs (1970), in her ethnographic portrait of an Eskimo family, came to learn how significant emotional control is in Inuit society by using her own feelings as sources of insight.

7. Fei-ling Wang demonstrates that in the reform of the *hukou* system (1997–2002), this relaxation targeted certain select groups such as "elderly parents, children, and highly educated 'talented people' and skilled workers." In particular, the localized practice often called *"hukou* for talents and investments" has been further polished and nationally encouraged (2004: 119).

8. Internal material of Harbin police bureau. The policy began in January 1998.

9. Three out of sixteen factories and shops were built by successful rural migrants who had already acquired urban *hukou*. Running small-scale factories in downtown Harbin and elsewhere, they entered Hadong in search of a place where environmental regulations were looser.

10. The average annual rent on land near Hadong was 300 yuan per *mu*. Migrants farming near Hadong rented out their land to their neighbors or relatives in the countryside at much lower rates of only 100 to 150 yuan per *mu* (1 *mu* = 0.1647 acres).

11. Officially I was a research fellow at the Harbin Institute of Technology (HIT) and a graduate student at Stanford University. Yet neither of these positions was understandable to local residents. Taking the advice of a professor at the HIT, I introduced myself as a college student who was visiting Hadong for the purpose of making a social survey. Because of an increase in the number of research projects, the social survey (*shehui diaocha*) has been a very common form of research among China's college students.

12. Sun Yufen's complaint should not be interpreted to mean that no pension scheme exists for peasants in China. After the market reform, both the collapse of communes and the crisis of familial support—partly driven by the one-child policy—led the state to consider implementing a rural pension scheme as early as the beginning of the 1990s. As Shih-Jiunn Shi demonstrates, the policy remains a morass owing to "the dominant idea that land, family, and market provision should remain the chief pillars of rural old-age security" (2006: 800). In Heilongjiang in 2006, the number of basic pension insurance participants was 1,807,000 in the countryside and 8,010,000 in the city. This means that 95 percent of urban employed persons but only 19 percent of rural employed persons participated in the pension scheme (ZTN 2007: 903, 908; HTN 2007: 63).

13. I borrow this expression from Karl Marx, who described society in terms of the sum of interrelations: "To be a slave, to be a citizen, are social characteristics, relations between human beings A and B. Human being A, as such, is not a slave. He is a slave in and through society" (Marx 1973: 265).

14. "Members of the collective economic organizations in rural areas shall, according to law, have the right to undertake rural land contracts with their own collective economic organizations that give out the contracts. No organizations or individuals may deprive the members of the rural collective economic organizations of their right to undertake contracts or illegally restrict such right." Law of the People's Republic of China on Land Contracts in Rural Areas (hereafter Law on Land Contracts), article 5. A person is a member of the collective as long as his or her *hukou* belongs to the collective. The Law on Land Contracts was adopted at the Twenty-ninth Meeting of the Standing Committee of the Ninth National People's Congress on August 29, 2002, and went into effect on March 1, 2003.

15. As of 2006, the per capita annual disposable income of urban households was 11,230 yuan (http://news.sohu.com/20070120/n247727852.shtml).

16. According to article 16(2) of the Law on Land Contracts, the contractor has the right to "obtain appropriate compensation for the contracted land that is requisitioned or occupied according to law."

17. As unbearable burdens on peasants aroused widespread riots, the central government implemented a major tax reform in 2002, completely rescinding compulsory fees for farmers, except for the basic agricultural tax. This major reform, in turn, was followed by the repeal of the agricultural tax in 2006. See Chen and Summerfield (2007).

18. Article 20 of the Law on Land Contracts.

19. For administrative purposes, Binxian is one of the seven satellite counties of Harbin.

20. *Pingfang,* typical public housing in the Mao period, was not merely a physical form of urban architecture. As Li Zhang emphasizes, it was intended "to create a collective form of social life and egalitarian social relationships through spatial reorganization, while maximizing the use of space and minimizing construction costs" (2004: 8). Elsewhere the same author traces the shift from public housing controlled by work units to the predominance of commercially developed, consumer-oriented private housing in China (Zhang 2010).

21. Holston and Appadurai (1996) explain this state of exclusion in terms of a significant gap between formal and substantive citizenship. Formal citizenship refers to a person's legal standing (for example, the right to vote), while substantive citizenship implies the de facto ability to enjoy public access.

22. I would never argue that my ethnographic account of Sun Yufen represents the general condition of China's rural migrants. The life trajectories of rural migrants follow different paths according to skills and resources that they gained in the countryside as well as the ability of some to strike it rich under the city's risky and often illicit market circumstances. For example, a shanty migrant village called Zhejiangcun, which was ruthlessly bulldozed by the Beijing government in the 1990s (Zhang 2001; Xiang 2005), has since become a gigantic shopping complex, created as evicted migrants succeeded in business. (Jeong 2011). Nevertheless, I have linked Sun's sufferings to rural migrants in general because I find that for them, a poverty-stricken urban life is still more predominant than stories of "success," and more important, because the government's gesture celebrating "successful wealthy migrants" prompts me to produce a counternarrative against such propaganda.

23. The original reads, "It is always possible to recruit from the working class an army against the working class" (Rancière 1995: 95).

6. Dividing the Poor

1. I borrow the phrase from Renato Rosaldo, whose notion of culture is useful for understanding state governance. Against a classic view that posits culture as a self-contained entity, Rosaldo conceptualizes it as "a more porous array of intersections where distinct processes crisscross from within and beyond its borders" (1993: 20). Such an emphasis on porosity as well as the intersections of distinct processes leads us to observe how state governance is not unidirectional but subject to the often contradictory and unexpected encounters of governmental interventions. See also Li (2007: 28).

2. Around the mid-1950s, the state processed a series of administrative actions for preventing free migration from the countryside to the city. For instance, the State Council passed the Directive Concerning the Establishment of a Permanent System of Household Registration in 1955. In the city, the state took control over food rations between 1953 and 1955, and in the countryside, 97 percent of rural households joined cooperatives by the end of 1956 (Selden and Cheng 1994: 652–61).

3. Li Debin and Shi Fang note how scrupulously the government organized the entire process, from the selection of migrants to their settlement in the countryside: "The Harbin Migration Committee undertook a propaganda campaign while making the rounds of every street. Work teams helped those who decided to migrate to dispose of their household goods and to settle debt-related disputes. They organized carriages and went to see migrants off at train stations. When migrants arrived in the countryside, they were warmly welcomed by local cadres. On their own, the cadres checked to see if migrants' houses were well organized, if their windows were equipped to prevent cold air from coming into the house, or if the migrants had enough firewood" (1987: 225–27).

4. After the end of the Cultural Revolution, the Chinese government officially admitted that the sent-down movement had increased the burden on the peasantry and stripped many urban youths of their opportunity for education. Nevertheless, the government worked desperately to control the massive return of sent-down youths owing to its great concern for security (Gold 1980: 756), for it was feared that an influx of youths returning to the cities would be a source of social unrest.

5. Scholars have noted the relational nature of fear, stressing that fear cannot be defined on the basis of any preexisting indicators (Rancière 1995; Ahmed 2004; Appadurai 2006). Instead, the source of fear must be sought in the *relation* that one group has to another. "Identity is first about fear: the fear of the other, the fear of nothing, which finds on the body of the other its object" (Rancière 1995: 64).

6. Appadurai examines the tension between majorities and minorities at the national level. "Minorities," in his work, are used as metaphors for those who threaten the purity of the national whole.

7. The state's new categorizations as well as the new conditions of living together have aggravated urbanites' anxiety about their downward mobility. The term "vulnerable groups" (*ruoshi qunti*), first used by premier Zhu Rongji in 1998, has been widely used to refer to urban laid-off workers and rural migrants, as well as poor retirees and peasants. The state that once fashioned urban workers as the "majorities" of the country has now remade them as "minorities," placing them in the same category with rural migrants and peasants. Whether because of the state's categorization or because of their squalid housing conditions, being lumped together with rural migrants has aggravated the fear of impoverished urbanites that their status is waning and that they are no longer "majorities" in society.

8. State Council, "Some Opinions on Resolving the Problems Faced by Migrant Workers," document 5, January 31, 2006.

9. The security fee was renamed the community management fee (*shequ guanli fei*) after many residents refused to pay it because robberies were occurring frequently in the neighborhood.

10. The security fee and the cleaning fee were imposed on individual families, while the service fee was imposed on local shops at rates ranging from 20 to 100 yuan a month.

11. Many migrants must visit the Community office to request a certificate of residence (*juzhu zhengming*), which is needed for official applications, such as for jobs or for the temporary residence permit (*zanzhuzheng*) needed to register children for school. Yet these migrants are reluctant to go to the office, knowing that Community cadres will try to get them to pay the fees for the whole year.

12. The enemy is not predetermined in this distinction. Schmitt emphasizes: "The political enemy need not be morally evil or aesthetically ugly; he need not appear as an economic competitor....Only the actual participants can correctly recognize, understand, and judge the concrete situation and settle the extreme case of conflicts" (Schmitt 2007: 27).

13. Mao Zedong once wrote, "You must first be clear on what is meant by 'the people' and what is meant by 'the enemy'" (1990: 45). The distinction between the friend and the enemy, specifically the very ambiguity inherent in distinguishing those who are with you from those whom you struggle against, became a source of fear in political campaigns in the Maoist era. According to Dutton, this friend-enemy binary has been displaced by the legal-illegal distinction as the new order of the post-Mao era aims not at continuing revolutionary struggle but at policing social stability (2005: 251–300). Dutton, however, fails to explore the possibility that this historical act of distinguishing the enemy from the friend can be newly conflated with the act of singling out any "dangerous" elements that may hinder social stability. In Mao's era, the friend-enemy binary was no mere tool for achieving political control but a form of *bio*-politics through which people lived their lives. Such a distinction does not entirely disappear with the post-Mao preoccupation with law enforcement and depoliticization. Instead, the dichotomy that distinguishes "the people" from "the enemy," though far from being as severe as in the Maoist era, is conjured up as a local style of separating "us" from "them."

REFERENCES

Agamben, Giorgio. *Homo Sacer: Sovereign Power and Bare Life.* Stanford: Stanford University Press, 1998.

Ahmed, Sara. "Affective Economies." *Social Text* 22, no. 2 (2004): 117–39.

Anagnost, Ann. *National Past-Times: Narrative, Representation, and Power in Modern China.* Durham: Duke University Press, 1997.

——. "The Corporeal Politics of Quality (*Suzhi*)." *Public Culture* 16, no. 2 (2004): 189–208.

Anderson, Perry. "Two Revolutions." *New Left Review* 61 (2010): 59–96.

Appadurai, Arjun. "The Capacity to Aspire: Culture and the Terms of Recognition." In *Culture and Public Action,* edited by Vijayendra Rao and Michael Walton, 59–84. Stanford: Stanford University Press, 2004.

——. *Fear of Small Numbers: An Essay on the Geography of Anger.* Durham: Duke University Press, 2006.

Asian Development Bank. "Low-Income Housing Policies: Lessons from International Experience." ADB Observations and Suggestions Series, 2009. http://www.adb.org/publications/low-income-housing-policies-lessons-international-experience?ref=countries/prc/publications.

Baek Seung-Wook, ed. Jungguk Nodongja'ui Gieok'ui Jeongchi [Memory of the Cultural Revolution by Chinese Workers]. Seoul: Poli-teia, 2007.

Bai Gang, ed. *Chengshi Jiceng Quanli Chongzu* [Studies on Community Building in Urban China]. Beijing: Zhongguo Shehui Kexue Chubanshe [China Social Sciences Press], 2006.

Barlow, Tani E. "Theorizing Woman: Funü, Guojia, Jiating (Chinese Woman, Chinese State, Chinese Family)." In *Body, Subject, and Power in China,* edited by Angela Zito and Tani E. Barlow, 253–89. Chicago: University of Chicago Press, 1994a.

——. "Politics and Protocols of Funü: (Un)Making National Woman." In *Engendering China: Women, Culture, and the State,* edited by Christina K. Gilmartin, Gail Hershatter, Lisa Rofel, and Tyrene White, 339–59. Cambridge: Harvard University Press, 1994b.

Bernstein, Thomas P. *Up to the Mountains and Down to the Villages: The Transfer of Youth from Urban to Rural China.* New Haven: Yale University Press, 1977.

Bian, Yanjie, John Logan, and Xiaoling Shu. "Wage and Job Inequalities in the Working Careers of Men and Women in Tianjin." In *Redrawing Boundaries: Gender, Households, and Work in China,* edited by Barbara Entwisle and Gail Henderson, 111–33. Berkeley: University of California Press, 2000.

Bian, Yanjie, John R. Logan, Hanlong Lu, Yunkang Pan, and Ying Guan. "Work Units and Housing Reform in Two Chinese Cities." In *Danwei: The*

Changing Chinese Workplace in Historical and Comparative Perspective, edited by Lü Xiaobo and Elizabeth J. Perry, 223–50. Armonk, N.Y.: M. E. Sharpe, 1997.

Biehl, João. *Vita: Life in a Zone of Social Abandonment.* Berkeley: University of California Press, 2005.

Blecher, Marc J. "Hegemony and Workers' Politics in China." *China Quarterly* 170 (2002): 283–303.

Bourdieu, Pierre. *Distinction: A Social Critique of the Judgement of Taste.* Translated by Richard Nice. Cambridge: Harvard University Press, 1984.

———. *The Weight of the World: Social Suffering in Contemporary Society.* Translated by Priscilla Parkhurst Ferguson, Susan Emanuel, Joe Johnson, and Shoggy T. Waryn. Stanford: Stanford University Press, 2000.

———. *The Social Structures of the Economy.* 1988. Translated by Chris Turner. New York: Polity Press, 2005.

Bourgois, Philippe. *In Search of Respect: Selling Crack in El Barrio.* Cambridge: Cambridge University Press, 1995.

———. "Understanding Inner City Poverty: Resistance and Self-Destruction under U.S. Apartheid." In *Exotic No More: Anthropology on the Front Lines,* edited by Jeremy MacClancy, 15–32. Chicago: University of Chicago Press, 2002.

Brandt, Loren, Jikun Huang, Go Li, and Scott Rozelle. "Land Rights in Rural China: Facts, Fictions and Issues." *China Journal* 47 (2002): 67–97.

Bray, David. "Building 'Community': New Strategies of Governance in Urban China." *Economy and Society* 35, no. 4 (2006): 530–49.

Briggs, Jean. *Never in Anger: Portrait of an Eskimo Family.* Cambridge: Harvard University Press, 1970.

Brown, Jeremy. *City versus Countryside in Mao's China: Negotiating the Divide.* Cambridge: Cambridge University Press, 2012.

Burawoy, Michael, and Katherine Verdery, eds. *Uncertain Transition: Ethnographies of Change in the Postsocialist World.* New York: Roman & Littlefield, 1999.

Cai, Yongshun. "Collective Ownership or Cadre's Ownership? The Non-agricultural Use of Farmland in China." *China Quarterly* 171 (2003): 662–80.

———. *State and Laid-Off Workers in Reform China: The Silence and Collective Action of the Retrenched.* New York: Routledge, 2006.

Cao Gui-hua, and Wei-juan Yu. "Jiejue Shidi Nongmin Wenti de Guanjian: Wanshan Tudi Zhengyong Zhidu" [Improving the System of Land Expropriation and Requisition to Resolve the Problems of the Farmers Losing Their Lands]. *Resources Administration and the Legal System* (November 2006): 27–29.

Carter, James H. *Creating a Chinese Harbin: Nationalism in an International City, 1916–1932.* Ithaca: Cornell University Press, 2002.

Chan, Kam Wing, and Li Zhang. "The *Hukou* System and Rural-Urban Migration in China: Processes and Changes." *China Quarterly* 160 (1999): 818–55.

Chatterjee, Partha. *The Politics of the Governed: Reflections on Popular Politics in Most of the World.* New York: Columbia University Press, 2004.

Chen, Feng. "Subsistence Crises, Managerial Corruption, and Labor Protests in China." *China Journal* 44 (2000): 41–63.

Chen, Junjie, and Gale Summerfield. "Gender and Rural Reforms in China: A

Case Study of Population Control and Land Rights Policies in Northern Liaoning." *Feminist Economics* 13, no. 3–4 (2007): 63–92.

Chen Weiding. *Shequ Zizhi: Zi Zuzhi Wangluo yu Zhidu Shezhi* [Community Self-Governance: Organization Network and System Installation]. Beijing: Zhongguo Shehui Kexue Chubanshe [China Social Sciences Press], 2004.

Chen Xiwen. "Xinxing Tudi Zhengce de Zhengjie" [Deadlock of the Current Land Policy]. *Nongcun Hezuo Jingji Jingying Guanli* [Rural Cooperative Economy Management and Administration] 12 (2002): 6–9.

Chen Yongsen. *Gaobie Chenmin de Changshi: Qingmo Minchu de Gongmin Yishi yu Gongmin Xingwei* [Citizens' Consciousness and Action from the Late Qing to the Early Republican Period]. Beijing: Zhongguo Renmin Daxue Chubanshe [People's University of China Press], 2003.

Cho, Mun Young. "From 'Power to the People' to 'Civil Empowerment': The Making of Neoliberal Governmentality in Grassroots Movements for the Urban Poor in South Korea." *East-West Center International Graduate Student Conference Series* 13 (2005): 1–12.

——. "Forced Flexibility: A Migrant's Woman's Struggle for Settlement." *China Journal* 61 (2009): 51–76.

——. "On the Edge between 'the People' and 'the Population': Ethnographic Research on the Minimum Livelihood Guarantee." *China Quarterly* 201 (2010): 20–37.

——. "'We are the State': An Entrepreneurial Mission to Serve the People in Harbin, Northeast China." *Modern China* 37, no. 4 (2011): 422–55.

Chung, Jae Ho, Hongyi Lai, and Jang-Hwan Joo. "Assessing the 'Revive the Northeast' (Zhenxing Dongbei) Programme: Origins, Policies and Implementation." *China Quarterly* 197 (2009): 108–25.

Cohen, Myron. "Cultural and Political Inventions in Modern China: The Case of the Chinese 'Peasant.'" *Daedalus* 122, no. 2 (1993): 151–70.

Comaroff, John, and Jean Comaroff. *Civil Society and the Political Imagination in Africa.* Chicago: University of Chicago Press, 1999.

——. "Millennial Capitalism: First Thoughts on a Second Coming." *Public Culture* 12, no. 2 (2000): 291–343.

——. *Law and Disorder in the Postcolony.* Chicago: University of Chicago Press, 2006.

Cook, Sarah, and Susie Jolly. *Unemployment, Poverty, and Gender in Urban China: Perceptions and Experiences of Laid-Off Workers in Three Chinese Cities.* Sussex: Institute of Development Studies, 2000.

Cruikshank, Barbara. *The Will to Empower: Democratic Citizens and Other Subjects.* Ithaca: Cornell University Press, 1999.

Davies, Gloria, and Gaby Ramia. "Governance Reform towards 'Serving Migrant Workers': The Local Implementation of Central Government Regulations." *China Quarterly* 193 (2008): 140–49.

Davis, Deborah. *The Consumer Revolution in Urban China.* Berkeley: University of California Press, 2000.

——. "From Welfare Benefit to Capitalized Asset: The Re-commodification of Residential Space in Urban China." In *Housing and Social Change: East-West Perspectives,* edited by Ray Forrest and James Lee, 183–98. New York: Routledge, 2003.

——. "Urban Chinese Homeowners as Citizen-Consumers." In *The Ambiva-lent Consumer: Questioning Consumption in East Asia and the West,* edited by Sheldon Garon and Patricia L. Maclachlan, 281–99. Ithaca: Cornell University Press, 2006.

Davis, Mike. *Planet of Slums.* New York: Verso, 2006.

Dean, Mitchell. "A Genealogy of the Government of Poverty." *Economy and Society* 21, no. 3 (1992): 215–51.

——. *Governmentality: Power and Rule in Modern Society.* London: Sage Publications, 1999.

Deleuze, Gilles, and Félix Guattari. *A Thousand Plateaus: Capitalism and Schizophre-nia.* Translated by Brian Massumi. Minneapolis: University of Minnesota Press, 1987.

Deng Xiaoping. *Deng Xiaoping Wenxuan, 1975–1982* [Selected Writings of Deng Xiaoping, 1975–1982]. Beijing: Renmin Chubanshe [People's Press], 1983.

Desai, Padma, and Todd Idson. *Work without Wages: Russia's Nonpayment Crisis.* Cambridge: MIT Press, 2000.

Ding Yizhuang. *Zhongguo Zhiqingshi: Chulan, 1953–1968* [A History of the Chinese Educated Youth: The Early Waves, 1953–1968]. Beijing: Zhongguo Shehui Kexue Chubanshe [China Social Sciences Press], 1998.

Dirlik, Arif. "Postsocialism? Reflections on Socialism with Chinese Character-istics." In *Marxism and the Chinese Experience: Issues in Contemporary Chinese Socialism,* edited by Arif Dirlik and Maurice Meisner. 361–84. Armonk, N.Y.: M. E. Sharpe, 1989.

Dixon, John E. *The Chinese Welfare System, 1949–1979.* New York: Praeger, 1981.

Duara, Prasenjit. *Rescuing History from the Nation: Questioning Narratives of Modern China.* Chicago: University of Chicago Press, 1995.

——. *Sovereignty and Authenticity: Manchukuo and the East Asian Modern.* Lanham: Rowman & Littlefield Publishers, 2003.

Duda, Mark, Xiulan Zhang, and Mingzhu Dong. "China's Homeownership-Oriented Housing Policy: An Examination of Two Programs Using Survey Data from Beijing." Joint Center for Housing Studies. Harvard University, 2005.

Dutton, Michael. *Policing Chinese Politics.* Durham: Duke University Press, 2005.

Ebrey, Patricia Buckley. *The Inner Quarters: Marriage and the Lives of Chinese Women in the Sung Period.* Berkeley: University of California Press, 1984.

Elliot, Mark C. *The Manchu Way: The Eight Banners and Ethnic Identity in Late Imperial China.* Stanford: Stanford University Press, 2001.

Elyachar, Julia. *Markets of Dispossession: NGOs, Economic Development, and the State in Cairo.* Durham: Duke University Press, 2005.

Escobar, Arturo. *Encountering Development: The Making and Unmaking of the Third World.* Princeton: Princeton University Press, 1995.

Fei Xiaotong. "Jumin Zizhi: Zhongguo Chengshi Shequ Jianshe de Xinmubiao" [Autonomy of Residents: New Target of Community Construction in Urban China]. *Jianghai Academic Journal* 3 (2002): 15–18.

Fenghuang Factory. *Fenghuang Ribao* [Fenghuang Daily], 1980–1995. Cited as FR.

Ferguson, James. *The Anti-politics Machine: "Development," Depoliticization, and Bureau-cratic Power in Lesotho.* Minneapolis: University of Minnesota Press, 1994.

——. *Expectations of Modernity: Myths and Meanings of Urban Life on the Zambian Copperbelt.* Berkeley: University of California Press, 1999.

——. *Global Shadows: Africa in the Neoliberal World Order.* Durham: Duke University Press, 2006.

Feuchtwang, Stephan. "Remnants of Revolution in China." In *Postsocialism: Ideals, Ideologies, and Practices in Eurasia,* edited by C. M. Hann, 196–213. New York: Routledge, 2002.

Fong, Vanessa L. Only Hope: *Coming of Age under China's One-Child Policy.* Stanford: Stanford University Press, 2004.

Foucault, Michel. *Discipline and Punish: The Birth of the Prison.* Translated by Alan Sheridan. New York: Vintage Books, 1977.

——. *The History of Sexuality: An Introduction.* Translated by Robert Hurley. New York: Vintage Books, 1978.

——. "Afterword: The Subject and Power." In *Michel Foucault: Beyond Structuralism and Hermeneutics,* edited by Hubert L. Dreyfus and Paul Rabinow. Brighton: Harvester, 1982.

——. "Governmentality." In *The Foucault Effect: Studies in Governmentality,* edited by Graham Burchell, Colin Gordon, and Peter Miller, 87–104. Chicago: University of Chicago Press, 1991.

——. *Security, Territory, Population: Lectures at the Collège de France, 1977–1978.* Translated by Graham Burchell. New York: Palgrave, 2007.

FR. See Fenghuang Factory 1980–1995.

Gao Guangzhi. *Nie Pan: Dongbei Laogongye Jidi* [Old Industrial Base in Northeast China]. Harbin: Beifang Wenyi Chubanshe, 2004.

Geremek, Bronislaw. *Poverty: A History.* Oxford: Blackwell, 1994.

Giles, John, Albert Park, and Fang Cai. "How Has Economic Restructuring Affected China's Urban Workers?" *China Quarterly* 185 (2006): 61–95.

Gold, Thomas B. "Back to the City: The Return of Shanghai's Educated Youth." *China Quarterly* 84 (1980): 55–70.

Goldstein, Daniel M. *The Spectacular City: Violence and Performance in Urban Bolivia.* Durham: Duke University Press, 2004.

Goode, Judith, and Jeff Maskovsky. Introduction to *The New Poverty Studies: The Ethnography of Power, Politics, and Impoverished People in the United States,* edited by Judith Goode and Jeff Maskovsky, 1–34. New York: New York University Press, 2001.

Gordon, Colin. "Governmental Rationality: An Introduction." In *The Foucault Effect: Studies in Governmentality,* edited by Graham Burchell, Colin Gordon, and Peter Miller, 1–52. Chicago: University of Chicago Press, 1991.

Gottschang, Thomas R., and Diana Lary. *Swallows and Settlers: The Great Migration from North China to Manchuria.* Ann Arbor: Center for Chinese Studies, University of Michigan, 2000.

Greenhalgh, Susan, and Edwin A. Winckler. *Governing China's Population: From Leninist to Neoliberal Biopolitics.* Stanford: Stanford University Press, 2005.

Guan Xinping. *Zhongguo Chengshi Pinkun Wenti Yanjiu* [Research on China's Urban Poverty]. Changsha: Hunan Renmin Chubanshe [Hunan People's Publishing House], 1999.

Guiheux, Gilles. "The Promotion of a New Calculating Chinese Subject: The Cast of Laid-Off Workers Turning into Entrepreneurs." *Journal of Contemporary China* 16, no. 5 (2007): 149–71.

Guo, Xiaolin. "Land Expropriation and Rural Conflicts in China." *China Quarterly* 169 (2001): 422–39.

Guojia Tongjiju (National Bureau of Statistics). *Zhongguo Tongji Nianjian* [China Statistical Yearbook]. Beijing: Zhongguo Tongji Chubanshe [China Statistics Press], 2007. Cited as ZTN.

Gupta, Akhil. "Blurred Boundaries: The Discourse of Corruption, the Culture of Politics, and the Imagined State." *American Ethnologist* 22, no. 2 (1995): 375–402.

——. "Governing Population: The Integrated Child Development Services Program in India." In *States of Imagination: Ethnographic Explorations of the Postcolonial State,* edited by Thomas B. Hansen and Finn Stepputat, 65–96. Durham: Duke University Press, 2001.

Gupta, Akhil, and James Ferguson. "Beyond 'Culture': Space, Identity, and the Politics of Difference." In *Culture, Power, Place: Explorations in Critical Anthropology,* edited by Akhil Gupta and James Ferguson, 33–51. Durham: Duke University Press, 1997.

Gupta, Akhil, and Aradhana Sharma. "Introduction: Rethinking Theories of the State in an Age of Globalization." In *The Anthropology of the State: A Reader,* edited by Akhil Gupta and Aradhana Sharma, 45–48. Oxford: Blackwell, 2006.

Hanser, Amy. *Service Encounters: Class, Gender, and the Market for Social Distinction in Urban China.* Stanford: Stanford University Press, 2008.

Harbin Difangzhi Bianzhuan Wenyuanhui [Harbin History Compilation Committee]. *Harbin Shizhi* [Harbin Gazetteer]. Harbin: Heilongjiang Renmin Chubanshe [Heilongjiang People's Press], 1999. Cited as HSZ.

Harbin shi Taiping qu Difangzhi Bianxie Bangongshi (Taiping History Compilation Committee). *Harbin shi Taiping Quzhi* [Taiping District Gazetteer]. Harbin: Heilongjiang Renmin Chubanshe [Heilongjiang People's Press], 1992. Cited as TQ.

Harbin shi Tongjiju [Bureau of Statistics of Harbin]. *Harbin Tongji Nianjian, 1990–2007* [Harbin Statistical Yearbook, 1990–2007]. Beijing: Zhongguo Tongji Chubanshe [China Statistics Press], 2008. Cited as HTNJ.

Hardt, Michael, and Antonio Negri. *Empire.* Cambridge: Harvard University Press, 2001.

——. *Multitude: War and Democracy in the Age of Empire.* New York: Penguin Press, 2004.

Hare, Denise, Li Yang, and Daniel Englander. "Land Management in Rural China and Its Gender Implications." *Feminist Economics* 13, no. 3–4 (2007): 35–61.

Harrell, Stevan. "The Changing Meanings of Work in China." In *Re-drawing Boundaries: Work, Households, and Gender in China,* edited by Barbara Entwisle and Gail E. Henderson, 67–76. Berkeley: University of California Press, 2000.

Harvey, David. *The Condition of Postmodernity: An Enquiry into the Origins of Cultural Change.* Cambridge: Blackwell, 1990.

———. *A Brief History of Neo-liberalism*. Oxford: Oxford University Press, 2005.

He, Henry Yuhuai. *Dictionary of the Political Thought of the People's Republic of China*. New York: M. E. Sharpe, 2001.

Heilongjiang sheng Difangzhi Bianzhuan Wenyuanhui [Heilongjiang History Compilation Committee]. *Heilongjiang Shengzhi* [Heilongjiang Gazetteer]. Harbin: Heilongjiang Chubanshe [Heilongjiang Press], 1991. Cited as HS.

Heilongjiang sheng Tongjiju [Bureau of Statistics of Heilongjiang]. *Heilongjiang Tongji Nianjian* [Heilongjiang Statistical Yearbook]. Beijing: Zhongguo Tongji Chubanshe [China Statistics Press], 1997, 2007. Cited as HTN.

Henderson, Gail E. et al. "Re-drawing the Boundaries of Work: Views on the Meaning of Work (*Gongzuo*)." In *Re-drawing Boundaries: Work, Households, and Gender in China,* edited by Barbara Entwisle and Gail E. Henderson, 33–50. Berkeley: University of California Press, 2000.

Ho, Peter. "Who Owns China's Land? Property Rights and Deliberate Institutional Ambiguity." *China Quarterly* 166 (2001): 394–421.

Hoffman, Lisa. "Autonomous Choices and Patriotic Professionalism: On Governmentality in Late-Socialist China." *Economy and Society* 35, no. 4 (2006): 550–70.

———. *Patriotic Professionalism in Urban China: Fostering Talent*. Philadelphia: Temple University Press, 2010.

Holston, James. *Insurgent Citizenship: Disjunctions of Democracy and Modernity in Brazil*. Princeton: Princeton University Press, 2008.

Holston, James, and Arjun Appadurai. "Cities and Citizenship." *Public Culture* 8, no. 2 (1996): 187–204.

Hong Dayong. *Zhuanxing Shiqi Zhongguo Shehui Jiuzhu* [Social Relief in China's Transition]. Shenyang: Liaoning Jiaoyu Chubanshe [Liaoning Education Press], 2004.

Honig, Emily, and Gail Hershatter. *Personal Voices: Chinese Women in the 1980s*. Stanford: Stanford University Press, 1988.

HS. See Heilongjiang sheng Difangzhi Bianzhuan Wenyuanhui 1991.

Hsing, You-tien. *The Great Urban Transformation: Politics of Land and Property in China*. New York: Oxford University Press, 2010.

Hsu, Carolyn L. *Creating Market Socialism: How Ordinary People Are Shaping Class and Status in China*. Durham: Duke University Press, 2007.

HTN. See Heilongjiang sheng Tongjiju 1997.

HTNJ. See Harbin shi Tongjiju 2008.

Humphrey, Caroline. *The Unmaking of Soviet Life: Everyday Economies after Socialism*. Ithaca: Cornell University Press, 2002.

Hung, Eva P. W., and Stephen W. K. Chiu. "The Lost Generation: Life Course Dynamics and Xiagang in China." *Modern China* 29, no. 2 (2003): 204–36.

Hurst, William. "Understanding Contentious Collective Action by Chinese Laid-Off Workers: The Importance of Regional Political Economy." *Studies in Comparative International Development* 39, no. 2 (2004): 94–120.

———. *The Chinese Worker after Socialism*. Cambridge: Cambridge University Press, 2009.

Hurst, William, and Kevin J. O'Brien. "China's Contentious Pensioners." *China Quarterly* 170 (2002): 345–60.

Jacka, Tamara. *Women's Work in Rural China*. New York: Cambridge University Press, 1997.

Jeffery, Lyn. "Marketing Civility, Civilizing the Market: Chinese Multilevel Marketing's Challenge to the State." In *The New Entrepreneurs of Europe and Asia: Patterns of Business Development in Russia, Eastern Europe, and China,* edited by Victoria E. Bonnell and Thomas B. Gold, 325–46. Armonk, N.Y.: M. E. Sharpe, 2002.

Jeong, Jong-ho. "Renegotiating with the State: The Challenge of Floating Population and the Emergence of New Urban Space in Contemporary China." Ph.D. diss., Yale University, 2000.

——. "From Illegal Migrant Settlements to Central Business and Residential Districts: Restructuring of Urban Space in Beijing's Migrant Enclaves." *Habitat International* 35 (2011): 508–13.

Judd, Ellen. "Land Divided, Land United." *China Quarterly* 130 (1992): 338–56.

——. *Gender and Power in Rural North China*. Stanford: Stanford University Press, 1996.

Judge, Joan. "Publicists and Populists: Including the Common People in the Late Qing New Citizen Model." In *Imagining the People: Chinese Intellectuals and the Concept of Citizenship, 1890 -1920,* edited by Joshua A. Fogel and Peter Zarrow, 165–82. Armonk, N.Y.: M. E. Sharpe, 1997.

Kalb, Don. "Conversations with a Polish Populist: Tracing Hidden Histories of Globalization, Class, and Dispossession in Postsocialism (and Beyond)." *American Ethnologist* 36, no. 2 (2009): 207–23.

Kernen, Antoine, and Jean-Louis Rocca. "Social Responses to Unemployment and the 'New Urban Poor': Case Study in Shenyang City and Liaoning Province." *China Perspectives* 27 (2000): 35–51.

Khan, Azizur Rahman, and Carl Riskin. *Inequality and Poverty in China in the Age of Globalization*. Oxford: Oxford University Press, 2001.

Kideckel, David A. "The Unmaking of an East-Central European Working Class." In *Postsocialism: Ideals, Ideologies, and Practices in Eurasia,* edited by C. M. Hann, 114–32. New York: Routledge, 2002.

Kim Kwang-ok. Hyukmyong'gua Kaehyuk Sok'ui Joong'guk Nongmin [Chinese Peasants in the Middle of Revolution and Reform]. Seoul: Jipmoondang, 2000.

Kipnis, Andrew. "Within and Against Peasantness: Backwardness and Filiality in Rural China." *Comparative Studies in Society and History* 37, no. 1 (1995): 110–35.

——. "*Suzhi*: A Keyword Approach." *China Quarterly* 186 (2006): 295–313.

——. "Neoliberalism Reified: Suzhi Discourse and Tropes of Neoliberalism in the People's Republic of China." *Journal of the Royal Anthropological Institute* 13 (2007): 383–400.

——. "Audit Cultures: Neoliberal Governmentality, Socialist Legacy, or Technologies of Governing?" *American Ethnologist* 35, no. 2 (2008): 275–89.

Kohrman, Matthew. *Bodies of Difference: Experience of Disability and Institutional Advocacy in the Making of Modern China*. Berkeley: University of California Press, 2005.

Kojève, Alexandre. *Introduction to the Reading of Hegel.* Edited by Allan Bloom. Translated by James H. Nichols. Ithaca: Cornell University Press, 1980.

Kondo, Dorinne K. *Crafting Selves: Power, Gender, and Discourses of Identity in a Japanese Workplace.* Chicago: The University of Chicago Press, 1990.

Koselleck, Reinhart. *Futures Past: On the Semantics of Historical Time.* Cambridge: MIT Press, 1985.

Kraus, Richard Curt. "Class Conflict and the Vocabulary of Social Analysis in China." *China Quarterly* 69 (1977): 54–74.

———. *Class Conflict in Chinese Socialism.* New York: Columbia University Press, 1981.

Lahusen, Thomas, ed. *Harbin and Manchuria: Place, Space, and Identity.* Durham: Duke University Press, 2001.

Lee, Ching Kwan. "The 'Revenge of History': Collective Memories and Labor Protests in Northeastern China." *Ethnography* 1, no. 2 (2000): 217–37.

———. "Pathways of Labor Insurgency." In *Chinese Society: Change, Conflict, and Resistance,* edited by Elizabeth J. Perry and Mark Selden, 71–92. Cambridge: Harvard University Press, 2003.

———. *Against the Law: Labor Protests in China's Rustbelt and Sunbelt.* Berkeley: University of California Press, 2007.

Lee Hyeon Jung. "Jungkuk Nongchin Yeosung'ui Jasal'un Guayeon Jeohang'yinka?" (Is Suicide among Rural Women in China a Form of Resistance?). *Korean Cultural Anthropology* 44, no. 3 (2010): 75–124.

Lee, James. "From Welfare Housing to Home Ownership: The Dilemma of China's Housing Reform." *Housing Studies* 15, no. 1 (2000): 61–76.

Legg, Stephen. "Foucault's Population Geographies: Classifications, Biopolitics and Governmental Spaces." *Population, Space and Place* 11 (2005): 137–56.

Li Dazhao. "Shumin de Shengli" [The Victory of the Ordinary Folks]. 1918. In *Li Dazhao Wenji* [The Selected Writings of Li Dazhao]. Vol. 1. Beijing: Renmin Chubanshe People's Press, 1984.

Li Debin, and Fang Shi. *Heilongjiang Yimin Gaiyao* [Outline of Migration in Heilongjiang]. Harbin: Heilongjiang Renmin Chubanshe [Heilongjiang People's Press], 1987.

Li Lulu. "Shehui Fenceng Yanjiu" [Research on Social Stratification]. *Shehuixue Yanjiu* [Sociological Studies] 1 (1999): 103–11.

Li Qiang. "Xiandaihua yu Zhongguo Shehui Fenceng Jiegou" [Modernization and Structural Changes of Social Stratification in China]. *Jiaoxue yu Yanjiu* [Teaching and Research] 3 (1996): 26–29.

Li, Shi. "Urban Poverty Research in China: Poverty Lines and Methodology." *World Economy and China* 4 (2000): 50–58.

Li Songhua. "Heilongjiangsheng Chengshi Ruoshi Qunti yu Zuidi Shenghuo Baozhang" [Disadvantaged Groups and the Urban Minimum Living Standard Scheme in Heilongjiang]. *Heilongjiang Shehuikexue* [Heilongjiang Social Sciences] 88, no. 1 (2005): 121–24.

Li, Tania Murray. *The Will to Improve: Governmentality, Development, and the Practice of Politics.* Durham: Duke University Press, 2007.

Li, Zongmin. *Women's Land Rights in Rural China: A Synthesis.* Beijing: Ford Foundation Office, 2002.

Lindquist, Johan A. *The Anxieties of Mobility: Migration and Tourism in the Indonesian Borderlands.* Honolulu: University of Hawai'i Press, 2009.

Liu, Jieyu. *Gender and Work in Urban China: Women Workers of the Unlucky Generation.* New York: Routledge, 2007.

Liu Zhaojun, and Yuqing Chen. "Lun Nongmingong Tudi Quanyi de Falü Baohu" [Legal Protection of Rural Migrants' Land Rights]. *Sannong yu Linye Falü Shijue* [Perspectives on Three Agricultural Problems and Forestry Laws] (April 2006): 44–46.

Logan, John R., Yiping Fang, and Zhanxin Zhang. "Access to Housing in Urban China." *International Journal of Urban and Regional Research* 33, no. 4 (2009): 914–35.

Lu, Aiguo, and Manuel F. Montes. *Poverty, Income Distribution, and Well-Being in Asia during the Transition.* New York: Palgrave Macmillan, 2002.

Lu Haiyuan. *Zoujin Chengshi: Nongmingong de Shehui Baozhang* [Toward Cities: The Social Security of Peasant Migrants]. Beijing: Jingji Guanli Chubanshe [Economic Management Publishing House], 2004.

Lü, Xiaobo, and Elizabeth J. Perry, eds. *Danwei: The Changing Chinese Workplace in Historical and Comparative Perspective.* Armonk, N.Y.: M. E. Sharpe, 1997.

Mann, Susan. "Work and Household in Chinese Culture: Historical Perspectives." In *Re-drawing Boundaries: Work, Households, and Gender in China,* edited by Barbara Entwisle and Gail E. Henderson, 15–32. Berkeley: University of California Press, 2000.

Mao Tse-tung [Mao Zedong]. *Selected Works of Mao Tse-tung*, vol. 1. Peking: Foreign Language Press, 1965.

——. *Selected Works of Mao Tse-tung*, vol. 4. Peking: Foreign Language Press, 1967.

——. *Quotations from Chairman Mao Tsetung,* San Francisco: China Books, 1990.

Marcus, George E. "Ethnography in/of the World System: The Emergence of Multi-sited Ethnography." *Annual Review of Anthropology* 24 (1995): 95–117.

Marx, Karl. *The Eighteenth Brumaire of Louis Bonaparte.* 1852. Translated by Daniel De Leon. New York: International Publishers, 1972.

——. *The Grundrisse: Foundations of the Critique of Political Economy.* 1858. Translated by Martin Nicolaus. New York: Penguin, 1973.

——. *Capital: A Critique of Political Economy.* 1887. Translated by Ben Fowkes. New York: Penguin, 1976.

Matza, Tomas. "Moscow's Echo: Technologies of the Self, Publics, and Politics on the Russian Talk Show." *Cultural Anthropology* 24, no. 3 (2009): 489–522.

McLaren, Anne. "The Educated Youth Return: The Poster Campaign in Shanghai from November 1978 to March 1979." *Australian Journal of Chinese Affairs* 2 (1979): 1–20.

Meisner, Maurice. *Mao's China and After: A History of the People's Republic.* New York: Free Press, 1999.

Meng, Lie. *Harbin Jiuying* [Old Photos of Harbin]. Beijing: Renmin Meishu Chubanshe [People's Art Press], 2000.

Mitchell, Timothy. *Rule of Experts: Egypt, Techno-Politics, Modernity.* Berkeley: University of California Press, 2002.

Müller, Birgit, ed. *Power and Institutional Change in Post-Communist Eastern Europe.* Canterbury: CSAC, 1999.

Naughton, Barry. "Danwei: The Economic Foundations of a Unique Institution." In *Danwei: The Changing Chinese Workplace in Historical and Comparative Perspective,* edited by Xiaobo Lü and Elizabeth J. Perry, 169–94. Armonk: M. E. Sharpe, 1997.

———. *The Chinese Economy: Transitions and Growth.* Cambridge: MIT Press, 2007.

Nazpary, Joma. *Post-Soviet Chaos: Violence and Dispossession in Kazakhstan.* London: Pluto Press, 2001.

Newman, Katherine S. *Falling from Grace.* Berkeley: University of California Press, 1988.

Ngai, Pun. *Made in China: Women Factory Workers in a Global Workplace.* Durham: Duke University Press, 2005.

O'Connor, Alice. *Poverty Knowledge: Social Science, Social Policy, and the Poor in Twentieth-Century U.S. History.* Princeton: Princeton University Press, 2001.

Oi, Jean C. *State and Peasant in Contemporary China: The Political Economy of Village Government.* Berkeley: University of California Press, 1989.

———. "Bending without Breaking: The Adaptability of Chinese Political Institutions." In *How Far Across the River? Chinese Policy Reform at the Millennium,* edited by Nicholas C. Hope et al., 450–68. Stanford: Stanford University Press, 2003.

O'Malley, Pat, Lorna Weir, and Clifford Shearing. "Governmentality, Criticism, Politics." *Economy and Society* 26, no. 4 (1997): 501–17.

O'Neill, Kevin. *City of God: Christian Citizenship in Postwar Guatemala.* Berkeley: University of California Press, 2010.

Ong, Aihwa. *Flexible Citizenship: The Cultural Logics of Transnationality.* Durham: Duke University Press, 1999.

———. *Neoliberalism as Exception: Mutations in Citizenship and Sovereignty.* Durham: Duke University Press, 2006.

Ong, Aihwa, and Li Zhang, eds. *Privatizing China: Socialism from Afar.* Ithaca: Cornell University Press, 2008.

Ortner, Sherry B. "Identities: The Hidden Life of Class." *Journal of Anthropological Research* 54, no. 1 (1998): 1–17.

Oushakine, Serguei. *The Patriotism of Despair: Nation, War, and Loss in Russia.* Ithaca: Cornell University Press, 2009.

Paley, Julia. *Marketing Democracy: Power and Social Movements in Post-dictatorship Chile.* Berkeley: University of California Press, 2001.

Pan, Tianshu. "Neighborhood Shanghai: Community Building in Five Mile Bridge." Ph.D. diss., Harvard University, 2002.

Park, Jeehwan. "School as Classificatory Machine: Sorting, Socialization, and Class in a Japanese Middle School." Ph.D. diss., University of California, Berkeley, 2011.

Perry, Elizabeth J., and Xun Li. *Proletarian Power: Shanghai in the Cultural Revolution.* Boulder: Westview Press, 1997.

Perry, Elizabeth J., and Mark Selden. "Introduction: Reform and Resistance in Contemporary China." In *Chinese Society: Change, Conflict, and Resistance,* edited by Elizabeth J. Perry and Mark Selden, 1–22. New York: Routledge, 2003.

Perry, Elizabeth J., and Christine Wong. "Introduction: The Political Economy of Reform in Post-Mao China; Causes, Content, and Consequences." In *The*

Political Economy of Reform in Post-Mao China, edited by Elizabeth J. Perry and Christine Wong, 1–27. Cambridge: Harvard University Press, 1985.

Pieke, Frank N. *The Ordinary and the Extraordinary: An Anthropological Study of Chinese Reform and the 1989 People's Movement in Beijing.* New York: Kegan Paul International, 1996.

Procacci, Giovanna. "Social Economy and the Government of Poverty." In *The Foucault Effect: Studies in Governmentality,* edited by Graham Burchell, Colin Gordon, and Peter Miller, 151–68. Chicago: University of Chicago Press, 1991.

Rancière, Jacques. *On the Shores of Politics.* Translated by Liz Heron. New York: Verso, 1995.

——. *The Philosopher and His Poor.* Translated by Andrew Parker, Corinne Oster, and John Drury. Durham: Duke University Press, 2005.

Rocca, Jean-Louis. "The Rise of Unemployment in Urban China: The Contradictions of Employment Policies." *China Perspectives* 30 (2000): 42–55.

——. "Modernity in China: The Need for a New Critical Approach." *China Perspectives* 42 (2002a): 54–61.

——. "'Three at Once': The Multidimensional Scope of Labor Crisis in China." In *Politics in China: Moving Frontiers,* edited by Françoise Mengin and Jean-Louis Rocca, 3–32. New York: Palgrave, 2002b.

Rofel, Lisa. *Other Modernities: Gendered Yearnings in China after Socialism.* Berkeley: University of California Press, 1999.

——. *Desiring China: Experiments in Neoliberalism, Sexuality, and Public Culture.* Durham: Duke University Press, 2007.

Rosaldo, Renato. *Culture and Truth: The Remaking of Social Analysis.* Boston: Beacon Press, 1993.

Rose, Nikolas. *Powers of Freedom: Reframing Political Thought.* Cambridge: Cambridge University Press, 1999.

Rose, Nikolas, and Peter Miller. "Political Power beyond the State: Problematics of Government." *British Journal of Sociology* 43, no. 2 (1992): 173–205.

Rosen, Stanley. *Red Guard Factionalism and the Cultural Revolution in Guangzhou.* Boulder: Westview Press, 1982.

Sachs, Jeffrey, and Wing Thye Woo. "China's Transition Experience, Reexamined." *Transition: The Newsletter about Reforming Economics* 7, no. 3–4 (1996): 1–5.

Sargeson, Sally. "Subduing 'the Rural House-Building Craze': Attitudes towards Housing Construction and Land Use Controls in Four Zhejiang Villages." *China Quarterly* 169 (2002): 927–55.

Schmitt, Carl. *The Concept of the Political.* 1932. Chicago: University of Chicago Press, 2007.

Selden, Mark, and Tiejun Cheng. "The Origins and Social Consequences of China's Hukou System." *China Quarterly* 139 (1994): 644–68.

Sharma, Aradhana. "Crossbreeding Institutions, Breeding Struggle: Women's Empowerment, Neoliberal Governmentality, and State (Re)Formation in India." *Cultural Anthropology* 21, no.1 (2006): 60–95.

Shevchenko, Olga. *Crisis and the Everyday in Postsocialist Moscow.* Bloomington: Indiana University Press, 2009.

Shi, Shih-Jiunn. "Left to Market and Family—Again? Ideas and the Development of the Rural Pension Policy in China." *Social Policy & Administration* 40, no. 7 (2006): 791–806.

Shi Weimin. "Jianshe de Guifanxing Wenjian" [The Normative Policy Documents on Community Building]. In *Chengshi Jiceng Quanli Chongzu* [Studies on Community Building in Urban China), edited by Gang Bai. Beijing: Zhongguo Shehui Kexue Chubanshe (China Social Sciences Press), 2006a.

———. "Shequ Jianshe de Falü Yiju" [The Legal Foundation of Community Building]. In *Chengshi Jiceng Quanli Chongzu* [Studies on Community Building in Urban China], edited by Gang Bai. Beijing: Zhongguo Shehui Kexue Chubanshe [China Social Sciences Press], 2006b.

Shin, Kwang-Yeong. "Globalization and Social Inequality in South Korea." In *New Millennium South Korea: Neoliberal Capitalism and Transnational Movements,* edited by Jesook Song, 11–28. New York: Routledge, 2011.

Siddharthan, N. S. "Regional Differences in FDI Inflows: China-India Comparison." 2006. http://ideas.repec.org/p/ess/wpaper/id438.html.

Sigley, Gary. "Chinese Governmentalities: Government, Governance and the Socialist Market Economy." *Economy and Society* 35, no. 4 (2006): 487–508.

Siu, Helen F. "Grounding Displacement: Uncivil Urban Spaces in Postreform South China." *American Ethnologist* 34, no. 2 (2007): 329–50.

Solinger, Dorothy J. "The Floating Population in the Cities: Chances for Assimilation?" In *Urban Spaces in Contemporary China: The Potential for Autonomy and Community in Post-Mao China,* edited by Deborah Davis, 113–39. Washington, D.C.: Woodrow Wilson Center Press, 1995.

———. *Contesting Citizenship in Urban China: Peasant Migrants, the State, and the Logic of the Market.* Berkeley: University of California Press, 1999.

———. "Why We Cannot Count the Unemployed." *China Quarterly* 167 (2001): 671–88.

———. "State and Society in Urban China in the Wake of the Sixteenth Party Congress." *China Quarterly* 176 (2003): 943–59.

———. "The Creation of a New Underclass in China and Its Implications." *Environment and Urbanization* 18, no. 1 (2006): 177–93.

———. "The *Dibao* Recipients: Mollified Anti-emblem of Urban Modernization." *China Perspectives* 4 (2008): 36–46.

———. "The Phase-Out of the Unfit: Keeping the Unworthy Out of Work." In *Work and Organizations in China after Thirty Years of Transition,* edited by Lisa Keister, 307–36. Bingley, West Yorkshire: Emerald, 2009.

———. "The Urban *Dibao:* Guarantee for Minimum Livelihood or for Minimal Turmoil?" In *Marginalization in Urban China: Comparative Perspectives,* edited by Fulong Wu and Chris Webster, 253–77. New York: Palgrave Macmillan, 2010.

Song, Jesook. *South Koreans in the Debt Crisis: The Creation of a Neoliberal Welfare Society.* Durham: Duke University Press, 2009.

Tang Jun, Lin Sha, and Zhenxing Ren. *Zhongguo Chengshi Pinkun yu Fanpinkun Baogao* [Report on Poverty and Antipoverty in Urban China]. Beijing: Huaxia Chubanshe [Huaxia Press], 2003.

———. "Who Shall Determine Who the Urban Poor Are." *Chinese Sociology & Anthropology* 36, no. 2–3 (2003/4): 115–41.

Thompson, E. P. *The Making of the English Working Class.* New York: Pantheon Books, 1964.

Tomba, Luigi. "Creating an Urban Middle Class: Social Engineering in Beijing." *China Journal* 51, no.1 (2004): 1–26.

TQ. See Harbin shi Taiping qu Difangzhi Bianxie Bangongshi 1992.

Unger, Jonathan. *Education under Mao: Class and Competition in Canton Schools, 1960–1980.* New York: Columbia University Press, 1982.

Volkov, Vadim. *Violent Entrepreneurs: The Use of Force in the Making of Russian Capitalism.* Ithaca: Cornell University Press, 2002.

Wacquant, Loïc. *Urban Outcasts: A Comparative Sociology of Advanced Marginality.* Cambridge: Polity Press, 2008.

———. *Punishing the Poor: The Neoliberal Government of Social Insecurity.* Durham: Duke University Press, 2009.

Walder, Andrew G. "The Remaking of the Chinese Working Class, 1949–1981." *Modern China* 10, no. 1 (1984): 3–48.

———. *Communist Neo-traditionalism: Work and Authority in Chinese Society.* Berkeley: University of California Press, 1986.

Wang, Fei-ling. "Reformed Migration Control and New Targeted People: China's *Hukou* System in the 2000s." *China Quarterly* 177 (2004): 115–32.

Wang Jingyao. *Canyushi Zhili: Zhongguo Shehui Jianshe Shizheng Yanjiu* [Participatory Governance: A Positive Study of Urban Community Building in China]. Beijing: Zhongguo Shehui Kexue Chubanshe [China Social Sciences Press], 2006.

Wang, Ya Ping. *Urban Poverty, Housing, and Social Change in China.* New York: Routledge, 2004.

Wedel, Janine R. *Collision and Collusion: The Strange Case of Western Aid to Eastern Europe, 1989–1998.* New York: St. Martin's Press, 1998.

Weston, Timothy B. "The Iron Man Weeps: Joblessness and Political Legitimacy in the Chinese Rust Belt." In *State and Society in Twenty-first-Century China,* edited by Peter Hays Gries and Stanley Rosen, 67–86. New York: Routledge, 2004.

Whyte, Martin King, and William L. Parish. *Urban Life in Contemporary China.* Chicago: University of Chicago Press, 1984.

Wolf, Margery. *The Revolution Postponed: Women in Contemporary China.* Stanford: Stanford University Press, 1985.

Wolff, David. *To the Harbin Station: The Liberal Alternative in Russian Manchuria, 1898–1914.* Stanford: Stanford University Press, 1999.

Won, Jaeyoun. "Withering Away of the Iron Rice Bowl? The Reemployment Project of Post-socialist China." *Studies in Comparative International Development* 39, no. 2 (2004): 71–93.

———. "The Making of Post-proletariat in China." *Development and Society* 34, no. 2 (2005): 191–216.

Wong, Linda J. *Marginalization and Social Welfare in China.* New York: Routledge, 1998.

Wu, Fulong. "The State and Marginality: Reflections on Urban Outcasts from China's Urban Transition." *International Journal of Urban and Regional Research* 33, no. 3 (2009): 841–47.

Wu, Fulong, and Chris Webster, eds. *Marginalization in Urban China: Comparative Perspectives.* New York: Palgrave Macmillan, 2010.

Wu, Fulong, Chris Webster, Shenjing He, and Yuting Liu. *Urban Poverty in China.* Cheltenham: Edward Elgar Publishing, 2010.

Wu Gang. "Xiandai Shehui Zuzhi Jiegouguan yu Changshi Shequ Jianshe" [Perspectives on Organizational Structure in Modern Society and Urban Community Building]. *Beijing Shehui Kexue* [Beijing Social Sciences] 1 (2001): 14–16.

Xiang, Biao. *Transcending Boundaries: Zhejiangcun—The Story of a Migrant Village in Beijing.* Leiden: Brill, 2005.

Xiang, Biao, and Shen Tan. "Does Migration Research Matter in China? A Review of Migration Research and Its Relations to Policy since the 1980s." Working paper no. 16. Center on Migration, Policy, and Society. University of Oxford, 2005.

Xiao Donglian. "Zhongguo Qishi Niandaimo de Jiuye Weiji yu Chengzhen Feiguoyou Jingji de Fazhan Qiji" [Employment Crisis and the Chance for Growth of the Non-public Economy in the Cities and Towns in the Late 1970s]." *Zhonggong Dangshi Yanjiu* [History of the Chinese Community Party] 1 (2006).

Xu Yong. "Lun Chengshi Shequ Jianshe Zhongde Shequ Jumin Zizhi" [Study on Community Self-governance amidst Urban Community Building]. In *Jiceng Minzhu yu Shehui Fazhan* [Grassroots Democracy and Social Development], edited by Zhang Zhirong and Yang Haijiao, 304–25. Beijing: Shijie Zhishi Chubanshe [World Knowledge Press], 2001.

Yan, Hao. "Urban Poverty in China: An Emerging Challenge to an Economy in Transition." Paper submitted to the Twenty-fourth IUSSP General Population Conference, 2001. http://www.iussp.org/Brazil2001/s70/S71_01_Hao.pdf.

Yan, Hairong. "Neoliberal Governmentality and Neohumanism: Organizing *Suzhi*/Value Flow through Labor Recruitment Networks." *Cultural Anthropology* 18, no. 4 (2003a): 493–523.

——. "Spectralization of the Rural: Reinterpreting the Labor Mobility of Rural Young Women in Post-Mao China." *American Ethnologist* 30, no. 4 (2003b): 578–96.

——. *New Masters, New Servants: Migration, Development, and Women Workers in China.* Durham: Duke University Press, 2008.

Yanagisako, Sylvia Junko. *Producing Culture and Capital: Family Firms in Italy.* Princeton: Princeton University Press, 2002.

Yang, Dennis Tao, and Cai Fang. "The Political Economy of China's Rural-Urban Divide." In *How Far Across the River? Chinese Policy Reform at the Millennium,* edited by Nicholas C. Hope et al., 389–416. Stanford: Stanford University Press, 2003.

Yang, Jie. "'Re-employment Stars': Language, Gender, and Neoliberal Restructuring in China." In *Words, Worlds, Material Girls: Language, Gender, Globalization,* edited by Bonnie S. McElhinny, 77–105. Berlin: Mouton De Gruyter, 2008.

——. "The Crisis of Masculinity: Class, Gender, and Kindly Power in Post-Mao China." *American Ethnologist* 37, no. 3 (2010): 550–62.

Yang, Mayfair. "From Gender Erasure to Gender Difference: State Feminism, Consumer Sexuality, and a Feminist Public Sphere in China." In *Spaces of*

Their Own: Women's Public Sphere in Transnational China, edited by Mayfair Yang, 35–67. Minneapolis: University of Minnesota Press, 1999.

Yin Haijie. "Pinkunrenkou de Jingji Zhichuwang" [Study on Economic Support Networks of the Urban Poor]. Ph.D. diss., Harbin Institute of Technology, 2006.

Yin Haijie, and Guan Shixu. "Jingji Zhuanxing yu Chengshi Pinkun Renkou Shenghuo Zhuangkuang de Bianhua" [How Does Economic Restructuring Impact the Life of the Urban Poor?]. *Zhongguo Renkou Kexue* [Chinese Journal of Population Science] 3 (2004): 61–67.

Zhang, Hong, Shaoqun Weng, and Xuan Zhou. "Housing Price Fluctuations across China: An Equilibrium Mechanism Perspective." *Tsinghua Science and Technology* 12, no. 3 (2007): 302–08.

Zhang Hongyan, and Jingsheng Yin. "Dangdai Zhongguo Chengshi Shequ Shehui Jiegou Bianqianlun" [On the Contemporary Structural Change of Chinese Urban Communities]. *Dongnan Daxue Xuebao* [Journal of Southeast University] 2, no. 4 (2000): 28–37.

Zhang, Li. *Strangers in the City: Reconfigurations of Space, Power, and Social Networks within China's Floating Population.* Stanford: Stanford University Press, 2001.

——. "Spatiality and Urban Citizenship in Late Socialist China." *Public Culture* 14, no. 2 (2002): 331–34.

——. "Privatizing Urban Housing and Governmentality in Reform-Era China." Paper presented at "Privatizing China" workshop, Shanghai, June 27–29, 2004.

——. "Private Homes, Distinct Lifestyles: Performing a New Middle Class." In *Privatizing China: Socialism from Afar,* edited by Aihwa Ong and Li Zhang, 23–40. Ithaca: Cornell University Press, 2008.

——. *In Search of Paradise: Middle-Class Living in a Chinese Metropolis.* Ithaca: Cornell University Press, 2010.

Zhang, X. Q. "The Impact of Housing Privatisation in China." *Environment and Planning B: Planning and Design* 26 (1999): 593–604.

Zhongguo Laodong he Shehui Baozhangbu [China Ministry of Labor and Social Security]. *Zhongguo Laodong he Shehui Baozhang Nianjian* [China Labor and Social Security Yearbook]. Beijing: Zhongguo Laodong he Shehui Baozhang Chubanshe [China Labor and Social Security Press], 1999–2007. Cited as ZLSN.

Zhongguo Minzhengbu [China Ministry of Civil Affairs]. *Zhongguo Minzheng Tongji Nianjian* [Civil Affairs Statistical Yearbook]. Beijing: Zhongguo Tongji Chubanshe [China Statistics Press], 2007. Cited as ZM.

Zhou Wenjie, and Sujin Zhao. "Zhongguo Nongcun Yanglao Baozhang Wenti Yanjiu" [Study of the Rural Pension Scheme in China]." *Jilin Gongshang Xueyuan Xuebao* [Journal of Jilin College of Finance and Taxation] 78 (2006): 67–70.

Zhou, Yu. "Heterogeneity and Dynamics in China's Emerging Urban Housing Market: Two Sides of a Success Story from the Late 1990s." *Habitat International* 30 (2006): 277–304.

Žižek, Slavoj. *Violence: Six Sideways Reflections.* London: Picador, 2008.

ZLSN. See Zhongguo Laodong he Shehui Baozhangbu 1997–2007.

ZM. See Zhongguo Minzhengbu 2007.

ZTN. See Guojia Tongjiju 2007.

INDEX

Note: Page numbers in *italics* indicate figures; those with a *t* indicate tables.

Affordable Housing Program (AHP), 63–66
Agamben, Giorgio, 7, 122, 141, 143
Ahmed, Sara, 157
alcoholism, 70, 76, 81, 153
Anagnost, Ann, 181n10
Appadurai, Arjun, 152, 183n21, 184n6
Asian Development Bank, 78

Beijing Olympics, 1–3, 160–61
Biehl, João, 181n5
black market, 48, 56
Bourdieu, Pierre, 49–50, 58, 62, 65
Briggs, Jean, 181n6
buyout policies, 29, 37–38, 48, 62–63, 128,
    177n27

cainong. See peri-urban farmers
Cao Guiying, 60–63, 65, 80, 171
Chan, Kam Wing, 181n2
Chatterjee, Partha, 175n14
Chen Yuhua, 46–59, 63–67, 112, 138–39,
    150, 156–57, 171
child care, 132
    elder care and, 127–30, 135
    gendered role of, 35–36, 97
    monetary assistance for, 77, 100
Chiu, Stephen, 56
citizenship, 16–20, 117, 142–43, 175n15,
    183n21
class, 5–9, 29, 40–41
    antagonisms of, 156, 174n3
    awareness of, 58–59
    Bourdieu on, 49–50
    consumerism and, 49, 59
    downward mobility and, 9–13, 59–60
    ethnicity and, 176n9
    subjectivity of, xvi, 5, 9–11, 50, 54–60,
        66–67
cleaning fees, 95, 113, 115, 144–45, 158–63,
    185n10

collective-owned enterprises (COEs),
    24–25, 34–39, 44, 178n3
    reclassifying of, 177n20
    wages at, 177n26, 177nn22–25
Comaroff, Jean, 48, 78
Comaroff, John L., 48, 78
community fees, 95, 113, 115, 144–45,
    157–63, 184n9, 185n10
Community Residents' Committee, 94–95,
    98–99, *103,* 104–18, 175n16
    government targets for, 68–70
    professionalism of, 108, 110–11
    salaries for, 106, 108, 112
community self-governance, 95–100, 112–18,
    181n11
computer literacy, 110–11
consumerism, 55–60, 178n2
    neoliberal, 49, 93
    waste disposal and, 93
corruption, 24, 65–66
    dibao policies and, 78, 84–85
crime, concerns about, 43, 153, 156, 157,
    161, 166, 184n9
Cruikshank, Barbara, 79–80, 95, 117
Cultural Revolution, 11, 31, 55, 121
    education during, 40, 109, 111,
        184n4
    urban unemployment and, 36–37,
        149–51

dangzheng jiguan. See party organizations
Daoli district, *22,* 23, 175n1
Daowai district, 23, 175n1, 176n13
    See also Harbin
Deleuze, Gilles, 179n10
democracy, 9–11
    community self-governance and, 95–100,
        112–18, 181n11
    grassroots, 181n11
    social contract theory and, 18–19

203

Deng Xiaoping, x–xi, 27, 34, 104
  on market pioneers, 56–57, 178n1
  on rich elites, 49
dibao. See minimum livelihood guarantee
Dirlik, Arif, 7
domestic violence, 60–61, 140
dongtai guanli, 80–82, 90
drug abuse, 76
Dutton, Michael, 160, 185n13
"dynamic management," 80–82, 90

Economic Development Zones, 28
education, 17, 60, 108–11, 164, 172, 179n5
  computer, 110–11
  during Cultural Revolution, 40, 109,
    111, 184n4
  expenditures for, 77, 100
  rural, 179n4
elder care, 127–30, 135
Elegance Life Garden condominiums,
    46–48, *47,* 64, 138–41
empowerment logic, 19, 20, 95–97, 116, 117
enterprises, 34–36, 56, 69, 182n9
environmental concerns, 106, 125, 169, 182n9

Falun Gong, 1
Fei Xiaotong, 181n11
Fenghuang Company, 42–43, 55
Fenghuang Cultural Palace, 21, 32
Fenghuang Service Corporation, 37,
    177n23
Fenghuang work unit, 35, 42, 54
  bankruptcy of, xv, 24, 31, 38, 101
  residential compound of, *22,* 30–31,
    39, 42
  welfare programs of, 100–102
"forty–fifty unit," 55–56, 58
Foucault, Michel, 14, 83
  on bio-power, 74, 77
  on governmentality, 16, 70, 71
  on sovereign-subject relationship, 18, 84,
    174n13
Fukuyama, Francis, ix

gambling, 60–62
garbage disposal. *See* waste disposal
gender, 106, 138
  division of labor and, ix, 24–25, 34–39,
    44, 97, 105
  land access and, 133
globalization. *See* neoliberalism
gongchang. See state-owned enterprises
gongsi. See collective-owned enterprises
gongyixing gangwei. See public posts policy

gray market, 48, 56
Great Leap Forward, 35–37, 55, 149
guanxi (personal connections), xiv, 56,
    65–66, 134
  dibao calculations and, 84
  See also corruption
Guattari, Félix, 179n10
Gupta, Akhil, 157

Hadong, xiv–xv, 21–45, *22*
  decline of, 29–34
  fieldwork in, xiv–xvii
  history of, 30–34
  real estate market in, 42, 46–67, *47,* 141–42
Harbin, xiv, 4, 21–25, *22, 26*
  demographics of, 176n12
  Migration Committee of, 184n3
  real estate market in, 46, 48, 54, 142
Harbin Institute of Technology, xiv, 21, 167,
    182n11
Hardt, Michael, xii, 164, 170
Harrell, Stevan, 105
Harvey, David, 48–49
health care, 31, 111
  allowances for, 76–78, 81–82, 100, 116
  hazardous jobs and, 61, 81
  insurance for, 38, 106, 155
  See also medical assistance
Hegel, G. F. W., 174n4
Heilongjiang province, *26,* 28, 176n7,
    182n12
Hoffman, Lisa, 178n8
Holston, James, 183n21
Hong Kong, x, 2, 25, 28
household registration system, 136, 146–49,
    159, 181n2
  changing status in, 126
  mortgages and, 64, 139–40
  origin of, 184n2
  peri-urban farmers and, 39–40, 43
  reform of, 124, 182n7
housing, 42, 46–67, 124, 136, 170, 183n20
  "affordable," 46, 51, 60, 63–66
  Bourdieu on, 49–50, 62, 65
  heating assistance and, 78, 82
  landlord rents for, 42, 44, 126, 142, 182n10
  monetary assistance for, 78, 156
  privatization of, 51–52
  real estate market for, 46–48, *47,* 51–54,
    62–67, 124
  worker, 21–22, *22,* 51–52, 60, 63–66
Housing Provident Fund (HPF), 63–66
Hsu, Carolyn L., 174n5
hukou. See household registration system

Hung, Eva, 56
Hurst, William, 173n2

Japan, 9, 23, 167
  during World War II, 27, 30
Jewish immigrants, 23
Jilin province, *26,* 28, 176n7
jingji shiyong fang. See Affordable Housing
  Program
job training, 69, 106, 155, 162–63
Judd, Ellen, 133

Kafka, Franz, 141
Kentucky Fried Chicken (KFC), 55, 58
Kernen, Antoine, 163
Kojève, Alexandre, 174n4
Kondo, Dorinne K., 101
Koreans, 23, 120, 136, 150, 167
Korean War, 26, 30
Kraus, Richard, 6

Land Contracts Law, 182n14
Lee, Ching Kwan, 19, 86
Lei Feng, x, xiv, 33, 176n16
Lenin, Vladimir, 174n7
Li Dazhao, 7
Li Debin, 184n3
Li, Tania, 97, 165
Li Yuming, 1, 95, 114–16
Liaoning Academy of Social Sciences, xiv
Liaoning province, 26, *26,* 28, 176n7
Lin Liping, 87, 106, 116, 161–66, 171, 178n31
Lin Yan, 72–73, 78–79
Lindquist, Johan A., 173n5
Liu, Jieyu, 35

maiduan. See buyout policies
Manchuria, 26, 175n4
Mao Zedong, 2, 27, 43
  on gender equality, 36
  on intellectuals, x, 27, 178n5
  on Lei Feng, 176n16
  nostalgia for, xi, 24, 29, 117, 169
  on "the people," 4, 8, 185n13
  on rebels, 86
  on self-reliance, 96, 112
  social relief policies of, 8, 71, 74, 75
marriage, 57–58, 67, 151, 164
  See also gender
Marx, Karl, 7, 182n13
medical assistance, 76–78, 81–82, 100, 116
  See also health care
micro-financing, 69, 155
migrants. *See* rural migrants

Migration Committee, 184n3
Miller, Peter, 97–98
minimum livelihood guarantee *(dibao),* xvii,
  17, 55, 71–92, 155
  appeals for, 83, 88
  calculation of, 79–84, 179n9
  disability and, 76–78, 116
  origin of, 73–74, 106
  recipients of, 76, 85–87, 90t, 106, 127
Mitchell, Timothy, 70
murder, 153

Nangang district, 23, 175n1
Negri, Antonio, 164, 170
neoliberalism, 7, 62
  community governance and, 96–98
  USSR and, 10–12
  welfare programs and, 48–49, 78
New Culture Movement, 174n6
Newman, Katherine S., 12
New Youth movement, 7, 174n6
nongmin. See peasants

O'Connor, Alice, 79
Olympic Games of 2008, 1–3, 160–61
one-child policy, 41, 56, 98, 106
  dibao criteria and, 76
  subsidies for, 100
Ong, Aihwa, 28
Ortner, Sherry B., 29, 176n9

party organizations, 34
peasants, 109, 126
  displaced, 132
  pension plans for, 129, 131, 182n12
  as "the people," 40–41, 43, 130
pension plans, 33, 38, 48, 127
  minimum livelihood guarantee and, 74
  for peasants, 129, 131, 182n12
  of peri-urban farmers, 40
  See also retirement
"the people," ix–xiii, 24–25, 130, 168–72
  the citizen and, 16–20, 117
  class and, 5–9, 40–41
  the community and, 110, 117–18
  definitions of, 4
  fear of, 84–88
  Korean concept of, ix–xii
  Mao on, 4, 8, 185n13
  national development and, 34, 49
  nostalgia for, 40, 110
  "the population" and, 17–18, 68–92
  rural migrants and, 163–64
  split within, 39–45

peri-urban farmers, 25, 39–45, 80, 126, 178n30
  See also rural migrants
Poland, 11
poverty, xi–xv, 9–16
  defining of, 13
  "deserving poor" and, 76, 89, 155
  differential, 148–51
  government managing of, 14–17, 68–71, 154–56, 166, 172
  neoliberal approach to, 48–49, 96–98, 116
  perceptions of, xi, 79–80, 154, 164–65, 168
  state policies on, 13–16
  See also minimum livelihood guarantee
public posts policy, 19–20, 69, 108–9, 162

Qing dynasty, 26–27, 75
qiye danwei. See enterprises

railway construction, 23
Rancière, Jacques, 9, 143, 184n5
Residents' Committee (RC), 98–99, 102–5
  See also Community Residents' Committee
retirement, 128
  See also buyout policies; pension plans
Rocca, Jean-Louis, 6, 163, 175n15
Rofel, Lisa, 76, 101
Romania, 11
Rosaldo, Renato, 183n1
Rose, Nikolas, 14, 16, 97–98
rural migrants, 41–45, 115–19, 121–43, 161–62
  categories of, 124–26
  community fees and, 144–45, 158–59
  demographics on, xv
  household registration for, 146, 148–49, 159, 173n4, 174n12
  as "peasants," 126
  peri-urban farmers and, 25, 39–45, 80, 126, 178n30
  prejudices against, 120–22, 152–54, 156, 157
  real estate of, 131–38, *134*
  return to countryside of, 131–38, *134,* 184n3
  "sent-down" movement and, 151
  union for, 155
  urban workers versus, 16, 25, 39–45, 138–41, 146–47, 154–57, 164–65
Russo-Japanese War, 23

Schmitt, Carl, 160
security fees, 144–46, 158–63, 184n9, 185n10
self-governance. *See* community self-governance
"sent-down" movement, 31, 36–37, 55, 72–73, 149–51
  consequences of, 184n4
service fees, 144, 158, 163, 185n10
sewage, 39, 53, 93, 113–15
  See also waste disposal
Shengli Peri-urban Farmers' Association, 39–41, 178n30
Shenyang, xiv, *26, 27*
Shi Fang, 184n3
Shi Shih-Jiunn, 182n12
Shi Weimin, 108
shoufei. See community fees
social contract theory, 18–19
  See also democracy
social surveys, xiii, 138
Song Xiaomei, 82–83
Song Xiaowei, 68–69
state-owned enterprises (SOEs), 24–25, 28, 34–39, 44, 178n3
  restructuring of, 27–28, 73, 177n20
  wages at, 177n26
suicide, x, 91, 128, 135, 153
Sun Yufen, 43–44, 118–20, 123, 126–43, 146, 171
Sun Yuming, 118, 120–24, 126, 128, 138–39, 142, 171
surveys, social, xiii, 138

"theaterization," 91, 92
Thompson, E. P., 10
Tiananmen Square massacre, x, 3, 177n18
Tibet, 1, 2

unemployment, 68–69
  allowances for, 80, 106, 155
  disability assistance and, 76–78, 116
  statistics on, 173n1
Union of Soviet Socialist Republics (USSR), ix, 10–12, 150
urban-rural divide, 16, 25, 138–41, 146–47, 154–57, 164–65
  See also rural migrants

violence, domestic, 60–61, 104
voluntarism, 19, 20, 95, 96, 115, 180n1

Wang Fei-ling, 182n7
Wang Xin, 36

waste disposal, 32, 39, 43, 93–95, *94,* 106,
    112–15, 118, 156
    cleaning fees for, 95, 113, 115, 144–45,
        158–63, 185n10
Wei Yonglan, 113–15, 159–60, 166
Wen Jiabao, 122
Women's Federation, 35, 162–63
workers, xi, 9–11, 58
    housing for, 21–22, *22,* 51–52, 60,
        63–66
    income of, 32, 33, 64, 177n26,
        182n15
    "subalternization" of, 11
    temporary, 80–81, 106–7, 124, 130,
        141, 165
    unpaid, 10, 48, 122, 153, 181n3

work ethic, 76, 88–89
World Bank, 78

xiaxiang. See "sent-down" movement
Xu Ying, 85, *103,* 103–5, 113

Yanagisako, Sylvia, 10, 50
Young Communist League, 162–63
Yu Jianhua, 83, 85

Zhang, Li, 59, 124, 181n2, 183n20
Zhu Rongji, 27–28, 174n11, 184n7
zhufang gongjijin. See Housing
    Provident Fund
zuidi shenghuo baozhang zhidu. See
    minimum livelihood guarantee